HIGH-VELOCITY CONSCIOUSNESS

Deprogramming from Fear and Societal Mind Conditioning in a Techno/Media World

REVIEWS

"Our minds have never before been presented with the overwhelming amount of fear-based information now available 24/7. Kaufman gives us an elegant and clear way to find our way through the fear and head toward our higher states of peace and wisdom."

—Richard Schaub, Ph.D., author, The End of Fear

"In "High-Velocity Consciousness", Joan Marinakis brings clarity and reassurance to self realization. As we approach the next step to understanding multidimensional levels of the Human Collective Consciousness, our greatest tool is an informed "knowing" of how the different levels of our role in cosmic evolution is revealing itself to us. We are finally understanding that 'Metaphysics, is but Quantum Physics... poetically expressed'."

—Montgomery Taylor, writer, lecturer, broadcaster, cultural consultant and host of "Living Consciously"

"Discouraged about the meaning of your life? Been to too many workshops? High-Velocity Consciousness can help you. Marinakis Kaufman, author and psychological goddess offers us ourselves as the way—to meaning, to health, to joy and to spirit."

—Elaine De Beauport, teacher, researcher, author, educational innovator, and founder of the Mead Institute

HIGH-VELOCITY CONSCIOUSNESS

Deprogramming from Fear and Societal Mind Conditioning in a Techno/Media World

Joan Marinakis Kaufman

Printed in the United States of America

Published by Higher Consciousness Press

Kaufman, Joan Marinakis
High-Velocity Consciousness: Deprogramming from Fear and Societal
Mind Conditioning in a Techno/Media World/ Joan Marinakis Kaufman.

ISBN: 978-0-9883908-9-8
First edition 2014
LCCN: 2013911579
1. Psychology. 2. Self-help. 3.Consciouseness. 4. Techno/media influence.

Visit us at www.HighVelocityConsciousness.com

Cover Design by Dan Peyton
Author Photo by Matt Scott
Interior Formatting by D. Bass

Dedicated to the freedom of the mind

CONTENTS

AUTHOR'S NOTE

I have been given permission by a few of my clients to include their stories. I have changed all the names and identifying details to maintain their anonymity. Most stories are composites of similar experiences from several clients combined together to illustrate a point or clarify a process.

ACKNOWLEDGEMENTS

I started writing this book some time ago. I want to thank the people who helped me during those first stages:

Robin Kormos, no longer with us, whose attentive ear and encouragement were there from the beginning.

Arthur Aronson, who has offered me steadfast loyalty and clear responses all along the way.

Eva Young, who through her kind editing may have thwarted a developing comma obsession.

Susan Fisher, my inspiring fellow writer and spiritual sister.

Other helpers and editors in that early process included Barbara Shor, Ellen Levine, Ed Levy, Sue Machlin, Elaine De Beauport, and my dear longtime friends Beatriz and Manuel Kohn, Ileen Kohn, and Alan and Laura Levy.

I thank Marcos and Turiya Levy, for their continuing deep support. Marcos's valuable website help was much appreciated.

I thank my wonderful goddaughter Tara Kelton for her keen, creative, and loving eye.

I relish the hours spent with Cheryl Woodruff in provocative exchanges, mixed in with valuable advice (and a lot of laughing).

I appreciate the editorial staff at CreateSpace for helping with the manuscript format.

I also want to thank the following people:

Nicholas Kotsianas, friend kéfi-maker, poet, and kindred Greek spirit.

Maria Papapetros, unique intuitive consultant and friend who many years ago simply said, Write! Write! Write!

Gary Heidt, an artist on many levels, an agent and friend who has been with me from the beginning and believes in the importance of waking people up.

Dan Peyton, who manifested my thoughts into elegant visions with his beautiful cover.

Matt Scott, who with a comforting smile, produced the wonderful back cover photo of me.

Timothy Sheard, mystery writer and workshop leader from the National Writers Union who has kindly guided me with book-business answers throughout.

Dave Bass, who helped me develop the wonderful interior book design and with whom I've enjoyed engaging in both tech talk and the puzzlements of life.

Rick Gioiello, multi-creative artist whose fun-filled photo sessions resulted in the author's photo on my website.

Suzanne Levinson, fiction writer and dear friend who has been gracious and forthcoming with valuable help.

Daniel Kaufman, excellent writer and copyeditor of my book, and also my son, whose love, advice, and support is immeasurable. I am grateful for his special kind of inner strength, intelligence, creativity, sense of humor, and tender caring.

Bob Kaufman, my husband who left this world years ago, but who appears in my dreams now and then with loving encouragement and sometimes a dance or two.

To all my clients, friends, and relatives who have offered me a perennial thumbs-up for this long project: thank you.

INTRODUCTION

I have been involved in the field of psychology for some time, and I'm still fascinated with the resilience and brilliance of the human psyche. We are so interesting. We have the ability to survive the most difficult times and reveal flashes of wisdom and certainty in the midst of all kinds of trouble. If given a chance, these high-level revelations can help us override lifelong fears and well-established negative thinking.

In the beginning, however, classical psychoanalysis focused on labeling problems, learning how to solve them, and adapting to society in order to lead a better life. It did not always relish strangeness, diversity, and esoteric experiences beyond ordinary reality. That made little sense to me. I came from an artistic and musical background, and I knew how important higher levels of consciousness were for the evolution of the human spirit.

In time, these realms began to be more acknowledged by some practitioners in the field. I explored them through various transpersonal psychologies, hypnotherapy, Tai Chi, Yoga, meditation, and other things. Each process offered a way of moving into dimensions of consciousness that expanded the possibilities of the mind. I learned how to reach these states more easily, and I incorporated them into my work with clients.

In a lot of the early New Age workshops I attended, I saw how some people could get immersed in pleasurable altered states that usually had little to do with their lives. In those early days, there was not much crossover effect between an awe-inspiring weekend exploring higher dimensions and then dealing with a miserable job or a difficult relationship. In some groups, people were also affected in dangerous ways because there were often rigid controls about how the practice was taught. Independence of mind and spirit outside the group was not always encouraged. In some situations, everything that was deemed to be an altered state was thought to be spiritual and wonderful. This was, and is, not always true.

Then, awareness of the body began to gain importance in psychological research. I had performed as a dancer in my early years, and so the idea of paying attention to physical experiences felt valid and appropriate to me.

Practitioners began to respect the body as an information-filled place of discovery. Tuning in to physical sensations was another way of unearthing traumatic memories that needed to be released. Also, the body contained creative intentions that needed to be fulfilled.

I received training for several years in alternative healing. This natural inner state is the ability to facilitate self-healing in others. It involves deep meditation with objective attention, compassion, and heart-to-heart communication.

My most direct and powerful experience using all of these modalities took place with my godson. For almost a year, I worked very closely with Carlos, who was twenty-three at the time and had suffered through several dangerous episodes related to bipolar disturbances. In addition to the necessary medical and pharmaceutical support, Carlos wanted to feel comfortable enough to experience and also to observe the intense states that he found himself in. He leapt into higher dimensions at times and also found himself in various unnerving altered states. He would have illuminating dreams, experience euphoric insights, engage in philosophical explorations and declarations, and then he would tumble down into the depths of anxiety, depression, and confusion. In time, this shifting of moods became more controlled and less overwhelming. He explored many levels of consciousness with the intention of slowly creating a balanced center so that he could function.

Carlos is a very talented musician and composer. Sometimes he played out his thoughts and feelings on the piano. He translated his anguish, anger, or euphoria into the music. At other times, he acted out various parts of his personality that were hiding under the surface of his awareness. Some of what we did together was just rational discourse. Later, he began to analyze what he was going through and talked about how to plan his future place in the world. His father, a chiropractor, worked on releasing the tension in his body, and this offered him relief as well as further insights. He had a friend who was a dance teacher, and she worked with him on movement.

We were all teaching him how to travel through different dimensions of consciousness, and in time, he was able to orchestrate these trips with relative safety and independent control.

That was many years ago. I felt so privileged to be part of this experience with someone I cared about so deeply. Carlos is now a successful musician and popular teacher. He is married to a wonderful woman and his son, at five, was reading, banging drums, and playing piano.

I continued incorporating what I was learning about traveling through different dimensions of consciousness into my practice and into my own process. And then 9/11 happened, and everything changed. In New York City, the tragic intrusion permeated every aspect of life. I looked at the strange atmosphere around me, and I began to question everything.

It was not that all the training I had had for so many years was invalid, just incomplete. Talking about problems was not enough. Positive thinking was not enough. Body consciousness was not enough. These were valid explorations, but something else needed to be addressed as well. I became aware of several things that were disturbing.

In any sudden catastrophe, media reports can be frightening, confusing, and often misleading. However, as time passed, information about the circumstances of the event and the actions around the Twin Towers disaster created more questions and became more problematic. My focus was not on who did what and when and how. Others were examining that. I became acutely aware of the power of the media/technology arena to affect large numbers of people through direct and subliminal means. Societal mind conditioning is certainly not a new thing, but today the ever-present media and new technologies are able to affect our thinking more than ever before. I became concerned about the freedom of the mind.

With 9/11, thousands of people in this city were bound together in a collective mind-set of victimization. This is a natural response embedded in our genetic makeup and activated when our lives are threatened. However, this victim mind-set was not passing. For many people, fear and apprehension just went underground.

I asked myself a lot of questions. How do we live in a world where threats can come from anywhere: from terrorist attacks, a volatile economy, rising oil and gasoline prices, floods, earthquakes, new diseases, and toxic food and air? How can we know what the truth is when deception is taking place in government proclamations, hypocrisy is found in religious establishments, and corruption is exposed in once-trusted corporations? Can we survive and flourish when the whole world seems to be going crazy?

The bad news is that it's worse than you think. The dark side of humanity is coming to the surface once again, and everyone is affected. People are dying in some parts of the world, and others are slowly letting their spirits die because it takes effort to keep hope alive today.

People in positions of power have used variations of mind manipulation for thousands of years. This is nothing new. Only now, it's possible to program our thinking very quickly and often without our permission.

The good news is that at the same time we are grappling with stressful news speeding around us every day, we are also waking up and searching for different ways to deal with all of this. Traditional methods need to be looked at more carefully. We can no longer spend five years in psychotherapy talking about what our mother did to us. Pharmaceuticals that help us suppress our fears can also damage our brains. Religious and spiritual practices that promote peace are limited if they don't also help us to release our hidden fears and examine today's real-life issues.

This era of information overload and crises at every corner is also heralding a transformation of consciousness that we have not experienced before. We are at the brink of a brilliant mind/body/soul expansion, but we need a new mode of awareness to deal with the complexities of a quickly changing world.

Scientific, medical, and technological progress continues at a mind-boggling pace. We need to match that with brain excellence and a more rapid integration of consciousness. Also, the persistent fear and anxiety that lurks beneath the surface of our awareness fragments our consciousness and makes it less possible to function in an integrated way. This is nothing new either. We've known for a long time that emotional stress blocks our overall energy and intrudes into our physical and mental functioning. We do our best, but there's so much to dissociate from these days that we look for quick fixes in order to feel safe and to experience life more fully.

The following is a list of what I hope the reader will learn from this book:

1. To notice how we are being conditioned, through various forms of the media and advanced technology, to keep our minds contracted and our choices directed by external sources.

2. To recognize that we are experiencing various degrees of mind dissociation, due to anxiety and societal mind conditioning, which affects our concentration and fragments our thinking.

3. To deprogram and release our repressed personal fears that are being triggered more easily by the collective anxieties of today's world.

4. To activate our intuitive abilities to discern between truths and counter-truths and be able to make the best decisions in everyday situations, especially during stressful times.

5. To match the accessibility of computerized information by downloading from our own infinite knowledge-filled higher states of consciousness.

6. To utilize a daily self-reflective cross-referencing process that promotes brain synchronization and body/mind/soul integration that helps us reconnect with our ability to access pure, unmediated experience and knowledge.

Part One presents what is happening today with regard to societal mind conditioning and our increasingly mediated reality. Some examples of general mind manipulation are given. We look at the natural process of dissociation and how and when it becomes destructive. Unresolved emotions, especially fear, deplete our energy, divide our consciousness, and keep us from accessing our higher states of mind. We look at the different forms of fear and anxiety and begin to research our own fear history.

Part Two explores how we can begin to free the mind by understanding the multidimensions of the psyche and the natural dynamic experience of movement and change. High-Velocity Consciousness is introduced. Through personal illustrations and client experiences, we look at the process in action: a mindspeed integration of consciousness that is sometimes spontaneous and at other times results from creative exploration.

Part Three illustrates how we use High-Velocity Consciousness on a daily basis. The seven step exercise and mind-orchestration tools are defined. With each exercise, we observe and communicate with the world around us, within us, and beyond us in a deeper, fuller reality. We examine the importance of each part of the process in our integration. We know more than we think we know.

Part Four offers some suggestions about how we can be more mindful in distinguishing between societal mind conditioning and information that increases our individual knowledge and respects our freedom of thought.

Can we survive and flourish when the whole world seems to be going crazy? Yes! We can use our minds to deprogram from fear, evaluate truth, and activate our intuitive process. When we magnify our vision, strengthen our personal stability, and nurture our creative resources, we change from conditioned thinking to a state of "knowing." That's an attractive way to live, and it can affect everyone around us.

Join me in this exploration, and please be open to everything and question anything in this book, in your life, in the world. Let's begin.

PART I

SOCIETAL MIND CONDITIONING

ONE

TECHNOLOGY, SPEED, AND QUICK FIXES

Speed is good only when wisdom leads the way.

—James Poe

How we speak, the way we think, how we dress, and how we act are conditioned first by the family we grow up with and then by the society that we live in. Societal mind conditioning, especially through the media, succeeds when we are convinced that taking some action, using some technology, or buying some product will make us healthier, more attractive, safer, smarter, or more successful. Societal mind conditioning is not necessarily a bad thing, but it becomes problematic when who we are and how we should be are defined more and more by external sources. It becomes threatening when certain kinds of technology begin to intrude into our private lives and affect our minds. We don't always notice or care because we are excited and drawn to new things, especially when they promise to make life easier and, in some situations, more interesting.

For the first time ever, in May of 2008, a four-foot-three shiny white metal robot clanked onto the stage and conducted the Detroit Symphony Orchestra in what was described "as a note-perfect, if passionless, performance. Not that the American audience seemed to care. There were enthusiastic cheers as the robot took a bow."[1]

Also in the same month, Chris Parry, the head of Britain's top private schools organization, predicted that within thirty years, children will learn by downloading information directly into their brains. Mr. Parry, a former rear admiral, said that "It's a very short route from wireless technology to actually getting the electrical connections in your brain to absorb that knowledge."[2]

In December of 2008, it was announced that Japan's ATR Computational Neuroscience Laboratories had developed new brain analysis technology that could reconstruct the images inside a person's mind and display them on a computer monitor. Further development of the technology may soon make it possible to view other people's dreams while they sleep.[3]

By the time you read this, there will be other dazzling and disturbing research made public. The technology revolution is moving swiftly, and we're trying to keep up with it. We live in a high-speed world that relishes fast-moving images, quick sound bites, and instant gratification.

The fast tempo of life probably had its beginnings with the invention of the clock during medieval times. We began to divide time into intervals. We became more aware of how long it took us to accomplish something or to travel somewhere. The Industrial Revolution, begun in the 1770s, accelerated the pace. Soon the car replaced the horse, machines replaced the workers, and the faster we could produce and sell material goods, the richer we became. We fell in love with speed. It tapped into something intrinsic in our nature—perhaps a genetic inheritance from our early beginnings, when quick thinking was a desirable and necessary trait as an animal or enemy approached suddenly.

Sociologist Todd Gitlin quotes historian James Truslow Adams, writing in 1931 about the variety of experiences we are subjected to compared with people thousands of years ago: "As the number of sensations increase, the time which we have for reacting to and digesting them becomes less...such a life tends to become a mere search for more and more exciting sensations, undermining yet more of our power of concentration in thought."[4] Gitlin adds, "The dirty little secret is that ours is a civilization that revels in the pure experience of speed. We share a yearning for the kinetic sublime."[5]

I believe that our attraction to speed, in large part, represents our need to be fully and passionately engaged, to feel the adrenaline rush of life. Perhaps in our craving for excitement and engagement, we are trying to break out of the analytical left-brain thinking that has operated for such a long time. We think we get it by speeding, but it's temporary, like an addiction that's never completely satisfied. And like every addiction, it contains some underlying fear.

Speed does several things. It stops us from feeling and thinking too deeply. We're afraid of what we might find if we have too much time to consider our personal questions or the problems of the world. While speed gives us the illusion of satisfaction, the subliminal discomfort that still remains under the surface is not really addressed. Speed takes us further away from integrating our consciousness. We avoid not only our subliminal fears but our creative capabilities as well. We are even less directly involved with our own process—and many people in power prefer that. They want us to keep busy, move faster, buy more, and think less.

Instead of feeling more authentic and promoting deeper emotional sensitivity, we move through life still primarily as spectators in a fast-moving, artificially created virtual reality. We are becoming addicted to manufactured excitement by scanning multiple websites, playing complex video games, or watching films about other people's lives. We indulge in couch potato interaction with reality programs where people quickly marry, divorce, get fired, hired, or survive adventures all in a matter of months or even weeks. We are reading fewer books and rushing through more headlines. Our minds are not using speed to its best advantage, and neither are our bodies. In the middle of our love affair with speed, we are getting overwhelmed and tired, exercising less, and becoming more immobilized, except for our fast-moving keyboard fingers.

We are speeding out of control. Even our technology has surpassed our capacity to handle that technology. In 2003, the Northeast power blackout in parts of the United States and Canada affected over fifty million people. It reminded us how dependent and vulnerable we are in the face of this technology that has to be continually updated in order to accommodate a fast-changing culture and a growing computerized world. It leaves us breathless, and sometimes we just want to disconnect and get away from it all.

The answer is not to dismiss technological progress and move more slowly, but to integrate our love of speed into our mind process. We should be able to catch an emotion that we're feeling more quickly, recognize immediately when we're lying to ourselves, know intuitively whether some food is good for our health, remember a dream automatically that gives us a valuable insight, and know how to travel up to the higher and more productive dimensions of consciousness and back again in a few minutes.

The Quest to Forget and Not Feel

While speeding through life is one way of feeling excitement, it also helps us escape from repressed anxieties and fears that we're reluctant to explore unless some immediate crisis forces our attention.

Our ability to dissociate from disturbing experiences is a very important part of our survival mechanism. We don't want to have vivid recall of every terrible thing that has happened to us. However, "the quest to forget," especially in dealing with painful memories, is an alarming trend. Forgetting so as not to feel pain has become the desired result for coping with anxieties and fears. This fosters mind dissociation and reliance on solutions outside of us to control our thoughts and emotions.

On a physiological level, the absence of the feeling of pain is called analgesia. It is an unusual but serious illness because experiencing pain is a wake-up signal from the body that tells the mind to take some action about a broken bone or a bleeding ulcer. We can also say that on a psychological level, the absence of the feeling of pain means that we repress disturbing memories so that we don't feel them consciously.

Clinical amnesia is defined as partial or permanent memory loss due to brain injury, shock, or repression. In general terms, it can also mean that we forget painful memories so that we're not affected by their full emotional impact. This is a natural survival mechanism. However, in Western culture we have chosen psychological analgesia and amnesia as acceptable intentions for life. We are encouraged to do anything so as not to feel pain or remember our fears. We are told: You feel anxious? Take Xanax. You have sexual problems? Take Viagra. You have insomnia? Try sleeping pills. You're overstressed? Have a drink.

Some of these suggestions may be helpful and sometimes necessary. But what is the effect of using them over a long period of time? Do they encourage us to think with our whole mind, be more authentic, feel more passionate about life, and better orchestrate our fears, or do they just let us escape by forgetting? While some of us can operate for long periods of time by numbing ourselves to pain and fear, we cannot do it indefinitely without suffering negative effects. At some time, perhaps years later, unresolved fears may compromise the immune system; change into liver damage, cancer, or heart problems; or result in a variety of psychological issues.

Every wonderful and terrible thing that happens to us is part of our human experience. Repressing and forgetting emotional memories little by little renders us less human, less self-reflective, and more able to be directed by outside influences. And this is what is happening to us.

With every event we go through, there is always a choice about how we perceive it, what we project onto it, what we can glean from it, where it takes us, and how we can use it.

I was hit by a car as I was crossing the street many years ago. I don't need to remember and relive everything I went through during weeks in the hospital and months of rehabilitation. But to blot out all of those memories would deprive me of all the experiences I went through. These included fear, guilt, impatience, uncanny calm, humor, wheelchair madness, warrior toughness—both horrific and wonderful insights that were threaded to that event that changed me forever.

And yet, medical researchers are working to diminish the emotional effect of traumatic memories and, in time, may even succeed in removing the memories themselves. Roger Pitman, a professor of psychiatry at Harvard Medical School, directed a study that involved administering the drug propranolol, a beta-blocker that interferes with the action of stress hormones in the brain. His interest was in using it for post-traumatic stress disorders. Subjects in preliminary tests who were given propranolol showed no physiological signs of stress when they listened to a tape to reexperience their personal traumas.[6]

Joseph LeDoux, professor of neuroscience at New York University, and his colleague Karim Nader studied the mechanism of memory reconsolidation in laboratory rats. He created a fear response in the rats by introducing a musical tone accompanied with a mild electrical shock. After twenty-four hours, he repeated the tone, activating the "fear memory." But instead of a shock, he delivered a dose of anisomycin directly into the rats' brains. This inhibited the synthesis of protein, which is needed to form new memory synapses. For a while, the fear memory persisted, but twenty-four hours later, the rats responded as if it had totally disappeared. Further testing showed that the physiological fear response still registered in the brain, but was blocked and buried, separated from conscious recall.[7] This suggests that while we can block out pain and stress with medication or psychological dissociation for years, the physiological effects may continue to accumulate and eventually cause illness.

Dampening emotional pain, and even erasing traumatic memories, is a controversial issue these days. In 2003, Eric Baard, writing in *The Village Voice* about the guilt-free soldier, interviewed Dr. Leon Kass, who was then chairman of the President's Council on Bioethics. Dr. Kass, referring to memory-blunting drugs and speaking as an individual and not on behalf of the council said, "It's the morning-after pill for just about anything that produces regret, remorse, or guilt."[8] Do we really want a pill that makes killing other people easier? On the other hand, should soldiers who face the terrible realities of war in order to keep us safe have to suffer endlessly?

The council expressed a host of concerns and troubling scenarios:

1. If someone committed an act of violence and then took propranolol, would they come to think of violence as more tolerable than it really is?

2. Would rape victims forget key details vital to the prosecution of their attackers?

3. Is there a social obligation for people to remember past events for the communal good, such as victims of the Holocaust?[9]

Dr. William B. Hurlbut, another member of the council, said, "The pattern of our personality is like a Persian rug. It is built one knot at a time, each woven into the others. There's a continuity to self, a sense that who we are is based upon solid, reliable experience. We build our whole interpretation and understanding of the world based upon that experience or the accuracy of our memories."[10]

In America, we seem to be fascinated with the subject of amnesia and the intricacies of memory. In a *New York Times* article, Terrence Rafferty saw this trend reflected in the movies of the recent past. Some of the films he mentioned that involve memory erasure and recovery are: *Mulholland Drive*, *The Bourne Identity*, *Eternal Sunshine of the Spotless Mind*, *Memento*, and the remake of *The Manchurian Candidate*.[11]

Rafferty refers to Philip K. Dick, whose dark science-fiction novels written over twenty years ago were prophetic in describing a strange mind-controlled world of rewritten histories, deliberate memory erasure, and fabricated reality. In most of Dick's stories, "Amnesia is particularly insidious because the mind isn't even aware that it's afflicted, except perhaps subliminally: a persistent rationally inexplicable feeling that you're living a lie...the distant suspicion that in some way our day-to-day lives, our very identities have been constructed for us, with wholly synthetic materials." Rafferty concludes, "that our past, as Dick warned, has been hijacked, and we want it back...Maybe we're all trying desperately to remember who we are."[12]

TWO

MIND MANIPULATION

What concerns me is not how things are, but rather the way people think things are.

—Epictetus, Greek philosopher

The technology revolution, our love affair with speed, and the quest to forget affect our lives every day. The world is changing rapidly, and our minds are also changing, not always for the better. Especially in Western society, there are many general forms of conditioning and mind manipulation that have an impact on our consciousness and our state of being. Some of these are overstimulation, entrancement, subliminal perception and propaganda, manipulation of information, and desensitization.

Overstimulation

We are saturated every day with visual and sound stimulation from hundreds of TV channels and Internet websites. We are deluged with spam e-mails, paper mail, telemarketing, radio, TV and film trailers, subway and bus ads, and flashing billboards. We have constant media reporting about health and disease, economic and political activity, and conflict in dozens of known and unknown places around the world. We also have local news about the latest car accident in our neighborhood, the free concert in the park, or the imminent teacher's strike.

Our easier access to music through the Internet is a wonderful thing, but we are also being subjected continually with music in elevators, shopping malls, restaurants, airports, health clubs, hospitals—actually everywhere.

Of course, we can tune out the external world and tune in to our iPods and cell phones. We are increasingly interconnected and technologically involved. We are also experiencing an atmosphere of overstimulation that becomes too much at times.

Dr. Edward M. Hallowell and John Ratey, an associate professor at Harvard and a psychiatrist with an expertise in attention deficit disorder, are among a growing number of physicians and sociologists who are assessing how technology affects attention span, creativity, and focus. They are asking whether it is counterproductive, and even addicting. They use the term "pseudo-attention deficit disorder" to describe situations where people are influenced by technology and the fast pace of modern life and develop shorter attention spans and less tolerance for long-term projects.[1]

Research by psychology professor David E. Meyer suggests that people who compulsively multitask with e-mail exchanges, Internet access, cell phones, etc., instead of being more productive, are making themselves worse businesspeople. They spend 50 percent more time on those tasks instead of working on them separately, completing one before the other.[2]

Overstimulation can result in confusion. Writer David Shenk observes: "A little information makes you smarter, but a ton of it leaves you confused. We're getting more plugged in, but the level of distraction is increasing." Journalist and NYU lecturer Chris Albritton, who claims an addiction to news sites, can actually feel himself getting stupider. He says, "I don't think I'm as smart as I used to be. I just think I'm reacting more quickly, which makes you appear to be smarter." According to Barry Schwartz, professor of social theory, experiments show that too many options can make us unhappy.[3]

There seems to be a general speeding up of images, instantaneous information, fast-track aerobic consciousness, and repetition of anything that seems successful. A moneymaking film immediately spawns five others. The exhilarating car chase in the 1971 film *The French Connection* has been duplicated endlessly for many years in action films. Dramatic fires and explosions happen with frequent regularity on the screen.

TV is saturated with reality shows that present people experiencing real circumstances. We watch nonactors going through situations that seem authentic, but are often contrived with participants who are not always who they appear to be. In other shows, celebrities invite us into their private homes to watch their daily routines. We seem to be hungry for reality and fascinated with the human process, but TV, the ultimate virtual reality, is not the best place to experience it.

We have hundreds of religions and spiritual practices to choose from, with new ones developing every day promising the best path, the only path, with the most enlightened leader.

So, what's the best energy drink, diet pill, or vacation spot? Sometimes the loudest or most repeated one attracts our attention. Often, however, we are influenced subliminally, and the media outlets that have the best techniques to appeal to our very basic needs and insecurities usually affect our decisions.

Entrancement

When things become too much to handle, we want to distract ourselves from the difficulties of life and move into a more peaceful state. What begins as a need to relieve stress can become a habitual way of escaping fear. Some of us choose to go into various altered states.

In the past thirty years or so, the New Age movement introduced Western society to Eastern religions and meditation in various forms. People learned how to chant, move into Yoga postures, or sit in silent contemplation. Some of these early disciplines taught how to achieve altered states, but not always how to translate these experiences into everyday reality. Emptying the mind in a meditative state can be centering and valuable, but it must also encourage us to be more active and conscious about our thought process. And most importantly, we must be careful that we don't use altered states to dissociate from the issues of the world.

Large groups of people in meditative states or prayer may affect the atmosphere in positive ways. In the late 1970s, Transcendental Meditation groups claimed that they could decrease the crime rate in cities with only 1 percent of the population practicing TM techniques. They called this phenomenon "The Maharishi Effect."[4]

However, being in an altered state can also open people up to all kinds of conditioning and negative influences because the analytical left hemisphere of the brain is turned off. The mesmerizing power of crowds can be enormous. Many organizations use group entrancement to indoctrinate their ideas on a willing audience. I have had experiences over many years with a wide variety of groups. Most have been well-intentioned, while others have resulted in negative outcomes for the participants. We want to believe people who tell us how to relieve stress and be in a peaceful state. But, mind manipulation through entrancement can exist in some spiritual and religious groups, and so teachers must be chosen carefully.

Some sensitive people can be conditioned easily in groups with subliminal messages not directly heard but nonetheless registered in their subconscious. Certain kinds of lights and sounds are especially effective for this purpose. Imagine being in a club, under a multi-mirrored rotating ball and flashing colored strobe lights, while the band plays loud, repetitive percussion-based music. If you're drinking and dancing and having a good time, you're not really listening to the words that may be anything from "I want to beat her up and kill her for cheating on me" to "Life sucks, and death turns me on." We may not agree with any of that, but our minds are taking in the ideas anyway, because we're not monitoring anything at the time. If you're twenty-one, depressed, and angry to begin with, you might be influenced by those sentiments on a subconscious level.

Gambling casinos are especially designed to induce people into hypnotic states to spend money. You walk into a multisensory overload of bright colors, loud music, and flashing lights, with slot machines clanking, coins dropping, roulette wheels crackling, and bells ringing. It's hard to resist and stay mind centered.

Clubs and gambling casinos are dramatic examples of entrancement, but being seduced into altered states is possible anywhere from shopping malls to sports events.

Group entrancement is a very old process. Ancient Egyptians used a wheel turning in bright sunlight to create flashes of light that induced altered states. Chanting has been known for thousands of years as a standard trance-making practice. Military marching with drums is still a training device used with soldiers to create a hypnotic state so that they can become part of a group energy and follow orders without disruptive thinking. The most obvious and extreme example from history is the hypnotic cadence and repetition of Hitler's voice in speeches, accompanied by thousands of chanting, marching goose-steppers.

The hypnotic power and influence of one person on a large group is enormous, from dynamic leaders to dramatic rock stars. I remember such a moment at a psychology training conference in the

1980s in Texas. A group of about five hundred of us were listening to a charismatic speaker who was telling us about psychiatrist Dr. Milton Erickson's therapeutic hypnosis work and how he could influence people with subliminal instructions without their awareness. After about ten minutes, the speaker then asked how many people had just crossed their legs. It turned out to be a substantial number. (I almost did.) He then explained how he had used subtle verbal and visual triggers to convince us to take this action.

Milton Erickson was an innovative psychiatrist who used hypnosis to help people separate out from their negative programming and into positive thinking. For example, Dr. Erickson would induce a peaceful, quiet state by speaking softly and pacing his speech to the person's breathing. He would gain their confidence by reflecting back what they were thinking and feeling. Then he would distract the person's dominant brain hemisphere by speaking in a confusing, vague way. This resulted in the person's conscious mind becoming distracted in trying to figure out what he was saying. Having done this, he was then able to give positive instructions to the person's subconscious mind, which received them.[5] Multilevel communication was an important aspect of Neuro-Linguistic Programming, known as NLP, a therapeutic technique to detect and reprogram unconscious patterns of thought and behavior in order to alter psychological responses. Some practitioners, corporate trainers, advertising executives, and politicians have utilized NLP techniques more for manipulation than for therapeutic purposes.

Since at least the 1960s, the CIA has been using NLP and hypnosis techniques for carrying out investigations in the interrogation process.[6]

Sometimes confusion becomes the end result of entrancement. When President Eisenhower's press secretary told him that the State Department was frantic over the islands of Quemoy and Matsu, which China was threatening to seize by force, Eisenhower replied: "Don't worry, Jim. If that question comes up, I'll just confuse them."[7] He was not the first president, or the last, to use confusion to throw an audience off guard.

Entrancement was prominent in a children's program called *Boohbah* that was on public television from 2003 to 2005. It was mesmerizing and eerily beautiful. Five big-eyed, gumdrop-shaped, brightly colored robotic blobs repeatedly floated and bounced around and made strange noises. They were surrounded by psychedelic colors and bright flashing lights.

It was supposedly geared for three- to six-year-olds, but was criticized by various pediatric groups and psychologists. They stated that the program clearly targeted younger children, from eighteen months to two years, and lured them earlier and earlier to the magic of TV and fogged their brains.[8]

Television is the most common and widely used entrancement device that shuts down our critical thinking and causes subtle disruptive psychological and physiological effects over a period of time. TV operates from a platform of deliberate, rapidly changing visual images with cuts, edits, and sudden noises. It places us in an immediate altered state that activates our right brains and minimizes left-brain activity. EEG studies with TV watchers showed passive relaxation and less mental stimulation than during reading. The sense of relaxation ends when the set is turned off, but the feelings of passivity and lowered alertness continue, and subjects feel depleted of energy.[9]

Right-brain activation from external sources renders us more susceptible to any kind of conditioning because our left-brain logical awareness is not operating adequately enough to filter out or even think about what we're experiencing.

Subliminal Perception and Propaganda

Subliminal perception means we are registering something below the threshold of our consciousness. If we quickly look around the room, our brains will take in many details: colors and shapes, the furniture and objects that surround us. If we are then asked to recall whether there is a book with an orange cover on the middle shelf, we may not know the answer consciously, but our brains have registered that detail somewhere.

Perception appears to be both total and instantaneous. Some theorists speculate that only one-thousandth of this is consciously registered and processed. We are influenced the most by visual stimulation, and there are various ways that the brain can be stimulated without our conscious awareness.[10]

Researchers have designed tests that measure the physiological responses of the body while subjected to subliminal stimuli. For example, subjects are asked to watch a blank screen that is periodically superimposed with emotional subliminal stimuli in the form of words or images. Although the subjects report having no conscious awareness of the stimuli, researchers find alterations in certain brain waves, subtle variations in heart rate, and higher electrical potentials on the skin.[11]

The brain can perceive subliminal images and messages at a subconscious level, even when these are presented upside down, sideways, or even backward. During hypnotic trance, many subjects read quite fluently textual material presented in this distorted fashion— an impossible task for most people while awake.[12] Media professionals and others have known about this for years. Magazine ads often have subliminal words or images embedded in various ways: in the fold of a dress, a tiny word upside down in a corner, or a cloudy figure in the background.

In 1985, Dr. Bruce Ledford at Alabama's Auburn University used subvisually enhanced paper. That is, paper with messages and images that could be very lightly printed, embedded in the paper stock, totally unavailable to conscious perception. Students were presented with The Rosenberg Self-Esteem Scale, a standard measurement test, printed in two versions: one on plain paper, the other on paper embedded with the words "I love you" and large hearts. Self-esteem test scores on the subvisually enhanced version increased an average of 34.7 percent in an underachieving group of students. Average students improved 13.1 percent. Ledford's early research demonstrated that human perception, especially at the subconscious level, is far more involved in decision making and value judgments than anyone had suspected.[13]

This means that we can be influenced by subliminal material without realizing it because the embedded message, word, or image is below the threshold of our conscious perception. For instance, three weeks later while we're shopping, subliminally stored information from a commercial may trigger us to buy one brand of digital camera instead of another.

In 1973, researcher Jacques Ellul wrote (quoted in Key 1992): "To be effective, propaganda must constantly short-circuit all thought and decision. It must operate on the individual at the level of the unconscious."[14] Subliminal advertising works best when it taps into a person's natural tendencies and proclivities. A subliminal message to buy a new microwave oven isn't going to work if you bought one last year and you're hardly home to cook anyway. However, all of us have repressed feelings, thoughts, and ideas that we label taboo on a conscious level that can affect us subconsciously.

We have several ways in which we hide information from ourselves to avoid anxiety, depression, confusion, or overstimulation. Repression seems to be our central perceptual defense mechanism. We dissociate from uncomfortable emotional material every day. Nevertheless, these pockets of repressed, compartmentalized ideas may affect our thoughts and beliefs and influence our decisions and our actions. What is left out (excluded from conscious awareness) can be far more significant to survival than what appears in consciousness.[15]

Dr. Wilson Bryan Key, best-selling author and early researcher in communication techniques, wrote that the intention of subliminal advertising is to stimulate the most basic repressed desires and fears that hide in our subconscious. Sex sells because it is the material expression of our craving for love, excitement, and connection, but in certain situations, death sells, too, when it taps into our fears and stimulates our self-destructive or violent fantasies.[16]

In national advertisements, certain subliminal words appear most frequently as reinforcement devices for commercial art. Two of these words are "SEX" (the most commonly utilized) and "DIE."[17]

The use of these verbal substimuli has been around for a long time and can be discovered embedded even in currency. Dr. Key revealed the secret of Lincoln's beard. We can find it if we look with relaxed attention at a new and unwrinkled US five-dollar bill. (With the newest pink-tinted bills, it's hard to perceive.) The word "SEX" has been ingeniously embedded in Lincoln's beard, and it was designed at least sixty-five years ago. As far as could be determined, no one outside the US Bureau of Engraving and Printing ever consciously perceived the word. Dr. Key concluded that the "SEX" embedded in the engraving actually increases the money's symbolic value. It relates the currency to sex, often considered the most powerful human drive.[18]

In 2000, during the Bush/Gore American presidential campaign, one of the more public cases of subliminal advertising was exposed. A political television advertisement placed by the National Republican Committee ran over four thousand times, in thirty-three markets nationally, for about two weeks. It had been discovered that when the ad was slowed down slightly, the word "RATS," in large letters, appeared briefly on the screen while a voice-over criticized Vice President Gore's prescription drug plan. Two Democratic senators brought it to the attention of the Federal Trade Commission. It was subsequently pulled off the air.[19]

On May 13 of 2008, before the American presidential candidates were chosen, it was discovered that *Fox 5 News* from New York was flashing up a subliminal image of presidential candidate John McCain and his wife, Cindy, during its TV introduction sequence. The image flashed up too quickly to be recognized consciously, but nevertheless, it was registered by the subconscious. Fox News claimed it was accidental.[20]

Subliminals can be found in the strangest places. In 2003, Blanche Skelton, while feeding her six-month-old baby, heard something strange coming from his crib toy. It made soothing sounds and music for the baby to fall asleep to, with an animated picture of a cartoon-style aquarium on the front. But, in between the white noise of ocean waves, a tiny babyish voice piped up with childish angst and quietly said, "I hate you." She and her husband went back to the Walmart store, and sure enough, all the toys of that type played the same creepy voice. The store was dumbfounded and had no explanation, but finally took all of them off the shelves. It's not known how that subliminal message became embedded in the toy.[21]

Death and self-destructive imagery have been frequent aspects of subliminal content, especially in advertisements for alcoholic beverages. Media professionals have used motivational analysis to discover an addictive drinker's most common vulnerabilities. For example, a researcher at an AA meeting might learn that alcoholics often have nightmares after trying to stop drinking. The researcher asking details about the nightmare images might then include them subliminally in a magazine ad. Many alcohol ads have revealed distorted figures and screaming faces hidden in ice cubes or elsewhere that trigger both the fear of stopping coupled with the stimulation to drink.[22]

Subliminals alert our subconscious mind to our most basic desires and fears without the awareness of our conscious mind so that we buy the product, agree to a policy, or vote for a candidate without adequate self-reflection and careful evaluation.

A four-part documentary film called *Century of the Self* describes how targeting the subconscious took hold in Britain and the United States in the 1920s. Edward Bernays was the American nephew of Sigmund Freud, and is known as the father of public relations. He was instrumental in promoting his uncle's theories about the subconscious fears and desires of the self. He saw that these might be controlled and manipulated on a vast scale for power and profit through advertising. Bernays was very successful in shaping the American mind. He had clients that included presidents, celebrities, large corporations, and many foreign governments.[23]

We are affected subliminally. We are fed information in a variety of ways that convince us to follow a path we might not agree with initially. Information can be deliberately designed to tap into our most urgent desires and our worst fears.

Manipulation of Information

One way to manipulate information is through repetition. Especially in Western culture, we hear and see repeated every day the idea that being thin is always better than being fat. The word "diet" appears on almost half the supermarket products these days. It's still our decision about what to buy, but the prevalence of the word keeps reminding us that diet products are preferable if we want to watch our weight and be healthy and more attractive.

In the early months of 2003, the idea that Iraq was harboring "weapons of mass destruction" was repeated endlessly in media reports all over the world. Many people believed it. It triggered the worst of our basic fears, resulted in a military invasion of Iraq, and plunged us into a lengthy war. The inaccuracy of the statement was revealed too late.

Another way of manipulating information is to send a communication with two different messages, with one overriding the other. Examples of this are various TV ads for pharmaceutical drugs. We see beautifully colored scenes with attractive, smiling people showing how their lives have been positively changed by using a particular pharmaceutical. A few seconds later, while the beautiful images continue, a voice-over warns about the possible side effects, which may include headaches, stomach cramps, blood clots, or suicidal thoughts. The iconic imagery is more powerful and dominant. It is usually received more easily and automatically than the spoken word.

Public speakers, especially political leaders, have a variety of styles, deliveries, and ways of seducing an audience to agree with them. One of the techniques that many of them use involves several steps. First, the speaker will say a number of things that everyone wants to hear and will agree with. Then he will make several statements that are true, facts that the audience will probably accept without disagreement because they are already in a receptive "yes" state. Then, after that, he will ask the audience to support him on some issue or proposal. At some point, the speaker will ask the audience to imagine or visualize what he wants for them. This is a technique directed at activating the right brain and circumventing left-brain thinking.

Another way of getting the audience on your side is to tire the left brain by answering a question with such lengthy detail that the audience gets lost. This is then followed with a emotional personal story that moves the audience (also promoting emotional brain activation) and results in group sympathy, avoiding further clarification on the subject but priming the audience to agree with the speaker.

At his press conference in the spring of 2004, President Bush referred four or five times to his gratefulness for American troops, and sympathy for loved ones who lost brave soldiers in the Iraq War.[24] This evoked understandable compassion (emotional brain activation) in his audience, but also seemed like an attempt to soften or deflect difficult questions about the war.

People in power know how to stimulate our consciousness and manipulate how we think, feel, and act. They know about the different parts of the brain and how to appeal to each one—through a television commercial, a film, a website, a certain kind of music, or a political speech.

Former psychotherapist, advertising agency CEO, and best-selling author Thom Hartmann offered an example from Dick Cheney's speech during the presidential campaign of 2004. Cheney responded to a comment about sensitivity taken out of context from a speech of John Kerry's. Hartmann felt it was a masterful psychological manipulation of all three brains: the neocortex (the thinking brain), the limbic (the emotional brain), and the reptilian (the fight-or-flight survival brain).[25]

"America has been in too many wars for any of our wishes, but not one of them was won by being sensitive," Cheney said, firing first the thinking brain ("too many wars") and then the limbic brain ("for our wishes"). And then he went for the reptilian brain ("but not one of them was won by being sensitive").[26]

Hartmann continued by telling us that the last comment resulted in an instant response of laughter. This is an emotional and involuntary response that's the result of the neocortex thinking it's moving logically in one direction ("too many wars") and then suddenly getting derailed ("but not one of them was won by being sensitive") from that thought.[27]

The "punch line" causes the thinking brain to be momentarily confused and triggers the laughter response that comes involuntarily from the limbic brain. After the punch line, Cheney spoke directly to the reptilian brain, evoking his listeners' most primitive survival instincts by saying, "Those that threaten us and kill innocents around the world do not need to be treated more sensitively, they need to be destroyed." [28]

Cheney was able to stimulate different parts of the thinking and feeling process and provoke everyone's conscious and unconscious fears. Manipulating our three brains is not the technique of a particular political party or group. It is everywhere.

With awareness, we can begin to recognize when and how we shift into the emotions of the limbic brain, the logic of the neocortex (which is not necessarily correct), or the reptilian brain, where various fear forms of survival are activated

.

Desensitization

Desensitization has become more common, especially through film, television, and the Internet. It happens when we become accustomed to disturbing ideas, images, or situations over time. We distance ourselves emotionally from uncomfortable experiences that at first are unacceptable but become less so as we get used to being exposed to them. For example, we become inured to seeing dead bodies as brutalized cadavers in autopsies on popular American TV crime programs like *NCIS*, *Criminal Minds*, and others. We see women objectified at an earlier age, as lipsticked five-year-olds are idolized and sexualized. The death of two people or ten is just another unfortunate happening on the ten o' clock news. We expect it these days and respond only if a thousand people drown or if one famous person is involved in a sensational, tragic event. The proliferation of child sexual abuse and pedophilia involving respected authority figures causes us consternation and confusion, but after a hundred reports, it also dampens our shock.

People in the media defend their responsibility to report the horrible truth of life and what is going on in the world. However, the disturbing images that we are exposed to, when repeated over a period of time, may be changing how we view disturbing events, especially having to do with violence. How does desensitization to negative ideas and images affect us over time?

Steven Johnson, author of *Everything Bad is Good for You*, writes that video games exercise minds in powerful new ways. They promote hand-eye coordination and also pose new cognitive challenges that encourage us to think in more complex ways. [29] That may be true, but it's also important to ask, *what else is happening at the same time?*

At the University of Aachen in Germany, Klaus Mathiak conducted a small research study to discover what happens in players' brains as they encounter violent situations while playing video games. His volunteers were thirteen men, aged eighteen to twenty-six, who were proficient at a game that required them to navigate a complicated bunker, find and kill terrorists, and try to rescue hostages. As they played, an MRI scan recorded changing brain activity. Mathiak found that as violence became more imminent, the cognitive parts of the brain became more active. And during a fight, emotional parts of the brain, such as the amygdala, were shut down. He suggests that video games are a "training for the brain to react with this pattern." Other researchers speculate that playing violent video games regularly would strengthen these circuits in the brain and, faced with a real-life situation, someone might be more primed for aggression.[30] There are many arguments for and against this position, and there is no definitive answer.

With repeated exposure to disturbing images, ideas, and events—whether in a video game, TV program, film, or on the Internet—we tend to dissociate emotionally from what we see. Nonetheless, our minds are still registering these disturbing scenarios.

All the above forms of general mind manipulation are operating every day. Whether we realize it or not, we are affected by them. They seep into our consciousness and move us further away from discernment and from using our minds for critical thinking.

THREE

MIND INTRUSION

How often, or on what system, the Thought Police plugged in on any individual wire was guesswork. It was even conceivable that they watched everybody all the time. But at any rate they could plug in your wire whenever they wanted to.

—George Orwell

In December 2011, it was reported in *Science* magazine that researchers are progressing in their efforts to download information into our brains like the characters in the *Matrix* trilogy. In these films, the main characters become superpowerful just from being plugged into a computer program that teaches them new skills.[1]

Scientists at Boston University and elsewhere call this process Decoded Neurofeedback, or DecNef. They have been studying how a functional magnetic resonance machine (FMRI) can "induce" knowledge in someone through his or her visual cortex by sending signals that change the brain activity pattern. The person does not even have to be awake to receive the information. The researchers believe that in the future, learning a new skill might involve nothing more than sitting in front of a computer screen and waiting for it to "upload."[2]

This and other technological body engineering is especially promoted by an international intellectual and cultural movement called transhumanism. The transhumanist movement believes that through technological manipulations, we can make life easier and more convenient, erase unwanted memories, expand our intelligence, activate our strength and mental powers, reproduce ourselves through cloning, prolong life indefinitely, and even transcend death. The name "transhumanism" was coined in the 1920s by British biologist Julian Huxley, brother of *Brave New World* author Aldous Huxley. He hoped that the term would represent a new age of enlightenment and possibilities for human nature. His ideas were ignored until recently.[3]

In late 2007, at a conference at company headquarters, a Yahoo executive talked about the current flawed system of the human brain. He said that we need computer chips monitoring our neural networks because evolution is not going to do this for us, and so our brains need to be rewired through technology.[4]

At the same conference, a biotechnician presented a step-by-step proposal for transferring human consciousness onto a computer. Later, a programmer discussed "The Future of the Singularity," a time in the not-too-distant future when humans and machines will be one.[5]

Some years before, in 2003, award-winning inventor, scientist, and engineer Ray Kurzweil wrote *The Singularity Is Near*. The Singularity, wrote Kurzweil, is "a future period during which the pace of technological change will be so rapid, its impact so deep, that human life will be irreversibly transformed."[6]

Transhumanists see the body as a machine, the brain as a computer, and all the information that makes us who we are—our knowledge, memories, habits, and secrets—as data encoded in the brain.

Kurzweil repeats many of the same optimistic scenarios popular among transhumanists: Technology will one day free the world. He forecasts that by the end of the 2030s, we will augment our thinking capacity with cybernetic implants. An artificial general intelligence, thousands of times smarter than the entire human race, will emerge by the 2040s.

Kurzweil perceives some dangers to technological acceleration. He states that just as the Singularity could go very well, it could also go very badly. Nanotechnology gone awry could disassemble everything on Earth, reducing the world to "grey goo." Machines empowered by artificial intelligence might seize control of the world's arms and turn them against humans. A cyborg army might decide to wipe out the human race. As Kurzweil's ideas—both the optimistic and the cautious ones—gain greater audience, doomsday scenarios have been spreading among some transhumanist circles.[7]

Each radical invention that changes the world forever, like the printing press, the telephone, or the airplane, evokes questions in the midst of all the excitement. How will this new invention be put into practice? How will the experience change how we think, who we are, and how we live? Who will have the authority to utilize this process in the best way possible for humanity? What are the potential benefits and dangers of this technology? We must ask these questions now and frequently because the speed with which technology is proceeding is unparalleled in human history. Yesterday's science fiction is today's science fact.

While the idea of downloading information directly into our brains so that we can play the piano or master geometry within a few sessions is exciting, we must always ask, what else is happening at the same time with regard to this subject?

What's happening in the area of brain/computer technology is microchipping, one of the most potentially dangerous mind intrusion processes confronting us today. Microchipping goes beyond the general forms of societal conditioning already mentioned and increasingly involves intrusion into our private lives and minds. It reflects an accelerating trend toward more information-gathering on individuals by business, corporate, medical, and government/military agencies, especially in the name of securing our safety. We need to look at it with eyes wide open. I will present an abbreviated discussion of the subject.

Radio frequency identification (RFID) is a microchip technology that uses tiny data-storing computer chips or tags that are smaller than a grain of sand to track items at a distance. RFID tags have been hidden in the packaging of Gillette razor products and in many other products, such as clothing, shoes, or bags that you might buy at a local Walmart, Target, or Tesco.[8]

Each tiny chip is hooked up to an antenna that picks up electromagnetic energy beamed at it from a reader device at a central source. When it picks up the energy, the tag sends back its unique identification number to the reader device, allowing the item to be remotely identified. The tags are tracked by scanners installed at checkpoints, such as office doors or warehouse loading docks. The systems are commonly used in highway tollbooths. Libraries use them for inventory procedures and tracking books. United States passports have been equipped with RFIDs since 2006. Some credit card companies have been using RFID tags for some time.[9]

Privacy Concerns

The main privacy concern regarding RFIDs is that the owner of an item is not necessarily aware of the presence of an RFID tag. The tag can be read at a distance without the knowledge of the person, and so it becomes possible to gather sensitive data about an individual without consent.

The use of RFID technology has engendered considerable controversy, and even product boycotts, by consumer privacy advocates. In 2003, there was a successful boycott against Italian clothing manufacturer Benetton. The resulting worldwide opposition forced the company to cancel plans to sew RFID tags into millions of women's garments.[10] However, as of this writing, Macy's, Inc. plans to be among the first retailers to implement RFID tags in their shoes and clothing on a broad national scale. One of the people who is asking important questions about this proposal is Dr. Katherine Albrecht.[11] She is the founder and director of CASPIAN (Consumers Against Supermarket Privacy Invasion and Numbering), and is a consumer privacy expert and prominent critic of the invasive technology.[12] Albrecht and Liz McIntyre co-authored a book titled *Spychips* that introduced the subject in 2005.[13]

During that same year, a grade school in Sutter County, California, required students to wear IDs around their necks containing chips to help monitor attendance. The move prompted privacy complaints from parents, and the school eventually stopped using the technology.[14] As of this writing, two schools in San Antonio, Texas have approved a plan to implant RFID-chip-laden tags into student ID cards for monitoring purposes. Parents and students are once again protesting.[15]

Security Concerns

A primary security concern is the illicit tracking of RFID tags. Tags that are world readable pose a risk to both personal location privacy and corporate/military security. If a tagged item is paid for by a credit card, then it would be possible to indirectly deduce the identity of the purchaser by reading the globally unique ID of that item (contained in the RFID tag). Hacking into credit cards with RFIDs is becoming easier and more sophisticated, and presents clear dangers to unsuspecting card owners.[16]

Health Concerns

RFID supporters envision a world where RFID reader devices are everywhere: in stores, in floors, in doorways, on airplanes—even in the refrigerators and medicine cabinets in homes. In such a world, we would be continually bombarded with electromagnetic energy. Researchers do not know the long-term health effects of chronic exposure to the energy emitted by these reader devices.

Microchips have been implanted in animals for identification and tracking for over ten years. In 2005, the US Food and Drug Administration approved implanting microchips in humans. The manufacturer, VeriChip, said it would save lives, letting doctors scan the tiny transponders to access patients' medical records almost instantly. The FDA found "reasonable assurance" the device was safe, and a subagency even called it one of 2005's top "innovative technologies." But neither the company nor the regulators publicly mentioned that a series of veterinary and toxicology studies stated that chip implants had "induced" malignant tumors in some lab mice and rats. "The transponders were the cause of the tumors," said Keith Johnson, a retired toxicologic pathologist, explaining in a phone interview the findings of a 1996 study he led at the Dow Chemical Company in Midland, Michigan.[17]

In September of 2007, a new report by CASPIAN showed a causal link between implanted radio frequency (RFID) microchip transponders and cancer in laboratory rodents and dogs.[18]

Leading cancer specialists like Dr. Robert Benezra, director of the Cancer Biology and Genetics Program at Memorial Sloan-Kettering Cancer Center in New York, reviewed the research and, while cautioning that animal test results do not necessarily apply to humans, said the findings were definitely cause for concern. He said he would not allow family members to receive implants, and urged further research before the glass-encased transponders were widely implanted in people.[19]

Mind-Control Concerns

The following contains some information reported in 1999 by Dr. Rauni-Leena Luukanen-Kilde, former chief medical officer of Northern Finland. She wrote that implanted human beings can be followed anywhere. Their brain functions can then be remotely monitored by supercomputers and even altered through the changing of frequencies. Prisoners, soldiers, mental patients, handicapped children, deaf and blind people, and the elderly have been used as subjects in secret experiments, often without their consent.[20]

Every thought, reaction, and hearing and visual observation causes a certain neurological potential, with spikes and patterns in the brain and in electromagnetic fields, which can now be decoded into thoughts, pictures, and voices. Electromagnetic stimulation can therefore change a person's brain waves and affect muscular activity and cause painful muscular cramps.[21]

The US National Security Agency's electronic surveillance system can simultaneously follow and handle millions of people. Each of us has a unique bioelectrical resonance frequency in the brain, just as we have unique fingerprints. With electromagnetic frequency (EMF) brain stimulation fully coded, pulsating electromagnetic signals can be sent to the brain, causing the desired voice and visual effects to be experienced by the person. This is a form of electronic warfare. US astronauts were implanted before they were sent into space so their thoughts could be followed and all their emotions could be registered twenty-four hours a day.[22]

The mass media have not reported that an implanted person's privacy vanishes for the rest of his or her life. He or she can be manipulated in many ways. Using different frequencies, the secret controller of this equipment can even change a person's emotional life. He or she can be made aggressive or lethargic. Sexuality can be artificially influenced. Thought signals and subconscious thinking can be read, dreams affected and even induced, all without the knowledge or consent of the implanted person.[23]

In 2006, Wisconsin and North Dakota enacted the first legislation banning human chip implantation without consent. In 2007, then California Governor Schwarzenegger signed a bill making it illegal to require citizens to accept RFID implants. This means that California employers cannot compel anyone to have an RFID device implanted under his or her skin as a condition of receiving something—such as a paycheck or government benefits.[24]

As of this writing, Georgia and Virginia have passed similar bills.[25] It is likely that as people become more informed, more states will ban implanted microchipping in humans without permission.

As the world becomes more techno happy with promises of greater freedom, protection, and convenience in everyday living, more people will *want* to be microchipped. It will be cool. Instead of standing on an endless line at the airport, you can simply wave your microchipped hand with your ID information and get through quickly.

While most people in this world are well-meaning and want the best for humanity, others will advance and promote a situation that renders them more powerful, especially one that includes the technological ability to control large groups of people through their minds. Let's not be seduced by the enticing technology that is slowly robotizing humanity. Please say no to human subdermal microchipping. It is the beginning step toward global mind intrusion and manipulation. Examine everything carefully, and at the same time, please open your eyes to the magnificent and sometimes unimaginable powers of the natural human mind.

FOUR

DEGREES OF MIND DISSOCIATION

The intuitive mind is a sacred gift and the rational mind is its servant. We have created a society that honors the servant and has forgotten the gift.

—Albert Einstein

Societal mind conditioning becomes more problematic when it triggers our personal anxieties and fears.

It's a special challenge today to experience our lives with curiosity and passion and to deal with our emotions—especially our fears—with courage and action. This doesn't mean that we must be aware of what and how and why every minute. Sometimes we need to get lost in our sadness. Sometimes fear or anger can be energizing. We don't need to psychoanalyze everything we do. But we can develop a mindful awareness so that society does not manipulate our passions and amplify our fears. We live in a culture that promotes mind dissociation and has a stake in keeping our subliminal fears activated by affecting our brain functioning.

Is it possible to go to work, see a movie, laugh with friends, and go through the pleasures and heartaches of life while, at the same time, part of our minds are being affected by other things without our conscious awareness? Does the brain contain information not only from our own past, but also from our ancestors through genetic inheritance? Can we take on other people's fears and not know it? Can we be affected by experiences and information from sources that we can't always define?

It's quite possible. To quote comedian George Carlin, "They say only ten percent of the brain's function is known. Apparently, the function of the remaining ninety percent is to keep us from discovering its function."[1] According to Princeton neuroscientist Dr. Sam Wang, we know a lot more now about the brain, and the popular idea that we use only 10 percent of our brain's capacity isn't really accurate. He says that neurons are firing all the time in many parts of the brain. This neuronal thought activity is sometimes regulated and ordered, and sometimes it's chaotic.[2] We will see in a later chapter that sometimes an instantaneous ordering happens in a moment of danger when we have to think and act quickly. Ordering is also reflected in an insight we have after a long period of creative struggling. So what blocks us from integrating our mind activity more efficiently? One of the things that may happen is dissociation, a necessary function that becomes a liability under certain circumstances.

Natural Temporary Mind Dissociation

When we dissociate, a part of our mind takes a vacation from our conscious self. This is a natural ability. In its mildest form, it happens when we're reading a book and we suddenly realize that we've been on the same paragraph for five minutes. Our minds went somewhere else in the middle of reading.

We can blank out in the middle of a conversation with someone. We seem like we're listening. We even murmur an "uh-huh" now and then, but we don't remember much of what the person said.

Sometimes the distraction is more elaborate. We're washing the dishes, and we begin to daydream about our vacation. We imagine going hiking and wearing new boots. We think of the snow on the mountain—then the telephone rings. We're suddenly back again and realize we've finished washing all the dishes.

We can dissociate from the pain of a swollen ankle until after walking a marathon or playing a game of racquetball.

We can get so involved in a movie that we cry, laugh, or become frightened or angry because our mind dissociates from our normal reality and moves into the fantasy of the story.

Most of us are familiar with these temporary withdrawals from the immediate present.

Mind Dissociation for Past Painful Events

With upsetting events, especially at an early age, we withdraw more completely from the experiences. We try to forget by tucking them away somewhere deep in our memory banks.

Gina, one of my clients, agreed to help her friend out with her son's fourth birthday party. Everything was going well, and then the entertainer arrived. He was a tall young man dressed in a colorful clown costume. His face was painted white, and he was wearing a big red nose. The kids loved him. But Gina got sick to her stomach and left soon after. In our next therapy session, she told me how embarrassed she was about her strong reaction.

"I really don't like clowns. I don't think they're funny. I know it's stupid, but there it is."

I asked her to focus on the "sick to her stomach" feeling and tell me when she had experienced that before. She went through a few memories, and then later in the session, she remembered that when she was about three years old, one of her uncles appeared suddenly from behind the couch in a clown mask. She was scared and confused. After she realized it was her uncle, she calmed down, but underneath she was still upset. Here was a person she really liked who suddenly became somebody who scared the hell out of her. The party situation that Gina encountered as an adult triggered the fearful reaction. She is not alone. There are many adults who are afraid of clowns. There are several websites online that welcome anyone who "hates clowns."

Early traumatic memories often remain in our minds more like scattered sensations rather than clearly remembered events. When you're three, you don't have the mental ability to evaluate the situation. You're frightened, and the moment gets stuck in your mind—and especially in your body—as a dark frozen experience that you want to forget. You dissociate from the event and the uncomfortable feelings connected to it.

Mind dissociation is a natural process of moving on by disconnecting from past pain. We all have painful memories that lie in compartments in our brains. We separate many of them from our conscious awareness so that we can survive.

So why should we want to get in touch with these pieces of our emotional history? Isn't life hard enough without uncovering shadow memories we want to forget? It is, but many of these pieces affect us anyway. They come to the surface in the form of uncomfortable emotions, subtle sadness, unusual fatigue, or general apprehension. And sometimes, as with Gina, external events trigger emotional responses that surprise us with their potency.

Pathological Dissociation

In its most extreme form, dissociation results in what clinical psychologists now call dissociative identity disorder, or DID. Often it results from childhood trauma, especially sexual abuse. A child is sexually exploited by an adult, usually a family member. Sometimes these secret actions include threats of violence or death if the child reveals to others what is happening. The drive to be loved and to feel safe, and the fear of separation and death, is very strong. In order to escape, the mind splits into two or more personalities. In effect, the child thinks, *This is not happening to me. It's happening to someone else.* As time passes, he or she creates other personalities to deal with the torture. These alternate identities may appear publicly and act in opposition to the predominant personality. They can be jarring to other people and confusing to the victim, who may not even recall switching from one personality to another. There might be a shy adult personality that exists alongside an angry teenager. Some internal or external circumstance can trigger the appearance of one personality or another. Sometimes, as the child gets older, this compartmentalization breaks down. The person may feel that something is terribly wrong. He or she may not be able to account for hours of missing time, or may just feel crazy.

The most well-known study of DID was the case history called "The Three Faces of Eve," which was made into a film in 1957.[3] This condition was also explored in the book *Sybil*, written by Flora Rheta Schreiber,[4] with whom I shared an office many years ago. I remember that she was continually impressed with "Sybil"'s courage and refusal to be imprisoned by her illness. Eventually, Sybil was able to function as an art teacher and prolific painter in Lexington, Kentucky, until she died in 1998.

There continues to be controversy in the psychiatric field regarding the validity of Sybil's diagnosis as a true multiple personality. We will probably never know the complete story. During those early years, my strong impression was that Dr. Schreiber genuinely believed that Sybil's traumatic experiences and complicated life were real.

Extreme and Deliberate Mind Dissociation

The most extreme and deliberate mind dissociation involves what is called trauma-based mind control. This is when our two basic drives—the craving for unconditional love, sexual expression, merging, and fulfillment; and the fear of pain, abandonment, separation, and death—are systematically used against us in the most drastic ways imaginable. The intention is to split the brain through deliberately induced trauma repeatedly so that the mind fragments into pieces, creating separate identities. These alternate personalities can then be used for specific purposes like sexual exploitation, espionage work, assassination training, or suicide missions. This can take place anywhere from secret government/military operations to cults that masquerade as religious or spiritual groups. The person takes part in prescribed acts usually without having any conscious memory of the experiences.[5]

A form of early trauma-based mind control and brain splitting was dramatically illustrated in the 1971 film *A Clockwork Orange*. The person is strapped to a chair, and his eyes are forced open with tape. He is fed conflicting visual images to both eyes simultaneously, which affect each brain hemisphere differently. High-speed films of terrifying scenes bombard one hemisphere, while the other one is presented with pleasurable, loving, and comforting settings. One side of the brain is desperately trying to dissociate from the fearful images, while the other part is trying to connect to the safe scenarios. The person feels insane, and the mind splits into two personalities. The predominant or front personality may believe that he or she is a moral, upstanding citizen while the split-off personality can be triggered to commit a violent act.[6]

"Manchurian Candidate" has become the popular label for a mind-controlled assassin ever since it was introduced in the 1962 film of the same name. Since then we have learned that deliberately dividing the brain into separate, individually working compartments can be accomplished with drugs. One side of the brain, let's say the right hemisphere, is injected with a substance that numbs it and shuts it down, making it impossible to communicate with the other side, which is awake. Torture, sometimes in the form of electric shocks, is then introduced to split the mind even further. The left hemisphere is then trained to speak a different language or memorize extensive passages of material without the consciousness of the other part of the brain. These dormant abilities can then be activated with a particular trigger: a word, a movement of the hand, or a sound.[7]

This is similar to what happens in public stage hypnosis when an audience member is put into a hypnotic trance, given an order, and then snapped out of the trance. The person doesn't remember what happened just minutes before. But upon command, and to their surprise, they begin to bray like a donkey, or find themselves making a speech about grapefruits. However, split-brain programming is much more severe and permanent than any public stage hypnosis. And contrary to popular belief, with extensive trauma-based mind control, it is possible to commit acts that on a conscious level, the predominant or conscious personality would never imagine doing.

Many people believe that Robert F. Kennedy's murderer, Sirhan Sirhan, was a mind-controlled assassin. When questioned by the public defender assigned to him, Sirhan said, "I don't remember much about the shooting, sir. Did I do it?" He said he felt like a "puppet" who was mind controlled. Sirhan's voice during initial interviews with psychologists was analyzed using a psychological stress evaluator. Charles McQuiston, a former high-ranking US intelligence officer, stated that he was "convinced that Sirhan wasn't aware of what he was doing. He was in a hypnotic trance when he pulled the trigger." Other experts, including Dr. Herbert Spiegel, a renowned medical hypnotist, agreed.[8]

It is unfortunate that certain groups of people with special intelligence, secret knowledge, ruling power, monetary means, and advanced technology use their status to experiment with large numbers of people.

Anything that is beneficial for human beings, any revelation, any new scientific discovery, can be exploited and used for negative purposes, from hypnosis to drugs to religion to nuclear power. What follows are just a few of the ways people have been experimented on without their permission and without full knowledge of the circumstances.

Some US Human Experimentation

1. 1932–1972, The Tuskegee Syphilis Study: For forty years, the US Public Health Service conducted an experiment on 399 black men in the late stages of syphilis. They were never told of their illness, were denied treatment, and instead were used as human guinea pigs in order to follow the progression and symptoms of the disease. They all subsequently died of syphilis. Their families were never told that they could have been

treated.[9]

2. 1945–1960s: Several secret US government projects included Project CHATTER (established in 1947), and Project BLUEBIRD (established in 1950), which was later renamed Project ARTICHOKE in 1951. Their purpose was to study mind control, interrogation procedures, behavior modification, and related topics. Some of these experiments used chemical-hypnotic techniques on humans, and not always with their permission.[10] Researchers involved with some of these studies were Nazi scientists. In 1945, after World War II, Project PAPERCLIP was initiated. The US State Department, Army Intelligence, and the CIA recruited Nazi scientists and offered them immunity and secret identities in exchange for work on top secret projects, including experiments with mind manipulation, in the United States.[11]

3. 1953, The CIA-initiated Project MKULTRA: This was a research program that began in the early 1950s, and continued at least through the late 1960s. Six of the subprojects involved testing on human beings. The published evidence indicates that MKULTRA used many types of drugs, as well as other methods, to manipulate individual mental states and to alter brain function.[12] On the Senate floor in 1977, Senator Ted Kennedy said:

> The deputy director of the CIA revealed that over thirty universities and institutions were involved in an "extensive testing and experimentation" program which included covert drug tests on unwitting citizens "at all social levels, high and low, native Americans and foreign." Several of these tests involved the administration of LSD to "unwitting subjects in social situations." At least one death, that of Dr. Frank Olson, resulted from these activities.[13]

To this day, most specific information regarding Project MKULTRA remains highly classified.

4. 1953–1966: Operation Midnight Climax was a subproject of MKULTRA. It consisted of a web of CIA-run safe houses in San Francisco, Marin, and New York. It was established in order to study the effects of LSD

on nonconsenting individuals. Prostitutes on the CIA payroll were instructed to lure clients back to the safe houses, where they were surreptitiously plied with a wide range of substances, including LSD, and monitored behind one-way glass. Several significant operational techniques were developed in this theater, including extensive research into sexual blackmail, surveillance technology, and the possible use of mind-altering drugs in field operations.[14]

5. 1965: The CIA and the Department of Defense continued the research of MKULTRA, now renamed Project MKSEARCH. This program experimented with the manipulation of human behavior through the use of various mind-altering drugs. The intention was to produce a perfect truth drug for use in interrogation, and generally to explore any other possibilities of mind control.[15]

6. 1994: Senator John D. Rockefeller issued a report revealing that for at least fifty years, the Department of Defense had used hundreds of thousands of military personnel in human experiments and for intentional exposure to dangerous substances. Materials included mustard and nerve gas, ionizing radiation, psychochemicals, hallucinogens, and drugs that were used during the Gulf War.[16]

Human experimentation is not new, and as technology advances, we must continue to be diligent and alert to the various ways mind intrusion and mind manipulation continue to be used with or without our consent.

Degrees of Mind Dissociation and Fragmentation

The process of mind dissociation has different forms. We can retreat from our immediate conscious self into a temporary distraction. We can repress and forget painful memories so that we can move on with our lives. We can experience such severe trauma early in life that the dissociation can become pathological and fragment our consciousness into different personalities. We can also be so overwhelmed with the troubles of the world that we develop a habit of dissociating from them. And in the worst possible scenario, we can be deliberately programmed to split into various personalities through psychological torture, drugs, and specialized brain technology.

I believe that most of us are experiencing various degrees of mind dissociation. It is not that we are mentally unstable, have histories of abuse, or suffer deliberate mind-control programming, but rather that we have fragmented parts in our consciousness. This fragmentation prevents us from using all of our mental and emotional faculties in an integrated way. Some of these fragments may be hidden from our awareness.

However, these negative emotional pieces affect us, more so now than ever before. With crises occurring more frequently and threats of instability in every corner, there is a collective experience of apprehension accumulating below the surface of our awareness.

Speeding through life, repressing and escaping from fear by looking for quick fixes, prevents us from facing, orchestrating, and integrating our fragmented selves so that we can better deal with the collective shadows of society. I believe that these dissociated parts formed through a genetic history of trauma over thousands of years have something to do with perpetuating fear, conflict, and violence in the world.

It's time to change that history.

FIVE

FEAR

One day at a time, we can leave our fears behind.
One day at a time, we can stare our hopes in the eye.
One day at a time we can live.

—Yusuf Islam

We begin our shift into self-awareness by looking at the different aspects of fear and how we deal with them. If we live near a troubled area of the world, our confrontation with fear is frequent, rather direct, and often explosive. However, most of us are enveloped in a cobweb of fear no matter where we live. This doesn't mean we're afraid to go out of the house or that we have panic attacks. It doesn't mean that we don't enjoy our work, our families, our partners, and our surroundings, but rather that some part of us feels more anxious and less safe than we did ten years ago.

Fear is an experience of anxiety or agitation about an impending real or imagined danger that may have to do with, among other things, financial loss and poverty, physical injury or pain, abandonment or isolation, betrayal, the wrath of God or some authority figure, or exposure of the self in some deep, humiliating way.

On a personal level, some fears may be obvious and direct, like being afraid of an abusive husband. Others may be more subtle, like anxieties underlying food addiction. And others may be quite hidden, like vague early memories of humiliation. Fear can be positive and motivate us into action—we study relentlessly to pass an exam, or exercise vigorously to lose weight. We change our lifestyle because of a health scare or drive more carefully after a near-fatal accident. But some subliminal fears hang out in compartmentalized places in our minds, just below the surface of our awareness. They may appear in the form of shifting emotions, fatigue, a feeling that something's just not right, or a general apprehension about the future.

When the body reacts with fear to an immediate danger, we know it as the fight-or-flight survival response. Our senses become sharpened, our strength is mobilized, and our brains help us decide what to do quickly. When we experience repeated childhood trauma, then this mechanism doesn't work as effectively. In order to survive, we try to dissociate from the negative experiences in various ways. Among other things, we place our attention somewhere else, or we repress our emotions. We may also develop undercover feelings of powerlessness that surface from time to time and cause us to feel nervous or depressed.

Fear permeates our personal and collective lives every day. In its most familiar form, we feel it as anxiety or worry. In its most dramatic form, it can result in panic or explosive anger. It can affect us by manifesting in accidents or illnesses that hinder our actions and confuse our minds.

In addition to our personal concerns, we are affected by the collective anxieties of the world. We question whether the stock market will plummet with more global instability. We worry about the permanence of health benefits. We wonder how safe we are from earthquakes or mass flooding. The more chaotic the world becomes, the more difficult it is to keep our balance.

Some of the Ways We Deal with Fear

Repression of fear can transmute into physical symptoms. Some digestive problems have their origin in childhood, when fear and anxiety were common accompaniments to dinner.

We may be so reluctant to look at some fear that we unconsciously choose another one to focus on instead. Let's say we impulsively did or said something hurtful to a friend. We feel guilty, but we're reluctant to examine what we did or take some action about it. Subconsciously, to divert our attention from the situation, we might develop a fear about having a physical illness. This temporary hypochondria allows us to experience some self-punishment because we feel guilty about how we acted with our friend. It also allows us to take some direct action about our health concern, which is better than doing nothing at all. We can see a doctor, take medication, get sympathy.

Sometimes we know we should take some action to release and resolve the fear, but we can't decide what to do. Every possible choice seems bad or wrong. We suffer the agony of indecision, which makes us even more anxious. Procrastination is often a surface expression propelled by fear.

And so is impatience. Here we feel as if time is running out. We want something to happen outside of ourselves so that the situation will change and we can relax. Or we want to take some action, any action, to relieve the anxiety. But impatience may force us into a hasty decision that doesn't solve the problem.

Sometimes we create different personalities or roles to cover up our fears. We can become bossy or controlling with other people because underneath we may be terrified of what might happen if we lose control of anything. Or we may become passive and submissive so as not to give anyone any reason to confront us with anything that triggers our anxiety. We can develop habits that safeguard us from feeling some unexplored fear. We watch TV or surf the Internet for hours, or use smoking, food, or drugs to escape from specific or generalized anxiety.

Unconscious fears can direct our behavior and affect our choices. A woman might want a serious relationship, but her unexplored fear of commitment may lead her to be attracted to men who, for a variety of reasons, are unsuitable or unavailable.

Fear can erupt in anger and violence when our physical or emotional lives seem threatened. Some relationship battles, even when love exists, can go on forever, with both parties taking turns bashing each other with various forms of psychological or even physical abuse. The anger directed at each other might be a temporary relief because at least anger gets the energy moving and out. But without honest examination, we create scenarios—consciously or unconsciously—that doom us to repeated failure.

When the anger is turned inward against ourselves, it can be unrelenting—punishing us for our weakness and inability to handle our emotions.

Some of us try to avoid deeper fears by purposely placing ourselves directly into challenging situations like vigorous sports, daring business transactions, or dangerous sexual encounters. But the bravery may be short-lived and relegated to that one activity unless the experience also helps us face and transform our internal fears as well.

Some of us like to scare ourselves by watching horror movies in a theater with others in a socially acceptable way. Fear puts us on the edge of our seats and can be exhilarating because it sharpens our senses and put us into a state of high-activated awareness. Perhaps it triggers the experience of a life-or-death choice programmed into our DNA that results in an immediate emotional response even though we feel generally safe in a movie theater.

We can also avoid looking at our personal fears by projecting them onto the world. "Everything would be fine if we only got rid of the ___ who are ruining this country." "All cops and lawyers are either corrupt, inept, or both." It's an understandable response to deal with fear by directing it at an outside group. But most generalizations become unproductive after a period of time and result in making us feel even more victimized, angry, and fearful.

The Physiological Expressions of Fear

Fear is usually felt in the gut, from the lower abdominal area to the navel. Sometimes we experience it as a kind of panic or hollow feeling in the chest. At other times, we may also feel it as a pressure or pounding in our heads.

When we are frightened, the amygdala, a structure in the midbrain, releases adrenaline into the body to alert us and to help us survive. A neurotransmitter from the amygdala brings the fear-filled information to the thinking part of the brain, where we try to make a logical decision about what to do. In a simple example, the choice may be obvious: "I'm taking a cab home because it's late, I'm alone, I'm anxious, I don't know where the subway is, and this creepy man seems to be following me."

When a fear becomes overwhelming, it means that there is an overabundance of adrenaline, which travels not only to the neocortex but also to many other parts of the brain. Emotional responses are released. Negative thoughts and body reactions begin to intrude and fight the logical brain. This happens especially when the current situation triggers traumatic emotional memories that have been incompletely processed in the brain. We don't always experience them as memories, but more like isolated sensory images or bodily sensations.[1]

We try to choose some reasonable way to deal with it. But when the fear is overpowering, the adrenaline—which flows into many areas in the brain—can result in heart palpitations, rubbery knees, and also fainting. The greater the chronic fear, the further removed we are from clearly evaluating the actual situation. We are no longer in the present moment and thinking about the things that might go wrong, but predicting the future and believing that something terrible will happen. We react as if there is inevitable danger with no way out.

Chronic fear traps us into assuming that there is no exit and no choice. This usually happens because we're reactivating our physiological fear memory from childhood, when we had little or no choice about what to do.

We always have choices, and there is always an exit from the terror, some way in which we can change the impact and effect of the emotion. With patience, we can unravel the constellation of memories that get threaded together, and view them with the perception of an adult instead of with the emotions of a child. In time, we can release the traumatic incidents from the past and view them as observers of our histories rather than as victims living with an immediate and continuing threat.

Mind Pattern

We needn't have experienced child abuse to have undercover fears that prevent us from living more fully. Most of us have been traumatized in one way or another. When these difficult early events are not acknowledged, they take residence in our psyches and create problems. Just remembering them is not enough. We also need to release the mind pattern that was formed with the fear. A mind pattern is a decision usually made in childhood out of choice or absolute necessity. It is not always a conscious one, but the mind pattern persists somewhere as an attitude, a fear, an anxiety, an unconscious reaction. For example, suppose we grew up with an alcoholic father who would change often from being in a good mood, funny, and involved, to being depressed, sullen, and disconnected. We need to understand the effect that those unexpected shifts of mood had on us, and especially the mind pattern that we used to deal with those situations. We may develop a variety of attitudes, from never expecting consistency from anyone, to repressing anger at most male figures.

When we look closely at the mind pattern of any persistent fear, there is usually some negative belief about ourselves operating.

According to national surveys, fear of public speaking ranks among Americans' top dreads, surpassing fear of illness, fear of flying, fear of terrorism, and often the fear of death itself.[2] This common fear can have thoughts connected to it like, *I'll lose respect if I don't do well. My identity will be threatened, and that will be publicly humiliating.* It's not always possible to be reasonable and think, *Whatever happens, it's not going to destroy me or ruin my reputation forever.* It's probably such a common fear because most of us have had experiences very early on about speaking in public in school situations. The younger we are when we experience anxiety about public speaking, the more likely it is that the negative emotion is stored in our bodies. When we speak publicly as adults, we trigger the physiological sensations we had as children before we could use logic to counteract the fear.

There's always some reason why we become frightened, some situation in our histories that our minds decided was threatening. It may have been one or more childhood incidents, or it may have been something dramatic that happened to us just last year.

Persistent Fear

Each persistent fear, no matter how slight, can be thought of as a habituated response to an event. It's as if our brains create a neurological pathway of fear that gets stronger with each incident that is similar to the original one. What may begin as a realistic fear becomes wedded to a series of memories that alter our perceptions. For example, in childhood, watching abusive fights between parents becomes etched in our minds with each repeated scene and may create anxiety that colors our own future relationships. If a sibling is consistently thought of as smarter, more attractive, or more successful than we are, our fear of never measuring up to anyone may follow us into adulthood.

Some experiences might not seem very abusive, like teasing from an older sibling. But they can collect and remain in our consciousness and result in sensitivity to judgments from other people later in life.

What makes a memory traumatic is not necessarily what actually happened, but the meaning that the event had for the individual. For one person, teasing by an older brother may be experienced as proof of his love and may result in building strength of character for that person. For another, it may feel as though the brother doesn't respect or care about him and create lifelong feelings of inadequacy.

Unless you are living in an active war zone, persistent fear is an idea, not a reality. It has, at its base, a feeling of powerlessness over some circumstance that we experience as threatening or dangerous. We can't always stop something from scaring us, but we can have some control over how we react to that fear and what we do with it.

Other People's Fear

We may have spent years in early childhood accumulating someone else's fears and anxieties without realizing it. I worked with a man who came from a caring family. Ben's childhood was uneventful, with the usual struggles of adolescence and what he called "normal neurotic anxiety" about life, love, and independence. But as therapy progressed, Ben also realized that an uncomfortable feeling that kept reappearing from time to time to haunt him was related to his parents' early lives. They had both been Holocaust survivors who chose never to speak about their experiences to anyone. Ben realized that throughout his childhood, and even as an adult, he had been affected by his parents' unexpressed feelings and tragic circumstances. He was finally able to speak to them about it, and communication began that brought some relief to both sides.

Another client of mine knew that during his early childhood, his mother had suffered from emotional illness. At first Ted was told that, "Mama is going to visit Grandma for a few weeks." As he got older, it became more obvious that she was going to the hospital. He never knew when it would happen. One day she'd seem fine, and then a few days later, she'd be gone again. As an adult, he had explored that difficult time in his life. What he discovered was that sometime during those early years, he had taken on her emotional illness. He felt her anxieties, her depressions, and her changing moods as if they were his own. None of this surfaced until Ted started to have a relationship with someone later in life. He revealed that sometimes he was afraid that he was really "crazy" like his mother. The closeness of the new relationship brought up his fears of abandonment by someone close to him, and also the underlying fear of his own mental instability.

As children, we are very vulnerable to other people's emotions, and also the unspoken secrets that they try to shield from us. We feel them anyway. They get locked in our psyches, and sometimes we don't even remember how they began.

Inherited Fear

Fear, long thought to be a learned response, may actually be a partly inherited trait programmed into our genetic makeup. Researcher Dr. John Hettema and colleagues studied ninety pairs of identical twins and eighty-three pairs of fraternal (nonidentical) twins. In relation to fear conditioning, the identical twins had the same responses, but the nonidentical twins had differing responses. Dr. Hettema stated that "Now we can say that the fear-conditioning process in humans is controlled, at least to some extent, by genetic factors. Between one-third and one-half of the fear conditioning appears to be inherited."[3]

So in addition to being affected by the emotions and attitudes of the people closest to us when we were children, we may also experience the fears of our ancestors. Most of us no longer live in the wilderness and feel the terror of wondering whether a ferocious animal or dangerous enemy might attack us during the night. However, we may have an inherited memory of those kinds of experiences. They remain somewhere in our DNA sequence as part of the fight-or-flight survival mechanism mentioned earlier. This response to fear can be reignited during an unexpected calamity and direct us to act in ways we never thought possible. It can cause a sweet seventy-five-year-old grandmother to successfully beat off a potential mugger with her umbrella, or cause a bystander to run spontaneously into a burning building to save a stranger.

This general survival mechanism activated by fear is inherited and lies dormant somewhere in our subconscious. Hopefully we never have to use it. But what about an inherited fear mind pattern that is more specific? Imagine an elderly African American woman. Her family's history of slavery, with all its cruel ramifications, goes back at least three or four generations. What kind of mind pattern will be passed on to her future generations? The inherited fear and subsequent response might have something to do with maintaining personal freedom and power, and an acute sensitivity to racial injustice.

Imagine now an Anglo-Saxon European woman of the same age. Her family's history of wealth and power, with all its ramifications of honor and privilege, also goes back at least three or four generations. What kind of fear mind pattern will her future generations inherit? It may involve maintaining privilege and power and include the fear of not living up to the expectations of the family culture.

How each generation deals with that inherited fear mind pattern depends also on what the influences are in the surrounding society. External political pressures can try to alter the collective mind pattern, as in the abolishment of slavery. External social pressures can also maintain the mind pattern by taking a position against marrying outside approved family bloodlines.

It is helpful to look at the cultures that we came from and how the traditions of those cultures may have influenced our ways of dealing with fear and survival issues. Also, what was going on in the world when we were born, and how were our family histories affected by the surrounding atmosphere?

Collective Fear

Our personal fears are influenced by the collective: the large group of people in an organization, a city, a country, or the world. Collective fear can activate our anxieties by mirroring or magnifying them, or introducing new ones for us to deal with.

Unexpected collective trauma can evoke and provoke our personal, inherited, conscious, and unconscious fears all at once. The World Trade Center tragedy on September 11, 2001, in New York City challenged everyone's perception of safety and control. I was with a client at the time, and we both watched in horror from my living room window as the towers disappeared before our eyes.

The danger was real, and the threat to lives continued for many weeks and months. Fear dark-blanketed everyone in the city and evoked different reactions in people. My cousin, whose close friend perished, strengthened his commitment to his spiritual group. A woman who barely escaped with her own life had to deal with her fear about an elderly man she was with, who disappeared in the rubble.

There were many reactions. Someone I know started drinking alcohol again. Someone else stopped drinking and decided to reconcile with his estranged wife. One family decided to leave the city and buy a home upstate.

Some young people's fear turned to patriotic anger, enough to consider military careers. Hundreds of people in the city volunteered to help wounded survivors, and hundreds more held candlelight vigils to honor the dead and also to object to violent retaliation. One block from where I live, crowds gathered in Union Square Park for several weeks after 9/11. They took turns standing on a small platform and talking about their fears and concerns. Some people refused to watch anything about the tragedy on TV. Others needed to watch every television report and read every article. A woman I know visited Ground Zero frequently. Watching the progress of the cleanup made her feel less frightened. Someone else I know refused to go back to that part of the city ever again.

Each of us deals with fear in a different way, especially during times of extreme circumstances. We do what we can to lessen the fear, to move through it, to live with it.

In New York City during that time, the emotions of shock, fear, anger, and grief combined to create a collective personality that included almost everyone. Now, years later, subliminal fear and apprehension continue in some form in people's consciousness and can be triggered by a sudden gas explosion or a 747 plane suddenly buzzing lower Manhattan.

In the past ten years or so, many different groups have promoted various forms of counseling, prayer, and meditation. These practices are helpful, but not if they result in just allaying fear instead of understanding it. Psychotherapy is important, but it must include looking at the physiological manifestations that accompany a traumatic event. We will explore this in a later chapter on somatic experience.

We must become familiar with our personal fears and look at what part they play in fragmenting our psyches and perpetuating the collective fear that has governed our world for such a long time.

Personal Fears Triggered by External Events

We begin our research from the outside in. What we are most afraid of in the larger world is in some way related to our personal fear states. Examining this opens a window into our deprogramming process. From now on, most chapters will include questions and exercises to help you with your personal exploration. Look at the following and respond as best you can.

1. What is your dominant and most persistent fear in the larger world? Examples: Stock market crash, a terrorist attack, getting stuck alone in an elevator, biochemical warfare.

2. Briefly describe the elements of that scenario and why it concerns you. Example: Mitchell's dominant fear was that a nuclear explosion would

take place in New York City. Though he blocked it out most of the time, it was surfacing more often with imagined alerts and terrorist threats. He thought of it as "a sudden, unexpected, and total devastation without survivors—nothing to be done."

3. Is there a possible relationship between that global situation and any of your personal fears or concerns?
Example: When Mitchell looked at how it might relate to him personally, he realized that the fear of nuclear explosion had something to do with his temper, which when unleashed, seemed uncontrollable. Mitchell was basically a non-abusive, gentle person, but his explosive anger, which sometimes erupted out of nowhere, terrified his wife and two young children, but most of all himself. As he explored the source of his outbursts, learned how to predict them, and found other ways of expressing his feelings, the fear of nuclear explosion weakened. He even said at one point, "Well, there are always people who survive the worst of disasters." He is still alert to possible danger, but is much less traumatized with each public threat.

4. Deepen and strengthen various aspects of your personal abilities by taking action in ways that feel productive and can support you in difficult situations.
Example: Mitchell is a martial arts practitioner and used his movement-meditation technique to center himself more automatically when he needed to calm down and gather his scattered energy. He began to trust his ability to change his anxious feelings by either releasing them or exploring them more creatively. He took action on a practical level and bought a new cell phone that gave him better communication with his family. He activated past memories of his own courage in the midst of seemingly uncontrollable and dangerous situations. Remembering his history made him feel more capable of handling whatever happens.

Programmed Fear

Programmed fear is deliberately induced fear conditioning by certain segments of society to convince us to follow a prescribed direction. We are encouraged to find external solutions in order to feel safer. We are told: You feel anxious? Take an antidepressant. You're worried that your child will wander off? Put a microchip under his or her skin. You're afraid of terrorism? Agree to more stringent surveillance techniques.

Certain government and military officials, medical authorities, religious and spiritual leaders, and media professionals help to perpetuate a fearful atmosphere and then offer us diversions and solutions. While all this is happening, we may find it difficult to choose what's best for us or even to evaluate the truth of the situation. We don't have time, things are moving too fast, we don't trust our own judgments, we follow the crowd, we shrug and feel powerless to go against the establishment, or worst of all, we deny that anything is really that bad. Life is just complicated, that's all. As some smart person once said, we are conditioned to believe we are not conditioned.

Researching Our Fear History

1. Place yourself in the role of a curious researcher gathering information. Make a list of your fear-based experiences from childhood to the present time. This can include things like failing a course in school, being punished, discovering an illness, or losing someone. Rate the severity of each experience on a scale from one to ten, with one being the least stressful to ten being the most traumatic.

2. After completing the list, look for repeated themes in the type of situation or the underlying emotional pattern.

> Examples
> Did competitive activities usually evoke anxiety for you? Is there a repeated pattern, like fear of humiliation, physical danger, or abandonment? What degree of control did you have in these situations, and how did you deal with what you felt? Did you ask for help? Did you get angry at yourself or others? Did you hide what you were feeling?

3. In childhood, how did your family handle fearful situations, either with you or amongst themselves? In your adult life, do you have people you can talk to when you feel anxious, or do you work things out by yourself?

4. Do you have any persistent fears? What is the negative belief you have that accompanies them?

Examples
- I'm not great with computers. (I'm stupid.)
- I'm afraid of losing my temper because it scares people away. (I'm a childish, angry person.)
- I'm always anxious about my children. (I'm a neurotic mother.)

Think about the mind pattern that might be related to this persistent fear. How did it originate? What is the positive realistic belief you would like to have about this situation?

Examples
- My brother was always better with technical stuff, and I felt intimidated by him. (I have a good mind. I can take a course and learn.)
- I was spoiled as a kid. I always got my way if I screamed loud enough. (It's okay to get angry sometimes, but I can find other ways to say what I feel. I can be in control of my own emotions.)
- My mother was ten times more neurotic with me. I guess I learned some of that from her. (I'm not that bad. As the kids get older, and even now, I'm learning how to be more selective about what I worry about.)

5. Think of your interactions with family, friends, partners, and people you know. Is your general anxiety level amplified or reduced when you are with each of them? Who makes you feel more relaxed, and who affects your mood negatively?

6. Do you think you have any inherited fears?

Examples
- I'm becoming an alcoholic like my father.
- I always worry about being poor no matter how much money I make.
- Divorces run in my family. I don't want to get married.

7. What part of your racial, ethnic, religious, or cultural heritage, or political beliefs, do you feel most connected to or most separated from and why? How do those feelings relate to your parents, grandparents,

great-grandparents, adoptive family, or other caretakers? Is there any element of anxiety or fear that you've experienced in relation to any of those groups?

8. Has fear ever propelled you into some constructive direction?

> Examples
> One boy dealing with racism in school and fears of physical harassment might decide to lift weights, join the boxing team, and successfully scare and repel bullies. Someone else might develop a keen, intelligent wit and humor that makes him or her popular and results in grudging admiration instead of racist assaults.

9. When do you feel you have been brave in your life? How did you override your fear, and what was the result? If you are not clear about this, ask one or two people who know you really well to offer their opinions about your courage.

10. What kinds of fearful dramas appear in your dreams? Is there a pattern or repeated theme? How do you appear in these dream scenarios, and how does this relate to your general personality?

> Examples
> Are you watching the story like an audience member in a theater? Do you become a superhero who defeats your enemy? Do you have a group of friendly fighters who save you? Do you become terrified and run away, give up, or wake up? Or do you cleverly talk yourself out of a dangerous situation?

Don't judge your dream actions. Just notice them. Watch to see if your dream personality stays the same or changes over a period of time.

11. What courageous characters, both real and fictional, have you been most attracted to or fascinated by?

> Examples
> James Bond, Joan of Arc, Batman, Martin Luther King Jr., Stephen Hawking, Amelia Earhart, et al.

What is appealing about the character or characters you chose? What aspect of his or her bravery or personality do you most admire? In what way can you include that aspect of his or her personality in dealing with your fears?

Examples
James Bond's cunning, Martin Luther King Jr.'s tenacity, Amelia Earhart's daring, etc.

Fear is a necessary ingredient in life. However, persistent fear narrows our view, contracts our energy, and keeps us in a victimized mentality. We can succeed in spite of fear, and sometimes because of it, but we also need to become aware of the undercover fears that quietly and consistently affect our lives and give us the illusion that we are exercising our free will.

Deprogramming from fear begins by naming the fear and its various forms and letting it unfold. Amorphous anxiety becomes less overwhelming when we can pinpoint what we are afraid of and notice when and under what circumstances it appears and how we react to it. When we understand it better, we can change our ways of viewing it. We can look at what upsets us in small increments rather than confronting and facing it head-on. Later, as we utilize all the dimensions of consciousness, we will see how fear diminishes when we change our perceptions about it.

PART II

FREEING THE MIND

SIX

FREE WILL, MOVEMENT, AND CHANGE

My first act of free will shall be to believe in free will.
—William James

Free will is probably located in the prefrontal cortex, and we may even be able to narrow it down to the ventromedial prefrontal cortex.
—Stephen Pinker

Free Will

The concept of free will is that we make personal decisions by evaluating the choices available to us. Sometimes we exercise our free will instantly and make a quick decision. At other times, our decision-making process takes longer. Here's an example of how we might use free will in a particular situation: Let's say you've been using a certain food product for a while. A friend tells you that she's switching to another brand. She heard that private researchers had discovered that some of the ingredients in the product were harmful if taken over a long period of time. Consumer complaints were made to the manufacturer, but not enough to result in a change in the product. The FDA has been contacted, but they have not responded as yet. Your free will to choose this food is based on limited information. At some point later on, you learn more about the harmful ingredients through a newspaper article. Now you know more. You can still choose to continue to use the food product. You can disagree with the research or ignore it. You can decide you like the food too much to stop eating it. You can tell yourself that your body is healthy enough to counteract whatever the negative effects might be. Or you may choose to stop eating it. Your decision is now based on more facts than you had initially.

Many of us are making decisions based on limited information, and often misinformation and propaganda. Free will can be exercised more fully when we are able to find out as much as we can about the external situation, but even more so when we use all the parts of our consciousness to make a decision. Sometimes our intuition proves to be right. Sometimes our reasoning serves us well. Sometimes our strong emotions lead us in the right direction. But it is also true that each of these approaches can be misleading. If we're not centered and mindful, seductive external conditioning, subliminal advertising, and various forms of misinformation can affect our choices. They may circumvent our ability to tune in to our internal evaluating process. We may eat something that's bad for our health or spend a lot of money on something we don't need. We can also agree to legislation we don't totally understand—legislation that can seriously affect our personal freedom.

We are less likely to be manipulated when we incorporate all the dimensions of our consciousness to make a decision. If we want to exercise free will, it's important to ask what influences us to move in one direction or another. Are we making decisions based on limited information? Is our free will contaminated by our histories with our mothers, fathers, or caretakers, or are we trapped by our own rigidity? What part of our personalities keep sabotaging what we do even when we think we're acting wisely? If our higher, smarter self knows better, then why isn't it operating more on our behalf? Even if we say to ourselves, "Life is not so bad," are we as fulfilled as we could be? Also, who is really running the show?

The intent of this questioning is not to feel victimized by the big bad world, but to use both our external and internal awareness to make better choices based on as much information as we can get. This doesn't always result in perfect solutions. Mistakes also give us important information. But when we're formulating ideas and making choices, we need to be utilizing our thinking process to its fullest capacity. How well informed are we when we choose a medicine, a couch, a lover, a political candidate, or a way of life? We are smart to begin with. We have the right answers somewhere. We just don't always know it or believe it.

We diminish our fears when we look at them with curiosity and courage. Doing that also melts the thick boundaries that block our access to important knowledge. Our free will has more dimensions of reality to explore.

Movement and Change

Everything flows. Nothing stands still.[1]

—Heraclitus

Using our free will to explore and expand consciousness involves movement. With the discovery of subatomic activity in quantum physics, we are beginning to understand that everything is moving and changing all the time. The emphasis is shifting from defining a predictable state to exploring the dynamics of a changing process. Movement is manifest in everything, and change is inevitable and organic.

No one's emotional experience remains the same or stays separate from another's for very long. How does this translate for us on a daily basis? We're enjoying the day, and then our wonderful mood suddenly changes with a confrontational phone call. We feel pretty good until a downpour catches us without an umbrella. The person we adored yesterday makes us feel dumb for loving him today.

The opposite happens as well. Our bad mood changes when someone sends us a really funny text message. We feel sad, tired, and lazy until our friend forces us to go to a new movie. We're not feeling very attractive, and then someone flirts with us at the coffee shop.

We live with an illusion of permanency as if that were a natural state. We do not realize that we are changing, moving, transforming all the time with our thoughts, our emotions, and our bodies. When we're happy, we want the moment to last forever. When we are unhappy, it feels like an eternity. Change makes us uneasy, especially when it moves us from a place of pleasure or peace to a place of uncertainty or conflict.

The process of High-Velocity Consciousness encourages us to shift more often from the stability and false safety of sameness to the adventure of change, movement, and diversity. Every conscious emotional/physical state eventually changes. The pleasure of an orgasm is limited. And although sexual intimacy is wonderful, at some point, sooner or later, you want to sleep, eat, or watch a movie. Emotional/physical states like fear, anger, guilt, and jealousy are also limited. Of course, some of us can stay depressed or anxious for months or even years. But unless we are experiencing severe clinical illness, negative emotions will change if given half a chance.

Knowing how to orchestrate and shift these states when they

happen is valuable because we are taking creative initiative in the immediate present about a debilitating feeling instead of thinking about it in the same old way. The ability to be centered and focused when needed, and then to travel at will among all the dimensions of consciousness, is the key to wellness. In the next chapter, we look at these multiple levels of reality and how we can become more conscious of them and use our free will to move among them.

SEVEN

DIMENSIONS OF CONSCIOUSNESS

Sometimes your only available transportation is a leap of faith.
—Margaret Shepherd

Dimensions, as they are used throughout this book, are not necessarily areas in a particular location or spaces of measurable proportions, static and unchanging. Rather, they can be thought of as levels of consciousness characterized by specific activities, inner experiences, or special focus. The following is a general idea about the levels of the psyche. It's based on a transpersonal psychology called psychosynthesis and was a major part of my early training.

Dr. Roberto Assagioli was a Jewish Italian psychoanalyst, a contemporary of Freud and Jung. He believed that at the basis of human activity was an impulse, an energy, a continuing message from the soul that tries to move us to higher states of fulfillment. Assagioli believed that each of us, in our own way, moves toward a synthesis, an integration of the various parts of our being. We experience life primarily from a state he called the middle unconscious. This is the place we are in most of the time. It includes our everyday activities, how we think and feel, what we choose to eat and wear, what work we do, and how we do it. Within this field is the conscious self and the various aspects of the personality. Surrounding this field is the middle unconscious that contains psychological elements similar to our waking awareness, like memories or ideas. This is the most accessible layer of unconscious material.[1]

He described the lower unconscious as the place of the elementary psychological activities that direct the life of the body—fundamental drives and primitive urges. He believed that it is filled with uncontrolled processes—various pathological manifestations such as phobias, obsessions, and paranoid delusions. Most of these have their origin in the experiences of childhood, which are often charged with intense emotions.[2]

He also defined an arena he called the higher unconscious, or, as it is better known, the superconscious. "From this region we receive our higher intuitions and inspirations—artistic, philosophical or scientific… It is the source of the higher feelings such as altruistic love, illumination… ecstasy." In this realm are the higher psychic functions and spiritual energies. Somewhere overseeing this realm resides the higher self.[3]

In Assagioli's theory, beyond these levels lies the universe, endless and eternal, containing the wisdom and knowledge of all human consciousness—past, present, and future. This is the collective unconscious.[4]

All the states mentioned above are permeable. This means that energies from any level of our consciousness, and beyond our conscious self, can move in any direction, at any time, and can affect our state of being.[5]

For example, one of my clients found himself reacting rather intensely to something a friend said at a gathering. It was a teasing remark that hurt him and made him quite upset. He later realized that the incident brought back the childhood memory of being mercilessly teased by his father in public. He experienced a flooding of energy from the lower unconscious, which for the moment transported him, like a time warp, into the painful past.

Another client had been in a depressed state for several days. She needed to make a decision about a difficult situation concerning her family. She seldom remembered her dreams, but one night she dreamt that a group of people she did not know carried her gently outside, into a field in the country, and counseled her. She could not understand what they were saying, but when she woke up, she realized that she had had an extraordinary experience. Her depression lifted, and she then understood how she could resolve the family problem. This was a flooding of energy from the superconscious, which sometimes manifests in a dream state.

The conscious self, housed in the middle unconscious, was dramatically affected in both of these examples. In the first, the upheaval of emotional content forced the man to look at repressed memories that remained dynamically potent just under the surface of his awareness.

The incident led him to reexamine the childhood interaction with his father that still affected him. Talking about the incident with his friend strengthened their relationship.

In the second example, the woman's dream helped her resolve an immediate problem. The peaceful feeling she had in the dream, and the receptive way she experienced the group counseling, indicated that this was advice coming from the higher dimensions of consciousness. Without understanding the words, she had downloaded information from her own higher self that could then be translated into positive action.

What happens when a person has greater access to one level or builds thick walls against another? Imagine a hypothetical situation in which a woman is living more exclusively in the lower unconscious. She would react to situations with an overly strong reference from the past. It would be difficult for her to experience the immediate present. Every man might remind her of her father, and if that memory is negative, she would have difficulty in relationships. She would be stuck in the past, experiencing a child's point of view. She might be overly emotional and vulnerable. She might have little access to logical reasoning. Less able to be introspective, she might be in touch with the superconscious, but she wouldn't know what to do with what she felt.

Now imagine a man living more exclusively in the middle unconscious. He might be successful, productive, practical, and intelligent. He would deal with things from a place of logic and reason. He might be very much in control of his emotions, and the past would be a distant, repressed, or intellectualized memory. He would have little time for abstract or philosophical musings. He might feel anxious when he was by himself and experience an emptiness from time to time that he would cover up with more work, sex, or football.

If a man lived primarily in the superconscious level of the psyche, he might be involved in religious or spiritual matters. He might be an artist. He might spend much of his time doing Yoga or practicing meditation. He would have access to so much information from the superconscious that it might be overwhelming for him, and he might sometimes feel out of control. In an altered state much of the time, it might be difficult for him to function in ordinary relationships or in structured situations.

Assagioli believed that these three levels of consciousness have no division at birth. They are not yet fully formed. The superconscious is merged with the lower unconscious. The middle unconscious is not yet a discrete area of awareness. All three levels are intermingled with the surrounding collective unconscious.[6]

As we grow and develop our personality and individuality, we become more divorced from the upper and lower levels. We create thicker boundaries, though the energies from these areas still affect us.

For Assagioli, a move toward synthesis, an integration of all levels of consciousness, was the intention of life—to move back to the merging at birth, but with full conscious awareness. He imagined the conscious self orchestrating the energies of the psyche with the direction of the higher self, which in turn would be receiving information from the collective unconscious, the universal fountain of infinite knowledge.[7]

High-Velocity Consciousness represents the natural ability of the mind to travel safely among different dimensions of consciousness. When we are able to do this, then the boundaries separating these levels become more permeable, and there is more automatic transmission and information when we need it.

One evening many years ago, after a very long day, I was meditating and fell into a deep sleep. Suddenly, a loud voice that seemed to be coming from somewhere in the room called my name urgently: "Joan!" It startled me, and I woke up. There was no one in the room or in the apartment, but the candle that I had forgotten about had burned down, and the flame was just about to ignite the pile of papers that were resting next to it. Where did that voice come from? Did my physical, sleeping nose smell the burning candle and tell my brain to wake up? Was my higher self protecting me? Was it a passing firefighter from the spirit world? I didn't care. Whatever it was, a disaster was prevented, and I was grateful. Later I realized that one level of my consciousness was simply competing with the other.

EIGHT

HIGH-VELOCITY CONSCIOUSNESS—MINDSPEED INTEGRATION

The mind makes choices based on millions of pieces of data and their correlations and projections, far beyond conscious comprehension, and with enormous rapidity.

—David R. Hawkins

They all heard and felt the tremendous explosion and saw the thick black smoke outside. The office was near the top of the tower. Dozens of people started moving and running around. The head administrator in the office tried to calm everyone down as the fear accelerated. "Everyone stay put," he ordered.

Maria felt her whole mind, body, and soul resist that order as she and other people tried to leave.

He continued, "If anyone leaves this office, don't bother to come back because you won't have a job. You'll be fired."

Maria thought, *F--- you. I'm leaving.* She was one of the few people from her office that survived the World Trade Center tragedy.

In a life-threatening situation, our senses are heightened. Ordinary thinking takes a backseat to adrenaline-propelled acute attention. Our mind seems to short-circuit irrelevant information, and we are often able to take action quickly to save our lives. What's going on in our consciousness when we experience a moment of flashing clarity and intuitive certainty, especially in the midst of danger?

Over thirty-five years ago, I had one of the first glimpses into this process. It was a lovely summer day. My husband was driving on a highway in Long Island. I was in the front seat with my infant son. Suddenly, a speeding car sideswiped us on the right and caused us to swerve to the left, toward the heavy metal divider. Then something strange happened. Time slowed down, all sound disappeared, and everything took on a luminous glow. I was in an altered state. I had all the time in the world as I experienced the following:

> I am putting my right arm and my whole body around the baby to shield him. My husband keeps moving the steering wheel to the left so we don't crash into the divider. We slide and scrape into it on the right, and stop. Now we are facing oncoming traffic. Somehow, I know that the cars will see us in time. While all of this is going on, I am noticing how blue the sky is and how green the trees look. Everything is beautiful, like a slow-moving ballet or some brilliant underwater scene.

All this took less than two seconds. The car was badly damaged, but miraculously we were all unhurt.

My perception of time slowed down, which is not uncommon for some people in life-threatening situations, while another part of my mind speeded up. I knew exactly what to do and how to do it, and what seemed to me most important was that I felt no fear.

Since that life-threatening event, I have also had wonderful experiences that involved altered states. Over the years, I became more interested in the internal process that results not only in clear perception during danger but also in valuable insights during the complexities of everyday life. I believe that this active mindfulness is a necessity in today's unbalanced world.

I call this process High-Velocity Consciousness. It is when all the different parts of our mind are operating together, integrating all the pieces of information that we need into a coherent picture. Our conscious mind is focused on our intention like a laser beam. Our thinking is alive and active, exploring multiple possibilities with curiosity, adventure, and in times of danger—urgency. Our emotions, instead of overpowering our thoughts, are consistent with them. Our visceral experience is activated, with a gut reaction that feels right. Somewhere in the middle of this dynamic flow, we download confirming information from our subconscious mind. There is a kind of quick mind traveling that takes place and a cross-referencing of information that comes together and becomes integrated.

Especially during times of danger, the mind acts like a high-speed supercomputer and runs through millions of files of all sorts: physical possibilities, emotional expressions, logical options, and pertinent information. Somewhere built into this computer is an organizing principle, our superconscious mind and higher self, that sifts through all these files and presents us with the best scenario to follow. We can then make a decision or take some action based on that insight. In those elongated seconds during the car accident, there was no guessing about what to do, no conflict of choice. I just knew and acted.

Everyday Insights

This process of mindspeed cross-referencing also takes place during non-life-threatening situations in everyday life. For example, one of my clients, Dorothy, met a man at a social gathering. He was attractive and fairly successful. They spent about ten minutes talking. Her first impression was, *He seems nice, but kind of boring.* He called her later, and they began a relationship even though his work took him out of town a lot. They fell in love, and after a year, he changed his work schedule so that they could spend more time together. He began to talk about getting married. The more they saw each other, the more nervous she became about making a commitment. Then Dorothy noticed that she was thinking about other men and began to panic about the idea of spending the rest of her life with a man who was not intellectually stimulating to her. They had little to talk about. With much difficulty, she finally broke off the relationship.

"He was a really nice guy, but I was bored much of the time." Her first impression was right—for her.

What was going on? Psychologist Dr. John Gottman, as quoted in Malcolm Gladwell's popular book *Blink*, would call it an example of "thin-slicing." This refers to the ability of our unconscious mind to make an accurate and truthful personal judgment in a short time based on very narrow slices of experience. Dr. Gottman has been studying married couples' conversations for nearly two decades. With only fifteen minutes of videotaped discussion, he can predict whether or not a couple will be married fifteen years down the line with 90 percent accuracy.[1] Dorothy's higher self knew within the first ten minutes that this man was not for her.

Advice From Above

Sometimes we don't want to hear or cooperate with the higher self. Years ago, I began to experience dizziness when I shifted my head from one position to another. It was subtle at first and then became more pronounced after two months. The doctor I went to ruled out an inner-ear infection or anything neurological. He thought it might be the result of some calcium crystals that had become dislodged—not an uncommon occurrence.

"Let's wait and see," he said.

I was not thrilled with that answer, as I continued to stumble around and feel unbalanced. The next day, just as I was waking up, still in a dream state, I heard a voice in my head say very clearly and directly, *"Whirl!"*

I thought, *Are you nuts? I'm dizzy enough and you want me to whirl? Forget it.*

Now, whirling was introduced by Rumi, the Sufi poet and mystic, in the thirteenth century as a form of sacred spinning meditation. We associate it with the whirling dervishes. I had mastered it about ten years before, but hadn't practiced in a long time. After a few days of continued dizziness, I said (to my higher self), *Okay, what have I got to lose?*

So I carefully whirled a few times during that day and the next for about five minutes at a time. Within two days, my dizziness was completely gone. Three years later, the vertigo returned. This time I decided to tell the doctor what had worked before and what I planned to do again. I expected a modified smirk. Instead he reacted with surprise and interest and described to me a machine that was shown to be effective for certain kinds of vertigo. The machine caused the calcium crystals to be reintegrated by stimulating certain kinds of rapid head movements.

What Was Happening?

1. My conscious mind was telling me to go to a doctor and get some medical information. That relieved some but not all of my anxiety.
2. The voice that I heard in my dream state seemed to be coming from my higher self and offered specific advice that I initially rejected and then chose to follow. The advice was within the scope of my physical capability and experience. I already knew how to whirl. I was not advised to snowboard or skydive.
3. Medical information about making certain kinds of rapid head move-

ments using machines or walking around to avert vertigo was already in the public domain. It was "in the air." My subconscious mind may have registered that information from somewhere without my conscious recollection of it.

4. Some inner impulse, some risk-taking part of me, despite my initial reluctance to whirl, compelled me to trust my intuition and take action.

Problem Solving

Sometimes when we consciously struggle with a problem, there is often a lot of mental effort that precedes a sudden insight or solution.

Psychologist James Vargiu used the model of an energy field to describe what happens when we try to solve an intellectual, emotional, or creative problem. We begin by consciously and purposefully trying to put together an answer, a solution that fits. We become involved in mental activity. We mull over bits of ideas, images, symbols, and abstract concepts. Our mind goes in many directions. At some point, in the midst of confusion and frustration, and often when we get tired of the mental process and we just give up, a solution appears in a flash of illumination. It seems as if all the substantial elements that we have been thinking about are moving and floating around in a kind of energy field. Then at some point, they simultaneously combine and organize into one coherent and meaningful pattern.[2] The organization seems to take place on a higher level of consciousness than our ordinary thinking state. It feels as if it's coming from outside of us, like the strong voice in my dream that told me to whirl.

The most famous example of this organization of elements and advice from above is the story of the nineteenth-century chemist Kekulé, who, in the middle of his frustrated attempts to solve a problem, described what he observed one day in a dream:

> Long rows, sometimes more closely fitted together; all twining and twisting in a snakelike motion. But look! What was that? One of the snakes had seized hold of its own tail, and the form whirled mockingly before my eyes. As if by a flash of lightning I awoke.[3]

This dream image gave him the long-sought-for clue to the closed structure of the benzene ring, which became the foundation of organic chemistry.

High-Velocity Consciousness can be thought of as a process that activates our mental elements more selectively so that organization into a sensible solution can take place more easily.

Blocks to Illumination

Somewhere in our minds, we have the right answers. They come to us during times of danger. We get insights sometimes while we're walking or showering. We get messages from a dream or after a long period of mental effort. So why don't we experience these high-level truths more often? Sometimes when we're in danger, we get too much adrenaline running through our bodies. Instead of an integration of consciousness, we panic and become immobilized. Sometimes we have an insight that we don't act on because our emotions get in the way, as mine almost did when I initially resisted the advice about whirling. Often we're blocked from accessing higher levels of consciousness because we're thinking in a limited way or we're just too busy.

Also, as technology has played a bigger role in our lives, our skills in critical thinking and analysis have declined, while our visual skills have improved. This was reported in research by psychology professor Patricia Greenfield of UCLA, who analyzed more than fifty studies on learning and technology.[4]

But the most important block to illumination is that conscious and subliminal fears—personal insecurities, negative obsessions, and apprehensions about the world—take up too much room in our minds and keep us stuck in the lower dimensions. Instead of mind integration and valuable insights, we have fragmented consciousness. This reflects the atmosphere of the twenty-first century. While there is more understanding about how our minds work, we're not always in touch with the different parts of our consciousness that can tell us what we need to know.

An example of this is a story related to the tragic tsunami event in Indonesia in 2004 that took so many people by surprise. There was a report about the Jarawa tribe from the Andaman and Nicobar Islands. They fled to a higher ground and safety just before the tsunami hit because they sensed the coming of a disaster. Their intimate connection to nature and focused sensitivity to their surroundings warned them.[5]

New brain research suggests that people subconsciously sense trouble ahead and that this early-warning system may exist in the anterior cingulated cortex, a brain area important in processing complex information.[6] Most of us have too much static going on to experience these warnings, though these abilities are possible for everyone and can be developed.

Parts Versus the Whole

When we make decisions based on just our conscious ego, we may be wrong. When emotions compel us to move in one particular direction, that may not be in our best interest, either. Our gut reaction may not always be right. (Strong emotions sometimes feel like deep insights.) Logical reasoning may ignore intuitive awareness. And persistent negative mind patterns, especially having to do with fear, may contaminate the reality of a situation. Training our intuitive sensibility means using all the parts of our mind.

The Physical Brain and the Infinite Mind

The brain can be thought of as the receiving station for the mind, which is vast and can tap into infinite knowledge beyond the confines of the physical brain and into the arena of the collective unconscious.

We have many levels in our brains, but three predominate. The reptilian brain is the oldest, and is primarily concerned with our survival instinct: the fight-or-flight response. The limbic brain represents our emotional needs and expressions. The neocortex, known as the thinking brain, is the largest and consists of two parts: the left and right hemispheres. We think of the left hemisphere as pertaining to logical, linear, and sequential thinking with attention to detail. The right hemisphere is usually associated with creative abstractions, spontaneity, timelessness, and seeing the whole picture. When we are deprogramming from fear and activating intuition, each part of the brain is important and can be utilized.[7]

The following personal example illustrates how these different parts of my brain were activated in a specific situation and how I tried to deal with anxious feelings by stimulating my imagination.

Some time ago, I noticed that I had a slight swelling in my neck. I tuned in to my higher self and felt that it was not serious and would probably go away in time. The doctor suggested an MRI.

At the medical center, I was handed a document to sign that listed the possible dangers of the dye they had to inject into my body. My reptilian brain and my limbic (emotional) brain became immediately activated, and I felt somewhat anxious. The logical left brain of my neocortex tuned in, and I asked the nurses questions like, "What's the percentage of people that develop allergic reactions or breathing difficulties, or actually die from this procedure?" (A small percentage.) I also learned that they had medication and equipment on hand should any of these infrequent events take place. I decided I was going to be fine even though I'd had previous allergic reactions to certain medications.

I had to lie down in the confining tunnel with my head in a vise for at least thirty minutes. My reptilian and limbic brains were reactivated. I am slightly claustrophobic, and it's also difficult for me to keep my body still for very long. I joked with the nurse a bit and mentally directed the cells in my body to counteract anything detrimental from the dye and to help me relax my head and body so I didn't move. I took a few deep breaths, and they slid me into the tunnel. I focused on my right brain and placed myself rather quickly into a meditative state.

I used the following mind-orchestration tools to stimulate my imagination.

One-Point Concentration

I closed my eyes, separated myself from my surroundings, and concentrated on one thing. I imagined lying on a beach and experiencing all the sensations: the feel of the sand under my feet, the sound of the waves, the sun on my body, etc. I was fully in the moment and enjoying the scene.

Two-Point Concentration

I did not want to get so entranced at the beach that I forgot where I was and moved my body. The MRI machine was very loud, clanking and banging. It was a challenge to stay in the beach scene and also to keep still. I had to be aware of both situations.

Changing Perception

I changed my perception by moving from one sensory modality to another. Instead of being totally silent whenever I exhaled, I hummed. When a wave of restlessness threatened my immobilization, I discovered that I could very carefully wiggle my toes without disturbing the MRI process. That was wonderful.

Mind Adventuring

I left the beach scene and let my mind wander wherever it wanted to go. My imagination placed me in front of an audience in the club where I sometimes performed, singing a selection of songs. I thought of some new ones, and I was trying to remember the words, when I was interrupted by the nurse, who told me that the time was up. The MRI report found nothing—score one more point for my higher self.

These mind-orchestration tools can be used in many situations. They are especially helpful when dealing with specific conscious fears or subconscious anxiety. We can use them to activate our intuition when we want to make a decision or solve a problem. Practicing them trains the mind to be more focused, flexible, and creative. We will examine them more closely later on. Different ways of stimulating the imagination are included in many of the exercises that are presented in the following chapters.

A Side Effect

When we are more fully and directly involved in utilizing all the parts of our brains, we develop a renewed excitement about trusting the power of our own minds. This doesn't mean that we always get exactly what we want when we want it, but that the roads we travel on become more interesting.

Jay had been practicing High-Velocity Consciousness for a while with some reasonable success. On this one day, he was sitting on the subway, somewhat anxious and upset because the store that he had just gone to was out of a particular book of poetry that he needed in order to write a paper for school. Jay was meditating and thinking about where to go next when a man who seemed quite inebriated came into the car. He was loudly reciting and half singing some kind of poetry.

Jay sighed, *Oh great! Just what I need right now, a drunk poet.*

The man was unsteady on his feet, and when the train stopped, he almost fell on Jay and the woman sitting next to him. They started talking, and it turned out that she had a copy of the book of poetry at home that he needed, and she offered to lend it to him. They began a relationship that lasted only three months, but he got a B+ on his paper, and the subway synchronicity renewed his faith in how interesting life can be. These "coincidences" can happen to anyone, but with High-Velocity Consciousness, they tend to happen more often.

Carl Jung coined the term *synchronicity* and defined it as follows: "Synchronicity is the coming together of inner and outer events in a way that cannot be explained by cause and effect and that is meaningful to the observer."[8]

I believe synchronicity happens more often when we practice High-Velocity Consciousness because we're traveling to and connecting with a wider range of consciousness that contains more information and knowledge than everyday reality. When we have access to that larger dimension, we have more opportunities available to us. There is also something about the combination of emotional need, strong intention, clear focus, and potent energy that promotes these meaningful occurrences. We will look at more examples of this later.

High-Velocity Consciousness represents the natural ability of the mind to travel safely among different dimensions of consciousness. When we are able to do this, the boundaries separating these levels become more permeable, and there is more automatic transmission and information when we need it.

Integrating Consciousness

In a crisis situation, like Maria's experience on 9/11, or my car accident, the mind short-circuits irrelevant information and integrates our consciousness more quickly.

Sometimes when we meet people for the first time, we have an immediate intuitive sense about them. They seem wonderful, but something is off or doesn't feel right. We can also be drawn to someone who doesn't seem to be our type, but something intangible attracts us to him or her.

We can receive information from our higher self through a hunch, a passing thought, or a dream. We can choose to pay attention to that experience or ignore it.

We become more aware of the process of mind integration when, during our struggle to solve a problem, everything suddenly comes together and a solution appears.

We can activate more parts of our brain and stimulate our

imagination when we are confronted with a specific situation like my MRI experience.

Or we can use our mind intelligence and introspection to understand what lies underneath persistent anxious feelings that are triggered by an external event.

Mind Freedom

We ensure the freedom of our minds when we tap into and actively participate with all the dimensions of consciousness on a continuing basis. This habitual mindfulness helps us become more integrated and centered. It connects us more often and more directly to our higher self, the designated CEO that's really smart and has our best interests at heart. We also need help, especially now, to evaluate what's happening in the outside world. We want to know that what influences us, what we believe in, and what decisions we make come from our personal inner exploration and not just ideas that we adopt without thinking from some "enlightened" guru, "down-to-earth" politician, or "electrically handsome" celebrity. We want to develop an ongoing sensitivity and resistance to the propaganda and technology that is being used to slowly control our actions and imprison our minds.

Our passionate intention to remain free and to achieve deep personal fulfillment is very strong and very possible, especially now.

Prolific author John Shirley writes:

So transcendence comes to fruition in the mind, in perception itself…You have to start somewhere, and you start with what's closest, by skeptically, fearlessly, examining your own experience of the world—and your own mind… Look around and question what you see, what you accept. And start with yourself. Know thyself.[9]

PART III

HIGH-VELOCITY
CONSCIOUSNESS

NINE

THE PRIMARY CENTERING PROCESS

Know yourself.

—Phemonoe, Greek poetess

Include the following primary centering process in your daily schedule. It takes only a minute or two. It is a prelude to some of the exercises and meditations that follow, especially in later chapters. It reminds your mind and body to relax. It helps you balance your emotions and thoughts before you turn inward to explore different dimensions of consciousness. It centers you when you're evaluating something from the outside world. Most important, it acts as a protective shield from external negative influences. According to some Eastern traditions, there are seven main energy centers in the body called the "chakras." They are associated with different colors. On a physiological level, they are related to the seven glands of the endocrine system. The seventh chakra is situated on top of the head and is known as the "crown chakra." It is believed to be an energetic connection to the superconscious and spiritual awareness.[1]

Go to the front cover of the book and look at the round violet-colored spot just below the title. It represents the color of the crown chakra. Become familiar with it so that you can visualize it as best you can with your eyes closed. If it is difficult to see the color in your mind's eye, just think of it. In time and with practice, you will be able to remember it more accurately.

1. Sit comfortably with your back supported, your legs uncrossed,

and your feet flat on the floor. Rest your hands on your lap with open palms facing either up or down. Relax your body, and close your eyes.

2. Begin with a few cleansing breaths. Breathe in slowly and deeply just through your nose, hold your breath for a count of three, and then exhale slowly and deeply through your mouth. Repeat this cleansing breathing process at least three times.

3. Place your attention now on the center of your forehead, on a spot between your eyebrows. This is known as the "brow chakra" or the "third eye," and its color is royal blue. This area corresponds to the pineal gland that is located deep near the center of the brain and acts as a balance between the right and left hemispheres of the brain. Visualize a small royal-blue dot in the center of that area on your forehead, breathe normally, and relax.

4. Now, imagine yourself in the center of an egg-shaped bubble made of the violet color of the crown chakra. It completely covers you and extends out somewhat beyond your body, above your head and below your feet.[2] Feel the comfort and protection of this beautiful color all around you for a moment or two, or as long as you like.

5. When you are ready to complete the process, place a small band of a brown-earth color all around, touching the outside of the violet bubble. This acts as a grounding completion so that though we are connecting to the higher dimensions, we are also rooted in this physical earth reality.[3]

Alternative Procedure

You can go through this primary centering process while lying down on your back, with your head on a pillow, and your arms at your sides or resting gently on your body. Close your eyes and repeat the above exercise.

In time, the primary centering process will become part of your daily routine. In the chapters to follow, it will be indicated in some of the exercises.

TEN

CROSS-REFERENCING: THE SEVEN STEPS

I have no special talent. I am only passionately curious.
—Albert Einstein

As we noted before, strongly felt emotions are not always reliable barometers of truth; neither is logical thinking. In the outside world, scientific research is not necessarily irrefutable. Religious dogma may be influenced by writers of history. Philosophical theories may not hold up over time. And psychiatrists and psychics are not always right. We may need a second or third opinion. Cross-referencing is strongly recommended, especially today, when societal mind conditioning is so prominent.

Not using all the dimensions of consciousness to understand and resolve conflicts is like trying to understand global warming when you have access to only one website dealing with ozone depletion in Canada in 2010. Sometimes we make decisions based on limited and dubious data. When we use the seven steps of cross-referencing, we have more perspectives and possibilities available to us. Instead of one view, we can look at a situation from several vantage points. We can use the seven steps daily so that paying attention to what's happening around us and within us becomes a familiar process.

Daily General Cross-Referencing

Step 1. Noticing Emotions and Moods

Now and then during the day, ask yourself how you are feeling emotionally and what kind of mood you are in.

> Examples
> - I woke up sad and stayed sad until I had that coffee during lunch. Then I was just irritable.
> - I'm feeling apprehensive all day, as if I'm waiting for something bad to happen.

Step 2. Noticing Personalities

Notice if your identity or role remains the same throughout the day and whether it changes with different people and situations.

> Examples
> - He touched me gently on the shoulder, and I felt like a dopey teenager.
> - I'm like everybody's surrogate mother. I don't like it and am certain other people don't like it either.

Step 3. Tuning In to Somatic Experiences

Get into the habit of listening to your body now and then, and pay attention to your physical experiences.

> Examples
> - My chest feels strange. Is it high blood pressure, or is my heart broken, or both?
> - I can't concentrate, and I keep bumping into furniture and things. I need space from everything and everybody.

Step 4. Observing External Fields

Become aware of the surrounding atmosphere and its effect on you.

Examples
- The meeting was held in a closed room. The air was stagnant, and so was the group.
- The people in the elevator were all silent, still, and serious until the two dachshunds came in yapping at each other, and then everybody started laughing.

Step 5. Observing Night Dreaming

Remember and record your dreams as often as you can.

Examples
- I opened the test booklet for my math exam, and when I looked at the questions, they were all Egyptian hieroglyphics, and I panicked.
- I was being chased by some gangsters who were pretending to be FBI agents. I suddenly stopped running, faced them, and squirted them all with Tabasco sauce.

Step 6. Activating Kéfi: Pleasure Experience

Once or twice during the day, close your eyes and remember a moment from the past that was pleasurable.

Examples
- I thought everybody forgot until I walked into the restaurant and heard "Happy Birthday" coming from the balcony from all my friends.
- I remember the time I tasted my first chocolate ice-cream soda.

Step 7. Accessing the Higher Dimensions

At least once during the day, close your eyes, place yourself in a meditative state, and move into higher dimensions of consciousness.

Examples
- All I saw were beautiful colors floating in and out of each other. I didn't see anything specific, but I felt good afterward.

- I don't remember much of the images except for a small dolphin, but my headache seemed to disappear, and I could finally go to sleep.

Cross-Referencing for Specific Issues

The following story illustrates how one of my clients used the seven-step cross-referencing process to deal with a difficult situation. Lena's mother had died of cancer several years before, and now Lena's breast exam showed a suspicious dark spot.

Step 1. Noticing Emotions and Moods
Lena was scared. Her husband was supportive and tried to calm her down, but his obvious attempt to hide his own nervousness didn't help. Now she had his anxiety added to her own.

Step 2. Noticing Personalities
Usually brave and in control, Lena felt like a frightened, angry child.

Step 3. Tuning In to Somatic Experiences
The fear felt stuck in her chest and was almost physically painful. She didn't want to be like her mother in any way, and she refused to give in to this awful possibility. She mentally and psychologically separated from her mother and reminded herself that she was different. Lena went to her aerobics class and danced out her emotions and began to feel stronger about all of this.

Step 4. Observing External Fields
One day she saw a card advertising a woman's health group that declared in bold letters: BREAST CANCER IS A FACT OF LIFE. That negative programming in the guise of helping infuriated her.

Step 5. Observing Night Dreaming
One night she had a dream about playing volleyball on the beach against a bunch of men in suits—and she was winning.

Step 6. Activating Kéfi: Pleasure Experience

Lena continued to go to her aerobics class whenever she could. She also remembered pleasure experiences from her past, especially in sports activities. That continued to make her feel healthy and strong.

Step 7. Accessing the Higher Dimensions

She connected with her higher self, beyond the fear, and resolved to use her power to deal successfully with anything that should come up.

Lena tuned in to her gut feeling several times during the next few days. During one meditation, she got an answer that surprised her: *"You don't have cancer, and you never will."* And she never did. After more tests, the spot was no longer there. The medical explanation was that it was probably a mechanical error on the screen.

What Was Happening?

Lena was able to travel back and forth among different levels of consciousness. She faced her specific fears honestly, uncovered her subconscious fears, respected her emotions, relied on her body strength and power, trusted her rational mind, tuned in to her intuitive self, listened to her dream, and refused to be intimidated by external conditioning.

Cross-Referencing When External Events Trigger Personal Issues

One of my clients used the seven-step process to deal with a situation where a world event triggered his personal anxieties and uncovered an old mind pattern.

Sam's work required him to travel several times a year to different parts of the world from New York. After 9/11, he became more apprehensive about flying. He felt anxious and agitated at the long delays. He was particularly uncomfortable with the military presence of soldiers at the airports.

Step 1. Noticing Emotions and Moods

Sam's persistent emotions of anger and resentment about the soldiers, even after several months, began to scare him. When he listened to his inner rage toward them, it was something like this: *I don't like you. You're probably not too smart. I hate what you stand for.*

There was another emotion that came up that he couldn't quite understand. He often felt somewhat guilty and anxious, like he was hiding something and *they* would find him out and take him away.

Step 2. Noticing Personalities

Sam noticed that he switched into a "tough guy" personality that was rather intense. His inner reaction was something like, *Who do you think you are? You're just young punks in uniform.*

One day, when one of the soldiers accidentally bumped his shoulder, he had a strong urge to punch him out. The other identity that also appeared was a "subversive personality." He had irrational thoughts that he was going to be suspected of something and stopped from going on his flight.

Step 3. Tuning In to Somatic Experiences

Tuning in to his body, he began to see that his stomach tightened until he passed through customs and could relax only after the flight took off. The mind pattern that seemed to be connected to it was something like, *Don't show what you're really thinking, or you're in for trouble.* It was not an unfamiliar feeling

.

Step 4. Observing External Fields

At first Sam thought that his agitation at the military presence had to do with his strong objection to the possibility of war with Iraq. His reaction seemed to be more pronounced at the airport, where he felt scrutinized. He also realized that groups of soldiers hanging out in twos or threes particularly irked him.

Step 5. Observing Night Dreaming

Sam had a recurring nightmare that he was being chased by Nazis at different times during his life. He grew up in a neighborhood with only three or four other Jewish families. In high school, he always felt on edge. Sometimes he was laughed at and picked on by a group of male students who wore sports uniforms. He hid his reactions so as not to draw attention to himself. The soldiers triggered his memory about the guys in school who picked on him. But where did the anxious feeling about being discovered and reprimanded come from?

Step 6. Activating Kéfi: Pleasure Experience

The most profound experience for Sam was when he watched his son take his first steps toward him without falling. Remembering the exhilaration of that moment always made him feel more hopeful about life and the future, even in a chaotic world.

Step 7. Accessing the Higher Dimensions

He asked his higher self about the source of the anxious feeling about being discovered. After several days, he began to put the pieces together. He had not been very kind to his younger brother when they were growing up. For eight years, he had been the only child, and though he loved his brother, he often picked on him. They were friendly now, but he still felt guilty about how he had behaved. He talked about it with his brother, who had actually forgiven him some time ago. Sam felt relieved.

What Was Happening?

Sam pinpointed the specific external situation (groups of soldiers) that continued to affect his moods. He was in touch with his emotions, physical responses, and the various personalities that were evoked during the orange-alert climate at the airport. From a conscious point of view, he objected to war, but when he looked honestly at his intense reactions, he saw that it was more than just that. The soldiers reawakened the memories of his school tormentors. The Nazi dreams corroborated that. However, on a deeper level, he was also identifying with the soldiers and needed to resolve his own guilt about being his brother's tormentor. He began to forgive the "young punk" in himself from those early days. Talking to his brother relieved a lot of the guilt feelings he had stored away for a long time. He also found himself being more sympathetic to the young soldiers. The Nazi dreams continued for a while, but now he began to confront his enemies instead of just running away.

Dissociated States and Hidden Energy

We may think of old issues and unconscious fears as frozen states better left alone, but they are potent and contain subterranean energy. Each time we explore our anxieties in some new way with critical and patient compassion, we tap into those dissociated parts and dissipate some negative energy. Instead of recycling an old mind pattern, we're more likely to use our emotions in a productive way. Sam was still angry about the possible war, but he used his traveling as an opportunity to gather ideas and opinions about it from various people outside New York, especially in Europe. He found his research sometimes disturbing, but also engaging and informative.

With practice, this cross-referencing process allows insights and interconnections to take place more easily and automatically, because the mind gets used to moving back and forth among the different dimensions of consciousness.

ELEVEN

STIMULATING IMAGINATION: MIND-ORCHESTRATION TOOLS

Imagination is everything. It is the preview of life's coming attractions.
—Albert Einstein

Here we review the mind-orchestration tools more carefully to understand why they are important and how they work.

One-Point Concentration

The ability to focus the mind more fully and automatically on one thing and to be able to screen out extraneous thoughts or unnecessary stimuli.

Why Is It Important?

When you are lifting a heavy box, you must use all of your effort and concentration on the action. Your body gets into position, and your intention is clear (how to do it and where to move it). If your cell phone distracts you, the lifting may not work. If you have thoughts like, *I should have asked my friend to help* or *I'm going to drop this*, you may also have trouble. What we say and think can influence our ability to successfully complete some action.

Similarly, if you are in some kind of crisis situation and you need to decide what to do, you have to be able to concentrate and place yourself into a self-reflective state beyond anxiety rather quickly. Interfering thoughts or emotions can create static between you and the decision you need to make or the result you want. Much of the time, thought interruptions from the past, or negative expectations about the future, hang out like chattering ghosts. Other times, we think we're paying attention, but our mind just goes blank. In the external world, there are many distractions: noises, climate changes that affect our moods, electromagnetic interferences that affect our bodies, subliminal messages that move into our minds, and general and deliberate societal mind conditioning.

In order to use our minds clearly to make the right decision, think our bodies into health, remember and release traumatic memories, activate hidden skills, or predict and change our futures, we have to know how to concentrate.

Everything we do in life usually has some thought-visualization process operating. When you decide to go shopping, somewhere in your mind is a thought, usually combined with an image, about which store to go to, how to get there, or what you want to buy. We're not always aware of this process because it's automatic, but learning how to focus intentionally with clear awareness gives us more direct control over what we want to accomplish.

In order to use our brains in the best way possible and to be able to move from sensory reality up to the superconscious and back again, to explore our emotions and then move on to a dream, we need to have control over our intention and to be more direct with our attention. We begin by focusing on a physical object without thinking of anything else. Then we practice conjuring up that image in our imagination. Later on, we can expand this to activate a specific memory or emotion. Let's begin with the following exercises.

Exercise

1. Choose a simple object from your home, like a coffee cup, a statuette, or a plant. Sit down somewhere, and place it in front of you. Take a deep breath, exhale, and relax. For at least a minute or two, stare at it intently and take it all in—the shape, the color, the texture, the size of it. Try not to let your mind wander to thoughts like how you got it, or what it means, just visually take in what you see as fully as possible.

2. Then, still with the object in front of you, close your eyes and imagine it in your mind with as much detail as possible. After a minute or two, open your eyes and check your accuracy. Then close your eyes and try again. Do this a few times until you remember how it looks and can do it more automatically. If visualizing is difficult for you, say the name of the object (e.g.., coffee cup) and describe how it looks in words, and think about what it feels like to the touch, or how light or heavy it is. Sometimes you will get a sense of it rather than a clear image.

3. Sometime during the day, close your eyes for a split second and get the picture of it in your mind's eye as clearly as you can, almost like a flash photograph. The more you do this, the easier it will be to bring it into focus. Experiment with different objects.

Alternative Exercise

Choose one letter from your name. Write it as a capital letter, and memorize how it looks. Several times during the day, close your eyes and visualize the letter in your mind's eye. Also try making it larger or smaller. You can also try this with a short word like "fix" or "will" or "hat." If you have trouble visualizing the letter or word, try tracing it with your finger in the air.

> Example
> I had a client who suffered from asthma. In addition to working on the psychological mind patterns related to the condition, she practiced focusing on a time in her childhood before she had asthma. Using one-point concentration, she was able to move back into her past and reexperience breathing normally, especially during gym class. She found that she could do this for several minutes, even in the middle of bouts of breathing discomfort, and then eventually for longer periods of time. After some time, she was able to stop taking medication and change her condition permanently.

Two-Point Concentration

The ability to focus our attention in two places during the same period of time.

Why Is It Important?

We can drive and listen to music on the car radio at the same time. If we are on a crowded highway, hopefully the driving takes precedence (especially over cell phones) with respect to attention. In actuality, we are experiencing both things but moving our consciousness back and forth between driving and listening to the music. We do many things like this, but not always with conscious awareness.

We get stuck in one way of thinking or feeling, and we often block out whatever else is going on. For example, we can be so busy talking and feeling sorry for ourselves and wanting sympathy that we don't notice that for the past few minutes the other person who started off being angry with us has been reaching out to connect with us and apologize. We are so involved with our own process sometimes we just don't notice what else is going on. Or, we can do the opposite. We can get so lost in another person's emotions that we ignore our own or become confused about what we really feel.

Addictions and obsessive thinking are ways we can get stuck in a persistent mind pattern. When we are in the midst of an addictive behavior—eating, drinking, or smoking for example—we are often in an altered state that ignores or rebels against thoughts from another part of our mind that tries to stop us. If we are smoking and at the same time could step back to notice what we're doing from a different perspective, we might be able to effect some change in that conditioned impulse.

Two-point concentration is especially helpful when we try to recall a disturbing event in order to resolve it. We can remember it, but at the same time view it as an objective observer without overwhelming emotions.

Exercise

1. Take a deep breath, exhale, and close your eyes. Keep your left hand still with palms open and faceup. Take your right hand and move the tips of your fingers gently back and forth on the palm of your left hand.

2. Continue to do that, but now ignore the left hand and place all of your concentration on your right hand as it moves back and forth, and especially focus on the physical sensation on the tips of the fingers.

3. Continue, only now ignore the right hand and place all of your attention on the left hand. Especially notice how the skin feels as it is being touched.

4. Switch hands and repeat the exercise.

5. Practice moving your awareness back and forth between the sensations of the right hand to the sensations on the left and see how close you can get to experiencing both sensations at the same time.

Alternative Exercise

1. When you are in a conversation with someone, take a deep breath and exhale.

2. Continue the verbal exchange, but also shift your attention now and then and notice how both of you are relating to each other through your body postures and gestures. Are you standing, sitting, facing each other eye to eye, or glancing away? Are you close enough to touch? How are you using your hands and arms during the conversation?

3. Continue talking with this added awareness.

> Example
> I was in a counseling session with a couple, Doris and Jack, who had been married for almost a year. They were in the middle of a conversation and were trying to iron out some problems that had come up during the week. Each one was trying to help the other understand what they were feeling and what to do about it. Doris then said that while she was listening and sympathetic to what Jack was saying, she also realized that whenever Jack pointed his finger to emphasize a statement, she felt herself getting annoyed. It was because whenever he did this, he became the professor teaching the student, and Doris objected to being put in that position. Jack had not been aware that he was gesturing in that way. He stopped, and that allowed for better communication.

Changing Perception

Changing the mode of perception or activity from one thing to another.

Why Is It Important?

Who we are, how we think, and what we feel is expressed in many ways. We're not always in touch with what our unconscious self or our higher self is trying to tell us. An example of this is a dream, which is a pictorial expression of what we may be feeling without realizing it on a conscious level.

We are all familiar with multitask learning in school. If we want to memorize a word, we can recall it better if we write it, look at it, and say it out loud. The Lozanov Method, developed by a Bulgarian physician and psychiatrist in the 1970s, is still used to teach languages by utilizing meditation, affirmative phrases, rhythmic breathing, and music all at the same time for better memory retention and recall.[1] When we use more sensory modalities, we are activating more parts of the brain. This helps expand our consciousness and may offer us more information about some issue we are grappling with. Mind shifting can interrupt the habitual ways of thinking that keep us stuck in negative mind patterns. It loosens our way of perceiving something; it moves us away from being too top-heavy with our thinking brain.

Exercise

1. Buy a small notepad, and carry it with you during the day. Select a simple problem, an issue that you've been thinking about. Describe it in one or two sentences in the notepad. Read it out loud. Now, without thinking about it too much, make a quick drawing (in pen or pencil) that represents the issue. It can be realistic or abstract, a letter, a symbol, a doodle, anything that is a visual expression of what you're thinking about.

2. During the next few days, as the issue comes up, or even if it doesn't, make some other notations and drawings without referring to the previous ones. You're keeping a pictorial journal of your particular concern.

3. At the end of the week, look at all the notes and drawings together. Are they the same? Are they different? What has this process been like for you?

Alternative Exercise

During the day, whenever you catch a passing negative thought of any kind, write down a word or two that expresses it on a piece of paper, and then tear it up and throw it in the trash. If it's not convenient to do this physically, then imagine going through the motions.

> Example
>
> Sandy woke up from a nightmare about a huge spider that was hiding in the walls of her apartment. She had dreamt of hidden spiders once in a while since her childhood, and they were always frightening dreams that affected her for days. This time she got up, splashed cold water on her face (water helps to shift negative energy), wrote down the dream, and drew what she thought the spider looked like and imagined what it was trying to say. What she came up with was something her mother used to say all the time: "You never know what's going to happen in life." While that was meant as a friendly warning, Sandy had incorporated her mother's anxiety and fear about the world, and she began to unravel other deeper levels about the dream that helped her process it.

Mind Adventuring

Allowing the mind to wander creatively to see where it goes and what it has to reveal to you.

Why Is It Important?

Repetition helps us strengthen neuronal pathways to the brain so that we can remember facts, skills, and ways of doing things more automatically and efficiently. However, the mind is always stimulated through novelty. The brain continues to grow in phenomenal ways the more it is engaged in new thoughts and activities. One way to encourage this mind adventuring is to notice how we perceive things around us and then play creatively with those perceptions. We are often projecting our ideas and our stories onto the world around us, but we don't always do it consciously. Noticing these projections may reveal to us what we're thinking and feeling on a deeper level. Giving our mind the freedom to wander is like creating a quick waking-dream story that satisfies the brain and also helps us uncover more information about ourselves.

Projecting quick stories onto things around us over a period of time reveals to us aspects of our unconscious ideas, concerns, and passions. Playing with our perceptions is good for our brain health.

Exercise

1. The next time you see your supervisor, neighbor, aunt, partner, or whomever, while you are talking to them, imagine each of them as a baby. How would they look? What would they sound like? How would they act? Do that with everyone you meet during the day.

Alternative Exercise

1. Look around you when you are at home, and choose some inanimate object at random, like a plate, a curtain, a shoe, etc. Imagine that this object has a gender and a personality and that it can speak. What would it say?

> Example
> Brad looked around my office to see what object attracted him. He chose a small statue of a carved wooden elephant with its trunk raised. He said it was a proud male, determined, slowly walking toward something. His trunk was raised because he was calling out to the rest of the herd, but nobody was around. He seemed to be alone, but still determined to find whatever he was looking for. Brad had been worrying about changing careers. He hadn't discussed it with his family yet and didn't know how they would respond, but felt that whether they approved or not, he had to do it anyway. The exercise brought this issue to the surface so that he could face it.

Each of these mind-orchestration tools can be used with any of the seven steps. You can experiment on your own with other variations. Each activity frees us from the restrictions of left-brain logical thinking. We activate the natural play activity of the right brain so that it can cooperate with the left instead of being overwhelmed by it. Deprogramming from fear doesn't mean we have to reactivate our anxieties in order to dissolve them. It means playing with our perceptions so that we arrive at some solution and release fear through our natural creative abilities.

High-Velocity Consciousness and Intuition

The seven step cross-referencing process stimulates our natural ability to travel multidimensionally and promote mindspeed integration when we need it.

When we find ourselves in various dimensions of consciousness, how valid is what we see, think, feel, and experience? Can we be duped into a false direction in the name of a god, a guru, an odd voice in a dream? Yes. Societal mind conditioning, subliminal propaganda, and advanced technology can affect our bodies and seep into our thoughts and our dreams. The more often we travel among different levels of consciousness and cross-reference our information, the less vulnerable we are to external conditioning.

Mindspeed integration is the experience of insight. As we saw in earlier examples, it may be felt as a certainty of action in a dangerous situation. We may experience it when a strong psychic prediction comes true. We may feel it in the middle of some startling synchronous event. It's when we *know* something. It's not just a thinking process that results from logical exploration. It includes all the levels of consciousness. Intuition is High-Velocity Consciousness in action.

Practicing the seven steps promotes our intuitive powers. With this multidimensional navigation, we learn how to shift not only between the rational and creative mind but also between the dream state and the physical state. We observe the past and the future and heighten our perception of the present. We respect sensory reality and welcome psychic reality. We shift from the emotional/psychological arena into the spiritual realm and back again. We reconnect with our ability to activate the full spectrum of our psyches and access our pure, unmediated experience and knowledge.

And one trip won't do it. For example, I know some people who had an insightful dream or experienced a sudden revelation. During that moment, their perceptions were affected dramatically. But then after a while, they went back to their usual routines as if that trip never happened. We need to be frequent flyers to all of the dimensions of consciousness, not occasional travelers to one or two.

In the following chapters, we'll examine each of the seven steps in depth and why they are important. Though they are listed in a certain order, they don't have to be used in succession. You may have a kéfi moment in the morning, remember a dream after lunch, or notice changing moods and body signals several times during the day. You can spend just ten minutes a day activating all the seven steps or take as much time as you like doing the various exercises. When you include these in your daily routine, you become automatically more aware of them, and in time, the process unfolds more naturally.

Included in each chapter are some examples of how societal mind conditioning can affect us in that particular arena. As we saw earlier, some programming is obvious and direct, and some of it is subliminal and indirect. Please become aware of the mind-manipulation atmosphere that is drifting into our lives. Look behind the pleasure-promoting and fear-provoking masks to explore *what else is happening at the same time*.

As you read through the book, ask yourself—what kind of societal conditioning particularly concerns you? Today it's a challenge for us to live in the world with both "healthy paranoia" and "infinite optimism."

Let's look at how to do that.

TWELVE

NOTICING EMOTIONS AND MOODS

Anxiety is the handmaiden of creativity.

—T. S. Eliot

Step 1. Noticing Emotions and Moods

Now and then during the day, ask yourself how you are feeling emotionally and what kind of mood you are in.

The first step of cross-referencing is to pay attention to our emotions and moods at different times during the day, especially the troublesome ones. We get angry when our friend shows up forty minutes late again. We feel guilty about yelling at a parent. These are pretty direct emotions, but there are also thoughts and feelings that move through us so automatically that we're not aware of them. They can last for a minute or two, or hang out in our subconscious fairly regularly. For example, if you have a well-established critical opinion about your appearance, that may be triggered every time you look in a mirror. We need to notice the positive emotional experiences as well, but we're not always aware of them either.

Why Is It Important?

Noticing what we are feeling gives us more information about who we are even though we think we know all about ourselves. Even just naming our emotions changes their effect on us. How often are our daily thoughts colored with anxiety? If a negative emotion persists, how do we break the circuit? How much time do we spend feeling really good about ourselves? In order to ask the questions, we must have a sense about what we're feeling and what we do with our emotions. Persistent negative thoughts need to be interrupted by deliberate action, especially today, when we are more easily manipulated through societal conditioning about how we should feel and what we should do about it. Let's look briefly at some emotions and how they affect us.

Anger

Anger is the intense feeling we have when we think we've been hurt in some way. It's our reaction to some kind of injury—to our body, our beliefs, our identity, or our power. When we're angry, we are provoked to exert some kind of action against the person, object, or situation that caused us to become unbalanced. Sometimes we think of retaliation. We look for a reestablishment of power or control over the initial situation so that we can relieve our frustration. Sometimes we take action; sometimes we don't.

Unwelcome intrusions of all kinds upset us. We feel angry when our physical or psychological space is invaded—someone pushes to get ahead of us in line; our parent or partner repeatedly interrupts our conversation. We get angry when someone or something blocks us from getting what we deserve, or stops us from doing what we want to do. We work hard, we're promised a raise—then we don't get it. We have an argument with our partner. We want to talk about it; he or she refuses and walks away from us.

We can become enraged when someone judges us harshly, humiliates us, or in some way diminishes our self-worth with open put-downs or underhanded manipulation.

Betrayal makes us angry. A friend we trust and confide in doesn't respect our privacy. Someone we think is supporting us suddenly becomes our enemy.

In the larger arena, injustice, insensitivity, or irresponsibility—being unfairly treated socially, medically, legally because we're not in a high enough economic bracket or we belong to a particular racial or ethnic group—makes us angry. We get angry when authority figures and institutions are not able to protect us from corporate corruption, terrorism, toxic air, or virulent diseases.

Anger can also be part of our inheritance. Just as we can unconsciously take on other people's fears, we can also inherit and repeat mind patterns of anger from parents and ancestors.

Anger is part of the human condition. It's healthy when it challenges us about something that we need to examine. It can be a positive form of self-assertion that leads to creative change. It can also be a distorted perception of reality, blaming and venting rage at the wrong people. When it is consistently repressed, it can result in dissociated states.

Persistent anger doesn't work too well when it's expressed explosively and indiscriminately, or when it's denied or camouflaged with positive thinking. It needs to be noticed and understood.

Questions and Considerations

1. Did you experience anger in your childhood? How was it handled in your family?

2. How do you deal with anger today? How often do you feel angry or irritated at something, someone, or yourself?

3. When you get angry, how long does the feeling last, and how do you experience it physically?

4. What action, if any, do you take either with yourself or with others to move through and release the emotion?

5. What kinds of things usually or always make you angry and why?

6. Think about some situations that triggered your anger that were valuable and constructive.

Jealousy and Envy

Jealousy begins as an attraction to, an enthusiasm for, or an excitement about someone or something that can turn into self-criticism.

The experience of jealousy goes something like this: You know someone or hear about somebody through some public source. You're impressed with who they are, or who you assume them to be. You become entranced for a moment. You wish you could be like that person, or have what that person has. Jealousy grows when the path between what you want and actually getting it seems long, difficult, and even impossible. The more intensely you want what the other person has, and the more inadequate you feel about getting it, the more jealousy takes root in the psyche. We get caught up in a frozen fantasy whose very existence in our imagination reminds us of our inadequacy. The contrast of these two polarities—the idealized goal and the feeling of impotency about achieving it—fuels jealousy and envy.

Jealousy is not just a personal issue. Especially in Western society, competition is keen, and more is better. We live in a culture of dramatic haves and have-nots, politically, economically, and socially—disparities that foster jealousy and envy from groups of disenfranchised people. Some jealousies immobilize people into self-loathing and hopelessness. Others result in violence. Some move people into action that turns into greed. They think, *I'll accumulate enough wealth and power until I'm safe from feeling envy.* But it's a false security unless internal integration accompanies the acquisition of external power.

A jealous feeling, an envious longing, can be transformed into a realized dream by examining our frozen fantasies. We need to challenge our own feelings of impotence about achieving that dream. Some kind of action, no matter how small, can change the fantasy from a persistent thought that goes nowhere to a feasible goal. In some instances, we need to let the fantasy go and move to a more realistic one that can be brought to fruition. Our fantasy about being the next singing sensation may not be realistic when five kind people independently tell us we can't carry a tune.

When a jealous feeling persists, we need to ask what it means and why it's so important. A client of mine consistently got angry with some homeless people in the city, especially the ones who seemed less troubled than the others. He finally admitted that he was jealous of their inactivity. He said that they had nothing to do all day—no job, no deadlines to meet, no mortgage to pay, and probably no family to feed. He was a CEO who was overworked, overstressed, and overburdened with responsibilities. Sometime later, he moved to a smaller firm and worked fewer hours, something he'd wanted to do for several years. He also found himself being less envious and angry with the homeless.

Many of us have secret jealousies. It helps to explore them and give them a chance to breathe. Some of our creativity is locked up in these secret places.

Questions and Considerations

1. Were there things that happened in your childhood that evoked jealous or envious feelings on your part or in other people? If so, how was it handled in your family?

2. Do you have any secret jealousies? If so, which ones are impossible frozen fantasies, and which ones represent possible dreams? What small action or actions can you take to begin to actualize the possible dreams?

3. How often do you notice someone who you believe is more attractive, successful, smarter, or luckier than you? What happens when you have this reaction, and where does it take you in your thinking? If this envy happens often or lingers too long, how can you use it to your advantage?

Guilt and Shame

Guilt is an experience of self-suffering. We feel guilty when we do something that goes against our conscience. We feel remorse about an action we took, some circumstance where we behaved badly with cruelty, misjudgment, intolerance, exploitation, or some other kind of insensitivity. Guilt means that we're going against a set of rules and regulations usually set up early in life by parental figures. We either agreed or disagreed with these rules, but nonetheless, we somehow internalized them. We feel guilty when we transgress these boundaries.

Guilt has been around for a long time and has been connected historically with the need for atonement by using ritual punishment for the transgressor. For thousands of years, public humiliation, physical torture, sacrifice of a limb or body part, or banishment out of the community were all ways of promoting guilt. (And still are in some places.) We all have within us the genetic memory of these horrific experiences, and conscious or unconscious guilt has been passed on to us from generation to generation.

The whole structure of society is based on rules and regulations and the cooperation of people to maintain these conditions. Underlying the idea about maintaining boundaries seems to be that we need to be frightened enough to feel guilty in order to remember what we are supposed to do and not do. So, fear surrounds guilt when we are punished by parents, partners, friends, or businesspeople. We're afraid of their anger, withdrawal of respect or love.

Shame, on the other hand, is different. Though it may also be related to something we do, shame is more of a feeling of failure about who we are on a deeper level, an exposure of ourselves in some mortifying way. With guilt, the admonition is, *Look what you did*, while with shame it's, *Look who you are*.

Guilt can be experienced in the privacy of our own minds without anyone around; shame usually requires an audience to be felt. Shame is often associated with sex and sexual feelings, embarrassment, and physical or psychological exposure of some kind. For example, both men and women may have hidden feelings of shame about some part of their bodies. We can feel shame when one of our hidden thoughts suddenly appears through a slip of the tongue or an unexpected exclamation that shocks everyone. It's as though the worst of who we believe we are is suddenly exposed. Behind the feeling of guilt is fear of anger, sadness, and disappointment from authority figures or people we respect. With shame, it's more like fear of contempt, a kind of disgust, from parental figures.

Of course, even though they're different, guilt and shame can also happen together. *I can't believe that you just said that terrible thing to her. You're not only selfish but a total idiot.*

Some people never feel guilty, which may not be a good thing, because nobody's perfect, and we all make mistakes once in a while. And some people feel guilty all the time, which is definitely not a good thing. It usually means that the person has too many "shoulds" and is not able to live up to his or her self-created values that may be unrealistic to begin with.

Guilt is not very productive when it becomes an end in itself and a reason to continue to feel terrible. It should be a prelude to action. The intention of feeling guilt and shame is to forgive ourselves by repairing, re-creating, and maintaining the boundaries that we have overstepped either within ourselves or in society.

Questions and Considerations

1. What kinds of things, if any, do you remember from your childhood that made you feel guilty or ashamed? How was this handled by parents, guardians, teachers, or religious leaders?

2. If there was some kind of punishment involved, what form did that take? Has that affected your way of dealing with feelings of guilt or shame today?

3. What kinds of things, if any, make you feel guilty or ashamed today? How do you handle these feelings?

4.When you need to forgive yourself for something, how do you do it?

Loneliness and Authenticity

An underlying theme that has come up with many of my clients over the years is loneliness. It has many forms: being alone and being afraid of some unnamed danger, not understanding why we can't find someone to love, turning people away from us because of our anger or depression, having an illness that separates us from life, experiencing emotions and thoughts that we don't want to share with anyone.

I believe that within our genetic memory, we remember an experience of feeling complete and connected, and we long for it: a time when we were part of the infinite source of creation, beyond the complications of a three-dimensional world. This memory of integrated wholeness is in contrast to the fragmentation many of us feel in everyday reality, especially now, in a time of accelerated change, confusion, and alienation.

Each of us wants to be authentic, to be in touch with ourselves and others in ways that feel real in the midst of the natural cycles of pleasure and pain. We want to participate in exchanges of truthfulness. When our insecurities and fears block these exchanges from taking place, we feel lonely.

In interpersonal relationships, we feel separated from someone who really isn't listening to what we're saying, or someone who listens, but has nothing to say in return. We feel it when we are with a person who speaks mechanically about beautiful or devastating experiences without any depth of emotion about them. We feel separated when we are with someone who might have important things to say, but who chatters on about superficial things.

We want to interconnect with people and be authentic, but we're sometimes afraid of being ourselves, so we put on an act. We develop roles that seem to work for a while. We project what we think is a functional style so well that we don't even realize we're doing it. Yet, we're always relieved when someone is real. Their honesty encourages us to be less afraid of being ourselves. In that moment, some of our loneliness dissipates and the promise of communion on some deeper level with ourselves and with others seems more possible.

Being real doesn't necessarily mean being a wonderful person. You can appear, for a moment, to be stubborn, ambitious, or angry. But there is something free about you when you are experiencing these emotions or attitudes—something honest that affects people positively. They sense the congruity of your words, actions, and feelings. People may not agree with you, or even like you, but for a moment, they are pulled into a place of feeling respect, and even compassion, for you.

I remember a counseling session where a husband and wife were arguing about an incident that had just happened. The husband had neglected to take care of something at home, and the wife was furious about it. It led to a familiar discussion about responsibilities. Both presented their versions of what had happened. They were like two intelligent but bitter lawyers stating their cases and getting nowhere. The emotional distance between them widened.

In the middle of a long, but reasonable-sounding argument by the woman, the man, who up until then had been quite composed, suddenly looked directly at her and screamed out in anguish, "You're driving me crazy. Everything I do is wrong! It's so hard."

His truthfulness cut through the air. She finally heard him. She reached out tenderly to touch his shoulder, and the real communication began.

The less pretense we have about who we are, the less lonely we feel. We want to be real with ourselves and with others. Living authentically means giving voice to all the parts of who we are without getting stuck in any one role or identity, and giving the other person the same freedom. At the same time that we are doing that, in the midst of an argument with someone we care about, we can try to keep some compassion alive, no matter how slight.

Loneliness begins to disappear with continuing awareness, and a repeated experience of being real and being heard. We all long for authentic communication.

Questions and Considerations

1. Were there times in your life when you felt lonely, especially during childhood? How were you able to change or shift that feeling? Did you try to do this alone, or did you have outside support and help?

2. What is the difference for you between a comfortable alone state and an uncomfortable lonely state? What internal dialogue accompanies each state?

3. Who do you feel most authentic with in your life, and why?

The Path of Uncomfortable Emotions

When uncomfortable emotions persist, even in subtle forms, fear can be found at their core. These personal insecurities are used by certain segments of society to influence our decisions and direct our actions. Our anger and fear can be activated by convincing us to agree to some government or military action, or diminished by encouraging us to take a pharmaceutical drug. Guilt and shame can be used to propel us to spend money to redeem ourselves through special religions, philanthropic donations, or long-term psychotherapy. Jealousy and envy are emphasized every day through the media to convince us to buy the perfect car, the best makeover, or the latest digital technology so that we can compete successfully. Loneliness can be alleviated through social networks, chat rooms or interactive video games, or so we are told.

Each of these emotions has value in its best form. Fear helps us to avoid danger, or learn how to confront it in some necessary way. Anger causes us to take action, express some hurt or fear, or correct an injustice. Guilt reminds us of our principles and standards and moves us to reestablish our boundaries. At their core, jealousy and envy represent some unrealized but persistent dream. Loneliness can move us to look for authentic communication with others. When we pay attention to what we feel, we can discover the hidden value of each emotion and use it to our advantage.

Fast Thoughts and Slow Emotions

In the best of circumstances, our emotions find their way to the frontal lobes of the cerebral cortex. This part of the brain helps us consciously explore, evaluate, and interpret our feelings and decide how to deal with them. However, as we learned earlier, this doesn't always work so efficiently. Our emotions, especially fear, can become overwhelming and affect our body and brain and interfere with our reasonable thinking process.

The ability of emotions to flood the brain and cause changes in many interrelated areas of the cortex and subcortex is linked to their relatively slow timescale. In general, feelings linger where thoughts do not. This mismatch between emotional duration and the quicksilver precision of thought and language is significant.[1] It means that when you are in the midst of experiencing something emotionally, even when it's not very intense, your mind is automatically triggered with memories, thoughts, and ideas about the situation. These are not necessarily helpful or valid and may even be unrelated to the topic. How quickly the mind becomes active in this way varies and depends on individual differences and emotional sensitivity. Instead of quick mind integration, we may have emotion-propelled haphazard thinking.

So what happens when we interrupt and amplify a negative emotion, visualize it in some new way, express it out loud with words, sounds, or movement? We are shifting it from the thought process and letting it unfold in another modality. When we do this, we are consciously moving through our emotions before they get entangled with our runaway negative thinking. Then we can orchestrate our emotions without recycling old and ineffective thought responses.

Anxiety-Reducing Exercise

The next exercise is effective for temporary relief from a stressful state by taking direct action and shifting into other modalities. The next time you are feeling anxious about something, try the following.

1. Choose an area where you can move around a little and have a watch or clock nearby within view. Begin the exercise in a standing position. Briefly describe out loud what is upsetting you.

Example
"I let him get away with that again. I got conned again. I thought I could stand up for myself, but I just wimped out."

2. Then, still standing, shift from thinking about the issue to noticing what you're feeling in your body at the moment. What is your physical experience, and where and how are you sensing it? Does your stomach feel tight? Is your heart beating faster? Do your legs feel heavy?

3. Decide on a limited period of time, anywhere from one to three minutes. Place the watch or clock in a place where you can glance at it so that you can stop at your decided designated time. Now keep the original issue in mind, along with the emotions and the physical experiences, and amplify or exaggerate everything. Let yourself do and say whatever comes to mind without analyzing it. Be spontaneous. Say what you feel out loud without censoring anything. At the same time, let your body become involved in some kind of movement as you speak. Shake your fists. Stomp around the room. Let yourself shiver. Don't think about it; just feel how your body is reacting, and go with it. Do all this as fully as you can for the designated period of time—no more, no less.

Examples
- "That was so stupid what I just did. I'm the world champion of dumb smart-asses trying to be funny…"
- "She's such a lazy bitch. I can't believe she got that promotion. I feel like grabbing her by the hair and…"
- "I feel like a know-nothing, do-nothing loser. Life sucks…"

4. Then, when the time is up, take a deep breath through your nose and exhale through your mouth. Sit down, close your eyes, breathe normally, and place your open hands, palms down, lightly on top of your head, toward the front, above your forehead and just above the hairline. Some of the fingertips of both hands may touch each other. Keep your hands there, gently pressing your open palms on your head, and count slowly to yourself from one to five.

5. Then, very slowly and carefully, remove your hands and feel the freedom of the air around your head. Tell yourself that now your mind will be cleared of all the previous emotions and thoughts so that you can

move on in a positive direction.

6. Take a deep breath through your nose, exhale through your mouth, and shift your attention immediately to some pleasurable activity. Go for a walk, take a shower, listen to a favorite CD, or eat something you like.

Emotions and Societal Mind Conditioning

Propagandists, or "influence technicians" as writer Kathleen Taylor calls them, know how to appeal to your emotional brain.[2] While you are in an emotional state and before you have a chance to stop and think, they influence you to feel a certain way and sympathize with their position.

In a public forum or on TV, notice when the speaker makes a statement that affects you and the audience emotionally and evokes, anger, compassion, sadness, or fear. At that moment, stop and ask yourself, how does this relate to the topic at hand, and what is the speaker's intention?

Some emotional presentations are obvious. In the first American presidential debate in 2008, Senator John McCain showed the audience a soldier's bracelet he was wearing that had been given to him by a mother whose son had been killed in Iraq. However, right after that, Senator Barack Obama showed the bracelet *he* was wearing given to him by another mother whose son had also died.[3] Both were emotional moments that evoked sadness and compassion and were presented by two people who had different intentions and viewpoints about the war.

Sometimes evoking emotions is valuable and makes sense. At other times it is manipulative. Know how you are responding at the moment. Ask yourself how authentic the person seems to be and what his or her intention is for presenting the idea in this way.

Cognitive Dissonance and Societal Mind Conditioning

When what we strongly believe in is called into question, most of us react with some degree of emotional discomfort. Let's begin with what happens to us on a personal level with this discomfort and then look at how some segments of society can manipulate us into resolving our upset to their advantage.

Social psychologist Dr. Leon Festinger developed the theory of cognitive dissonance in 1957. It refers to the uncomfortable feeling and emotional stress that happens when we are faced with two contradictory ideas at the same time.[4] For example, Harry, a forty-two-year-old man, believed that he was and had always been healthy. However, he had been drinking more alcohol every night after work. When he went for his yearly checkup, he found out for the first time that his blood pressure was quite high, and his liver and kidneys were not functioning well. The doctor told him that he might be in for further health problems if he didn't curb his drinking or try to stop it altogether. Harry had two opposing thoughts (cognitions) in his head now. The first was his belief that he was healthy, and the other was that he was given medical information that he might not be healthy.

Cognitive dissonance threatens our identity and challenges our belief in ways that we don't always want to face or admit. The two contradictory ideas put us into a state of distress that compels us to do something to reduce the tension. So what can Harry do?

For one, he can take the medical information seriously and change his drinking habits...but Harry didn't choose to do this.

He can also reject the information as untrue and ignore it, which is what happened. Harry said that the blood pressure report didn't seem accurate, and even if it was, it was probably temporary because he still felt pretty healthy.

Further, he can find ways of justifying his behavior (the drinking) by modifying his belief pattern in some way ("I'm healthy") to match or be more consistent with his behavior.

Harry said, "I'm in good condition physically. I'm just under a lot of stress right now. Drinking relaxes me. It never interferes with my work during the day. I know my father was an alcoholic, but that doesn't mean I am. I'm not like him at all."

We have choices about how to deal with information that questions our behavior, identity, or established belief. Most of us don't like to admit that we're wrong or that we made a mistake. Facing something that is opposite to what we believe requires examination and change that can make us even more uncomfortable.

Harry justified his drinking by holding on to his belief that he was healthy and that the drinking wasn't affecting him. Admitting he might be wrong meant that he had to change his habits, and that would bring him more anxiety. He was also in a work situation where going out and drinking with business associates was expected. The group around him supported the drinking lifestyle. He chose to alleviate his cognitive dissonance by disputing and dismissing the medical reports. Put another way, he dissociated from that new information. He modified his belief somewhat by admitting that he was under stress, but that drinking relaxed him and never interfered with his work. He declared that he was in control by separating himself from his father. But later, as his health got worse, he finally admitted he had a drinking problem and went for help.

Changing your belief system is harder when people around you support your position and justify your beliefs. Religious and spiritual cults are dramatic examples of how difficult it is for people to break away from them when they are confronted with serious evidence from the outside that contradicts their beliefs and commitment to the group.

Using the example of cults, Dr. Festinger said that beliefs are more likely to be retained in the face of massive contrary evidence when the following is involved:

1. The belief is deeply held and has affected how the believer has acted and behaved.

2. Action must have been taken because of the belief that is not easy to undo—like giving away your money and possessions and/or severing ties with your family. The general rule is that the more extreme the actions, the more people will cling to the belief that prompted them.

3. Clear and irrevocable evidence must occur to show the believer that the belief is in error. This creates the cognitive dissonance between belief and experience.

4. An individual will find it more difficult to ignore or explain away the obvious belief/experience contradiction, and so the more people there are with the same belief to support each other's position, the more likely it is that the belief will survive, no matter what the experience.[5]

Cults are extreme examples. However, most of us experience various degrees of cognitive dissonance all the time, especially today, when many of our beliefs are being questioned as new information is revealed. If we harbor a weak belief, we can be flexible and change our thinking and behavior. For years, Janet added raw spinach to her salad, until she found out that pesticide residue doesn't wash off spinach leaves, making it one of the dozen fruits and vegetables that carry the highest levels of pesticides. She was upset because she had always believed that spinach was very healthy. It is, but now she buys organic when she can. She always steams or boils it because cooking vastly reduces pesticides, and still retains most of the nutrients.

With respect to cognitive dissonance, weak beliefs like Janet's are easier to change because they are usually not threaded to other personal emotional beliefs that would be affected. She could admit that she was wrong about raw spinach being healthy. This was not a big deal. She took in the new information and changed her behavior.

However, if the belief that is being challenged by new information is strongly held, the outcome may be different, especially when it is deeply embedded with other beliefs. As Kathleen Tasylor points out, a devout believer in God does not hold this conviction in isolation from all his other beliefs; rather, it provides the emotional bedrock for much of his existence. Such beliefs can be extremely hard to change.[6] For example, many Christians today do not accept the Gnostic Gospels, the supposed teachings of Christ discovered in 1945, which present viewpoints that are different from long-established traditional Biblical writings.

Sometimes we are shocked out of strongly held beliefs. People who suffer extensive losses in times of financial crises begin to question their belief and trust in investment advice, banking institutions, and government. The important decisions we make are based on strongly held beliefs. When large numbers of people agree with us, it's easier to hold fast to what we believe in, even when that's challenged. We try to avoid cognitive dissonance by dissociating from the new information. Sometimes we just don't want to hear it at all.

Our states of cognitive dissonance can be exploited by people in authority who offer to relieve our anxieties with solutions that are not always in our best interest. Our belief that we were relatively safe from terrorist attacks was shattered with 9/11. Just six weeks later, in October, with virtually no debate, the Patriot Act was swiftly passed by both houses of Congress. Despite widespread congressional support, it was criticized for weakening protections of civil liberties. An unsatisfactory revision of the bill in 2006 was criticized by senators from both political parties. The bill passed Congress and was signed into law by President Bush on March 9, 2006. It still contains significant flaws that threaten our fundamental freedoms and privacy.[7] The Patriot Act was a quick-fix solution that was supposed to relieve some of our anxiety about feeling vulnerable and unsafe. I don't think it succeeded. What it did accomplish was to open the door to an era of extensive government surveillance and control over our lives. With regard to cognitive dissonance, the Patriot Act generally asks us to accept two contradictory ideas: that in order to maintain our liberties, we need to lose some of our freedoms.

Writer and international speaker David Icke points out how language can shape reality. He cautions that more and more we are moving into a global society where cognitive dissonance is being eliminated through the process of doublethink. Doublethink is what happens when people accept two mutually contradictory ideas as correct without examination.[8] It's an integral concept of George Orwell's famous novel *Nineteen Eighty-Four*. In this mythical totalitarian society, the idea was that everyone could be controlled and manipulated through the alteration of everyday thought and language. To create doublethink, the government programmed people to deliberately forget the contradiction between two opposing beliefs. After that, the people were then programmed to forget that they had gone through the process of forgetting the contradiction. This went on until ultimately and automatically they accepted the statement as being true without even thinking about it. This intentional programmed forgetting, once begun, continued indefinitely. Orwell described it as "controlled insanity."[9] Bombarding the people with constant mind-control propaganda made it possible for the government to make doublethink proclamations that the population automatically accepted, such as "War is Peace; Freedom is Slavery; Ignorance is Strength."[10]

Nineteen Eighty-Four, and its terms, language, and author, are bywords in discussions of personal privacy and state security. The adjective "Orwellian" describes actions and organizations characteristic of the totalitarian society depicted in the novel, and the phrase "Big Brother is watching you" refers to mind conditioning and invasive surveillance.

A few years ago in the United Kingdom, groups of people outraged by the continual attack upon civil liberties in their country decided to take some interesting action. Sponsored by the Libertarian Party, a copy of *Nineteen Eighty-Four* was sent to every member of Parliament. Each book was inscribed with the words "This book was a warning, not a blueprint" and arrived at Parliament on November 5,

2008,[11] to no doubt coincide with the annual British commemoration of controversial historical figure Guy Fawkes.

Since *Nineteen Eighty-Four* was published in 1949, the word "doublethink" became synonymous with relieving cognitive dissonance by ignoring the contradiction between two views. A national example might be, "We fight wars in order to preserve peace." A personal example of ignoring contradictions might be a person who has strong beliefs about animal rights but also wears fur. Another example of cognitive dissonance might be a person who is pro-life (anti-abortion), but believes in capital punishment.

So, how do we deal with the stressful emotions of cognitive dissonance? We begin to notice how we react when our beliefs or ideas are challenged—when we are faced with contradictory facts or new experiences. Though what we hear may be unwelcome, it can also be an opportunity to reexamine our emotional beliefs. We must dare ourselves to risk error in the name of creative expansion. We all make mistakes. Nobody is right all the time. Beliefs and truths can be altered with new information. Utilizing all the steps of High-Velocity Consciousness allows us to use cognitive dissonance to grow through the contradiction and learn from it instead of using it to maintain a rigid belief system.

Look at your beliefs and notice which ones are strong and solid and which ones require more examination. Especially look at the beliefs you have that evoke fear or anger in you when someone challenges them. Pay special attention to people who make public statements that throw you off-kilter emotionally, create cognitive dissonance, and then propose questionable solutions to alleviate your anxiety. Always cross-check the information you receive in the outside world, and also evaluate and compare the information you receive from your internal world through the different dimensions of consciousness.

Healthy Dissociation Technique

Sometimes when we try to explore a situation that really upsets us, the emotional impact from the scene interferes. We get overwhelmed with the anxiety, anger sadness, etc. The following exercise is not a way of resolving the problem necessarily, but a way of training yourself to look at it with less intense emotions.

1. Choose a specific stressful scene that happened to you in some

interaction with another person.

2. Sit in a comfortable position, close your eyes, and go through the primary centering process: take a few cleansing breaths, surround yourself with the violet color, and center yourself by visualizing the royal-blue dot in the middle of your forehead, between your eyebrows.

3. With your eyes still closed, imagine that you are sitting comfortably in an empty, darkened movie theater.

4. Visualize the specific situation on the screen as if you are watching a movie. Begin with a still shot, then slowly continue the scene as it evolves to a stopping point, and then end with another still shot.

5. Now, imagine the scene once again, beginning with the still shot, but this time speed everything up. Move through the scene in fast motion and end with the last still shot again.

6. Now, play the whole movie backward in normal time, beginning with the still shot at the end, until you come to the beginning scene again. Conclude with the opening still shot.

7. Once again, play it backward, starting at the end and going to the beginning, but speed it up.

8. Now, watch the whole scene again in normal time from the beginning to the end and see whether your emotions have changed in any way. Also notice if you had any thoughts during this process that you didn't have before. Take a deep breath, exhale, surround yourself with the grounding brown-earth color, relax, and open your eyes.

Questions and Considerations

At different times during the day, take a moment or two and notice what you are feeling. Which emotions predominate in your daily routine? What triggers your different moods? How long do they last, and what event, thought, or action causes them to shift? Also, become aware of the absence of emotions. Does this mean you are feeling comfortably balanced? Does your work schedule or life situation make it necessary to separate from your feelings, or do you habitually repress them anyway? Most of all, notice what makes you feel good and how often you feel good on a daily basis.

Say this to yourself now and then: *I maintain the freedom of my mind by noticing, respecting, and learning about my emotions with patient evaluation.*

THIRTEEN

NOTICING PERSONALITIES

We are dominated by everything with which our self becomes identified.
We can dominate and control everything from which we disidentify.
—Roberto Assagioli

Step 2. Noticing Personalities

Notice if your identity or role remains the same throughout the day and whether it changes with different people and situations.

We are a composite of different selves that are formed around physical attributes, inborn drives, creative possibilities, and manufactured survival mechanisms. A woman who is six feet tall may develop an identity that is related to her height. An innate personality trait may be an early talent and ability to draw or paint. A survival mechanism can be learned. If we grow up with an angry, controlling mother, we might develop a similar personality as we get older. Or we might do the opposite and become passive and compliant when confronted with strong women. We have many personalities—various public and private roles that we slip into consciously or unconsciously.

The complexity of our minds and the variety of our personality traits can be compared to the compartments of a Rubik's Cube. Each side of the cube is separated into nine small squares, each with a red, blue, orange, green, yellow, or white color. There is a central inner core around which the different segments of the cubes can be turned and rotated to form various combinations. The puzzle is solved when you can, through various manipulations, reach a point where each side of the large cube shows nine squares creating one solid color.

We usually present to the world the more solid or constant aspects of our personality, but there are other parts of us that combine together, like different colors, to reveal more hidden aspects of who we are. We have an infinite mind that can operate in a myriad of ways with many combinations of memories, emotions, and thoughts that come together to define who we are.

Assagioli called these parts "subpersonalities." He felt that there is a need to recognize and accept them through increasing awareness through the observing self.[1]

Why Is It Important?

Noticing and being objective about our various personality traits gives us a fuller picture of who we are and what emotions and mind patterns are contained in these different roles. The intention is to be able to experience this or that part of our identity when needed so that each role we find ourselves in contributes to the harmonic integration of our whole being.

We have a multitude of personalities. This ensemble of characters calls for our attention, especially when we disregard them or disown them. Sometimes we cut off parts of ourselves and relegate them to secret places in our psyches, and we explain the segregation in several ways. We may feel that these aspects of ourselves are so powerful that if allowed to take center stage, they might get out of control. We may be ashamed of some part and want to keep it from public view. We may not know how to handle people's reactions to it. We may be afraid that this part is who we really are and we don't want to face that. Sometimes we feel all of these things at the same time.

The moment you isolate that part from your conscious self, no matter how distasteful it is, you are disowning a piece of yourself. There is always, then, a part of you that is the enemy, that is not loved, accepted, approved of, acknowledged by you. You exist day after day with a continuing duality in your own psyche. When we become more aware of the different aspects of our personality traits, how we feel, think, and act becomes more congruent with who we really are.

Awareness of Our Multipersonalities

Most of us develop a general personality. When we move away from that predominant identity, sometimes we feel momentarily thrown. We know that we are generous and compassionate, but sometimes we become intolerably grumpy and selfish. We may dismiss that as our shadow part, an exception to the rule, something to be ignored—or we may dwell on it, privately believing that's who we really are. We also have hidden personality parts that contain unspoken wisdom, unexpressed visions, or unrealized power.

Clinical psychology has popularized the idea of connecting with our inner child, that identity formed when we were young. As adults, and under certain circumstances, we may find ourselves slipping into being a defiant kid, a spoiled child, or a shy teenager. But there are many more personalities than the inner child, and we have different degrees of awareness about them. I like to separate them into four general groups: predominant personalities, subpersonalities, alternate subpersonalities, and collective personalities.

Predominant Personalities

Predominant personalities are those temperaments, attitudes, traits, actions, talents, and interests that we are usually aware of and present to the public. They represent our primary identification.

Examples
- I think of myself as an artist. I'm very visual. I love to be surrounded by beautiful things. I'm sort of a private person.
- I get impatient with sitting still too long or reading. I'm very physical. I enjoy sports. I'm a good father. I love playing with my kids.
- I guess I'm a caretaker. That's an automatic role for me. I like to take care of people. I always did. I was the oldest one in my family.

We also define other people's predominant personalities as we perceive them.

Examples

- Jerry is a very funny guy and a really supportive friend.
- Celia is a good person, but sometimes she can be controlling.
- Edward is a brilliant writer, but rather aloof personally.

With predominant personalities, there is usually some agreement between how we view ourselves and how other people see us, but not always. Sometimes we're not the best judge of our own personalities. A client of mine who perceived himself as being a sensitive and caring person was shocked to hear from two people independently that he was seen as someone who presented himself in a caring way but often acted insensitively.

Each of us perceives another person through our own filters. Sometimes we project onto them who we think they are. A client told me about this man she liked who had a habit of telling jokes, often very corny ones. Most of his friends groaned when he started telling them, but she found him endearing. He reminded her of her father, who was also a corny joke teller. (There is someone for everyone.)

Questions and Considerations

1. What is your predominant personality? Ask some friends or family to describe you in one or two sentences. How do they see you? What is the predominant personality of some people you know?

2. Did you have a nickname growing up? What did people call you, and how did you feel about that?

3. In addition to nicknames, make a list of different names people called you from childhood to the present time. (Jimmy, Jim, James, Jimbo, dude, darling, Daddy, Bozo, etc.)

4. In the privacy of your home, take about five minutes and say as many of those names as you can remember out loud. Repeat each one several times, and go back and forth in no particular order. Notice if any memories come up and how you feel as you say each one out loud.

5. If you don't like your given name, what would you change it to and why?

Subpersonalities

If I were two-faced, would I be wearing this one?[2]

—Abraham Lincoln

Subpersonalities are somewhat less public. They may exist alongside our predominant personalities and appear occasionally, triggered by certain circumstances or certain people. We may shift into them consciously or unconsciously. We don't always accept them or let ourselves look at them too carefully. They can represent temporary emotional feelings or persistent secret identities.

Examples
- I feel competitive with my wife, and I need to be more successful than she is.
- I'm against S&M pornography, but sometimes I'm excited by it.
- I write romantic poetry that no one ever sees.

A male client had an administrative position in a large firm. His predominant personality was one of cool, unwavering, but thoughtful authority. He was well respected. He lived alone. One day during a therapy session, he revealed that once in a while, when he was really distraught, he would take out an old toy that he had hidden in his closet at home and place it on the table in front of him for a few minutes. It helped him experience whatever he was feeling, and it calmed him down. His mother had given him the toy and had died when he was about seven. He associated it with the loving comfort she had always given him. No one knew about his sensitive child subpersonality. Sometime later, he had a relationship with a woman who understood and respected his secret. In time, the ritual became less important as he learned how to share his emotions more honestly with her.

We all have secrets, and they need not always be shared. But we can ask ourselves how a subpersonality is helping us and how it's blocking us from advancing. Subpersonalities can be transformed and changed to be more effective as we begin to understand how they might have developed and what purpose they serve.

Questions and Considerations

1. Name some of your subpersonalities (the Bickering Bitch, Paul the Pompous, the Benevolent Manipulator, etc.).

2. Describe them briefly in a paragraph. How long have they been around, and how often do they appear?

3. Notice which of your subpersonalities appear with which family members, friends, and other people.

4. Are you the same age during the day, or does that shift with the activity or the person you are interacting with? When do you feel the same emotional age as your partner, child, teacher, pet—and when do you feel like a baby, teenager, or parent with them?

5. Notice when and why certain personalities appear and disappear. Name them and describe them.

> Examples
> - I went from a charming, sensitive guy to sexual predator in five minutes.
> - My brother comes near me, and I become Rambo.
> - Most of the time, she makes me feel like Mr. Stupid.

Subpersonalities Try to Reveal Themselves

Let's suppose that you have a subpersonality that is sarcastic. It only appears occasionally. You don't care for that characteristic very much, especially since you may have picked it up from your father. You try to keep it in check. However, your sarcastic subpersonality has its own agenda. It tries to get your attention in a variety of ways. You may find yourself reacting quite strongly in a group where someone makes sarcastic remarks. You feel angry and annoyed. If your reaction lasts for more than a few minutes or if it ruins your evening, then the likelihood is that your own sarcastic part is quite separated out from your awareness. We often project onto others the distaste that we feel for our own unexamined parts. If, however, you are secretly amused by the person's sarcasm, it may mean that you are closer to looking at that aspect in yourself.

You may find yourself in a situation that unexpectedly produces sarcasm from the deep regions of your mouth. This time, the subpersonality slips out before you can stop it. You may have a strange dream where you appear as a sarcastic stand-up comedian. Subpersonalities often live in dreams. The sarcastic part of you is trying to get your attention so that you will look at it and find out what it has to say.

Sarcasm usually has a negative connotation. It suggests a taunting, sneering, cutting remark, a kind of bitter, ironic laugh. When you look at this subpersonality more closely, you begin to uncover what it's trying to convey. This message may not be the same for everyone. For example, two of my clients independently discovered that they each had a sarcastic part.

I asked the first woman to act out her sarcastic part verbally and physically and to imagine what kind of character she was. As Ingrid talked and moved around the room, she became powerful and tough. I then played the role of someone in her life. We improvised together for a while. When I tried to respond to her verbally, she interrupted me before I could finish what I was saying. And she was having a wonderful time doing it. Ingrid was in a situation in her life where everyone was giving her advice. Her family and her friends felt free to criticize her and tell her how she should deal with things. She was too nice to tell them to stop. Her sarcasm was a distorted form of something she felt and couldn't express, like, *Hah! You think you're helping me? What you're saying may be fine for you; it's ridiculous for me. Stop telling me what to do.* She literally needed to cut people off and think for herself.

When the other client, Nadine, began to act out her sarcastic part, she became a character who turned out to be quite funny. She became a trickster who challenged people's statements with humor. In her usual communication with people, she was too serious. Underneath, she had a sharp, inquisitive mind that wasn't being utilized in her job or in her personal life. Her sarcastic subpersonality was urging her to question things more and to allow her natural humor to come through in her relationships.

When undercover personality traits are explored creatively, they can be integrated more into our conscious personality or utilized in a more authentic form. We have wonderful and terrible characters waiting in the wings to take center stage. Some never see the light of day. They just hover around, waiting to be heard.

Questions and Considerations

Select one of your subpersonalities. Give it a name. Close your eyes, take a few cleansing breaths, and invite this subpersonality to present itself to you on a theater stage. Invite it to speak and tell you about itself and its purpose in your life. Try not to create it deliberately; just wait and see what happens; allow the character to unfold. Watch how it moves, and listen to what it says. If nothing appears (it may be shy), try the visualization on another day or watch for it to appear in your dreams. Write down what you experience.

Alternate Subpersonalities

Alternate subpersonalities are the most hidden. We're not usually conscious of them. They are the ones that are the most separated out from our predominant personalities. They represent the identities that may be the most threatening to us. We are usually aware of them when something dramatic happens or when we find ourselves experiencing something that is out of character with the rest of our identity.

Examples
- I've always been a very sexual person. I've never, ever had a problem with getting an erection, and all of a sudden, for no reason, I can't do it, and I don't know why. I feel humiliated. It really scares me.
- I suddenly had this overwhelming feeling that I hated my kids and wished they'd never been born. I was horrified. What kind of a mother am I to have those thoughts? Is that how I really feel? I love my kids—most of the time.
- Oh my God. Yesterday, I actually felt myself being sexually attracted to my own sister. She doesn't know. Am I sick or what?

Each of these alternate subpersonalities, when examined without judgment, can help us begin to understand the emotions that precipitated the unexpected reactions that challenged our identities.

After many months of therapy, a client revealed something that was very upsetting to him since he had always thought of himself as a rather caring and sympathetic person. Henry told me that sometimes when he saw a disabled person, especially on crutches, he felt a sudden annoyance and rage at the person. One time he even had an urge to kick away the person's crutches. He was shocked and ashamed at his unexpected emotional reaction.

Admitting and facing that "mean" part of himself led him to discover that he was angry at disabled people because he was jealous that they were getting automatic sympathy and attention, something that he had craved all his life. Henry spoke about having a "crippled soul." Allowing that disturbing personality to emerge helped him uncover those hidden lifelong feelings and begin to work on them.

Questions and Considerations

Do you have any alternate subpersonalities, those aspects of you that are the most hidden? Examine them without judgment. Invite them to appear in a visualization, and see what they have to say to you. What is the mind pattern that is being challenged here? What needs to be explored and understood about the hidden emotion in this alternate subpersonality?

Collective Personalities

A collective personality is one that we usually experience as part of a group in our community, city, or country. It may reflect any of the categories already mentioned. We can think of it as part of our personality, public or private, that shares an attitude, activity, belief, or passion with a larger group. It may be evoked in a temporary way, like applauding with a thousand others after a political speech, or it may be a more permanent identification, like being a member of a choir.

Examples
- I'm an alcoholic. I've been going to AA meetings for several years in my neighborhood. We have a core group, and we've been through a lot of stuff together. They're like my real family.
- I'm a military man. My father and my uncle both fought in Vietnam. Ever since I was a kid, I loved flying. Pilots were always my heroes, and the air force was my second home.

- I'm an actor. When I'm involved in the theater with a group of people, I feel alive. We all become like a close, sometimes dysfunctional, but mostly supportive family with a common intention and passion—to make the play work.

The above examples are more or less chosen identities made by the individual to belong to one group or another. Sometimes external circumstances force us to become part of one collective personality or another. One of my clients went to a spiritual group at the urging of her friend. The chanting of a hundred people around her placed her in a kind of hypnotic state that she had never been in before. It was an uncomfortable experience because she felt transported, against her will, into an altered state by the power of the group.

Many of us know situations like that where we can get carried away, a music concert, sports event, or any situation where there is an intention to unify a group of people into a collective personality. In its best aspects, it can create a positive atmosphere of interconnection among large groups of people. In its worst aspects, it can lead to a group experience that may erupt into panic and even violence.

Questions and Considerations

1. Do you have a collective personality, a part of you that identifies with a certain group? List some organizations or groups that you've been a part of in your life. Which ones were temporary, and which ones are more permanent and why?

2. How do you imagine the general collective—groups of people you don't know very well—primarily experiences you? (An Asian person, a sexy woman, a smart lawyer, etc.)

Personality Polarities

When examined, each personality trait in all the categories usually contains both a positive and negative aspect.

For example, imagine a woman whose predominant personality is analytical. The positive aspect of this trait is that she is good at using her mind to examine details and pull abstract thoughts together to solve intellectual puzzles. She is a researcher propelled by curiosity, thrilled when she discovers the cause of the effect. She trusts factual evidence and tangible experiences.

In its negative aspect, her analytical side may cause her to insist on order and control for herself and everyone around her. It can result in a perfectionism that is unrealistic and stressful. She can get caught in the details of logic and miss experiencing the freedom and spontaneity of life.

This woman may emphasize one or the other aspect of her analytical self, either the positive or the negative one. In different circumstances, she may even shift from one to the other.

Suppose a man has a predominant personality that is creative. The positive aspect of this personality trait allows him to enjoy sensual, creative activities. He relishes the freedom of his mind that can travel anywhere and imagine anything. He can experience insights and feel the pleasure of endless possibilities.

In its negative aspects, this part might cause him to be so enraptured by his creative process and to move in so many different directions that he loses his initial focus or intention. Or he might compartmentalize his experience, like a precious treasure, instead of translating it into something tangible.

Each aspect of our personality traits is important. Each part is a way of being in the world. When we are respectfully aware of them, we notice when the negative aspects of these identities begin constricting our view instead of expanding our vision.

Questions and Considerations

Choose one of your personality traits that contains both a positive and negative aspect. Describe each aspect and ask, which one is more dominant? What kinds of situations bring out one or the other?

Collective Personalities and Societal Mind Conditioning

Collective personality conditioning means that outside sources directly or subliminally influence us to adopt a certain attitude, follow a directed path, or develop a specific style. The fashion industry is an obvious example, especially for women. One year it promotes T-shirts, bare bellies, and jeans; the next year it's flowered dresses and tights. Fashion presents us with changing ideas about color and style and lets us experiment with different aspects of our personality. The underlying message is "Follow the crowd. Try this. Don't be left out."

The societal mind conditioning that is the most disturbing today is the collective personality that developed after 9/11 in New York and elsewhere. It is a victim mind-set that is not diminishing. The uncertainty in the world with the global financial crisis, disastrous environmental situations, and continuous public fear programming keeps reminding us that we are all potential victims. When our trust in the people who run the show is compromised, the feeling of victimization grows. Fear is contagious. This is a natural response. We are hardwired to experience fear as a survival mechanism so that we can prepare for future danger. But today, threats can come from anywhere, and technology brings them to us instantly. It's a dangerous collective identity when it results in a continuing feeling of powerlessness. Large groups of people who are apprehensive and feel victimized are more easily influenced and controlled.

Each of us needs to change our way of being in today's world. And that change must come from within, through inner decision making that keeps us moving in a hopeful direction. We can refuse to stay victimized no matter what is going on around us. We need to build up a set of courageous experiences that counteract the victim mind-set and prevent it from becoming entrenched as a collective personality. These experiences should contain some element of risk and include actions that are not automatic and familiar. Taking a risk means something different for each person. There can be small risks as well as big ones. One of my clients dared himself to talk briefly to a stranger in an elevator, something he had never done. Someone I know decided to get advice from a second financial consultant in addition to the first one, and she also contacted a psychic adviser, something she had never done. Another client confronted her employer about an incident that had been bothering her for some time. She took the risk of being fired. She wasn't. A recently divorced man I know withstood the laughter of his business partners and took dance classes anyway.

Developing a habit of taking small and big risks helps to break down the collective victim personality, even when the result doesn't turn out exactly as you want it to. If you already take chances and they never work, then you may need to reexamine your choices and why they continually produce unsuccessful results. Sometimes we take risks but subliminally sabotage ourselves with negative expectations before we even take any action.

Find an aspect of your personality that's heroic and use it to take a risk on something once a week. There is always hope, there are always choices, and there are always changes of perspective that can move us in a new direction.

Personality Integration

The intention of cultivating awareness about the different roles we play is to integrate and direct them instead of being dominated by them. Our personalities—especially the difficult ones—are dynamic representations of our struggles and conflicts in everyday reality. In the higher dimensions of consciousness, we are beyond the intricacies of these various personality traits. We exist more in the purity of our essential beings. Understanding our multipersonalities moves us closer to this unifying center and helps counteract the societal mind conditioning that thrives on the fragmentation of our psyches.

Personality integration means working toward a more direct relationship between our conscious self and our higher self. In Assagioli's psychosynthesis work, the image of an orchestra is often used to promote this relationship.

Imagine a brilliant conductor who acts as our higher self. Our various personalities represent the different instruments, the potentials for producing a harmonious musical composition. However, sometimes the drums (the angry narcissist?) are too loud, or the violin (the reluctant lover?) isn't sweet enough, or the flute (the intelligent rebel?) doesn't show up at all.

Name some of your subpersonalities, and mentally place them in the orchestra facing you on a stage. You can have them represent different instruments or just be themselves. Close your eyes, take a few cleansing breaths, and watch how your ensemble interacts. Visualize the conductor orchestrating the various parts of your personalities in the best way possible for your benefit. The interaction and composition may be different from one time to the next. Tune in to this scenario every once in a while, and see what's happening. Each time you do this, you strengthen and deepen the communication between your conscious self and your higher self.

Observations and Declarations

Become the objective observer, and notice what kinds of personalities appear in your daily routine. Doing this regularly lessens the possibility of being overwhelmed by the emotions related to each role.

We can feel, *Oh, I'm so discouraged. I feel terrible. I'm such a failure, blah, blah, blah...* This emotional downward spiral can continue and get worse until we dissociate from it and take some action. What works better is to say, *Oh, here comes the doom-and-gloom part of me again, trying to take over.* Noticing and naming the subpersonality helps us distance from the negative aspect of that role. It makes it easier to remove its influence on us at that moment. We can look at it more objectively or put it aside and work on it later.

One time at a weekend workshop, we named our most troublesome subpersonalities and decided to send them away to summer camp. That was a welcome relief. However, most of them showed up again the following day. Integration takes time.

Say this to yourself once in a while: *I stand at the center of myself like a conductor, and I am able to bring my multipersonalities together to create interesting harmony and dynamically changing and evolving music.*

FOURTEEN

TUNING IN TO SOMATIC EXPERIENCES

The body is a marvelous machine…a chemical laboratory, a powerhouse.
Every movement, voluntary or involuntary, full of secrets and marvels!
—Theodor Herzl

Step 3. Tuning In to Somatic Experiences

Listen to your body now and then, and pay attention to your physical experiences.

The body is a tangible expression of many levels of consciousness. Persistent emotional stress may result in drooping shoulders. A subpersonality may reveal itself in a gesture. A trauma may manifest in a physical symptom, and the spirit of the higher self may be reflected in the eyes.

Why Is It Important?

Repressed and unresolved fear and anxiety can become blocks of frozen energy that compromise our functioning and fragment our consciousness. We also suffer when we don't fulfill our creative impulses. For some time, the physical body had been ignored in favor of analyzing the mind. We now know that traumatic events and repeated stresses manifest in our bodies—often in very specific ways that may reveal to us what's going on psychologically.

Our body tries to express what it knows, and most of us are not listening. Practicing direct awareness of body sensations goes beyond spending twenty minutes exercising or paying attention when we have a cold or break an ankle. Staying healthy and deprogramming from fear and emotional stress needs to include discharging energy from the body.

Releasing Frozen Energy

Dr. Peter A. Levine has been a stress consultant for NASA, a researcher in psychology and medical biophysics, and is the developer of "Somatic Experiencing." In 1997, Dr. Levine wondered why animals in the wild, though they are threatened routinely by predators, rarely get traumatized. Two of the familiar survival responses available to reptiles and mammals are fighting or fleeing. There is a third that physiologists call the "immobility" or "freezing" response, where the animal instinctively freezes and "plays dead." In this altered state, the animal experiences no pain, so it will not have to suffer if torn apart and eaten. Freezing has other advantages as well. The predator may lose interest in the fight and go away if the animal seems already dead. The freezing response may momentarily startle the predator and give the animal an opportunity to escape. When out of danger, the animal will literally shake off the residual effects of the freezing state, gain full control of its body, and return to its normal life as if nothing happened.[1]

Dr. Levine concluded that humans also use the immobility response, which is involuntary. The physiological mechanism governing this response is not under our conscious control. Many of us have experienced variations of this dynamic. Someone or something suddenly frightens us. We become immobilized. We can't move or catch our breath. When the danger is over, our hands may tremble, or our whole body may start shaking.

Most of us have been traumatized in some way, either with a dramatic event or an accumulation of stressful situations. Dr. Levine emphasizes that persistent traumatic symptoms are not caused by the triggering event itself. They stem from the frozen residue of energy that has not been resolved and discharged; this residue remains trapped in the nervous system, where it can wreak havoc on our bodies and spirits.[2] We want to release this frozen energy, but we don't always know how to do it. Sometimes, on an unconscious level, we repeat scenarios in order to reenact the scene, release the energy, and reestablish our power. This happened to me many years ago, quite unexpectedly.

I mentioned earlier that I was hit by a car. It happened as I was crossing the street and a taxi ran a red light. I had severe injuries, and for months after, I was hypervigilant every time I encountered traffic. On this one day, I was still using a cane, and I was about to cross the street. There were four or five people crossing with me, when suddenly a car jumped the light and almost hit us.

Instinctively, and out of character for me, I screamed at the driver, "You stupid a——! You just ran a red light!" I banged my cane on his front fender. He cringed as he slowly drove by, and I heard clapping from the group behind me. I wasn't so anxious crossing the street after that. I had unexpectedly completed the process.

Sometimes the reenactment and discharge of energy is symbolic. A few days after 9/11, my friend was both initially horrified and then fascinated as he watched his five-year-old son playing with a classmate. With blocks, they built the Twin Towers and then dramatically knocked them down, and then built them up again. They were expressing and releasing their fearful energy and also reassuring themselves that even if something is destroyed, it can be built up again.

Deprogramming from fear is difficult when we're just talking about traumatic events or evoking the emotions related to the issue. Body sensations can be remembered, and sometimes even resolved, with some actual or symbolic reenactment that releases the frozen energy. This can be complicated, and may require professional help. But we can do some of it ourselves.

When you've gone through a frightening event or a difficult interaction and it keeps resurfacing in your thoughts, it helps to be aware of the internal physical feeling that's related to the event. When you change from the thinking process to the body process and take some physical action, you have a better chance of releasing some of the past frozen energy. We try to do this any way we can to get some relief. We lash out at a cashier, we bump into someone by accident, or we spend sixty minutes on a fast treadmill instead of twenty. It doesn't always work.

Reframing the past event in some symbolic way is better. Being aware of the somatic experience related to it is an important element in recovery.

Observations and Considerations

Think of some symbolic way that you can safely release frozen energy from your system through some physical action or movement. Explore this idea gingerly and mindfully.

For example, one of my clients had gone through a terrible episode in his life that resulted in continuing depression and sadness. He wanted and needed to express it, but couldn't allow himself to cry because he had always associated that with weakness. That mind pattern was very strong. I asked him if there was someone he respected who, in a moment of anguish, had needed to express his pain before going on with his life. He chose a military friend he could identify with. He also played a piece of music that made him feel sad when he heard it. He was finally able to cry and release the frozen energy, which helped him slowly begin the process of moving on.

Gestures, Movements, and Body Language

Our gestures, movements, and body language often reveal what we're feeling and thinking subconsciously. Sometimes, what we're expressing physically is incongruent with what we're saying.

In a beginning therapy session, a young woman was telling me that she wanted to be in touch with her feelings and was ready to explore her past. However, she was sitting with her arms tightly folded over her chest and her legs crossed. Her conscious self was willing, but her body was saying something else. Later sessions revealed that she had been sexually molested as a child. She had not consciously remembered all the details of her past in the beginning, but her body did, and was protecting her.

Sometimes gestures and movements represent experiences or subpersonalities that the conscious self is uncomfortable with. They tend to disappear quickly when someone points them out. But sometimes they want to be noticed, even though they're not always so eager to be exposed.

One man I worked with had a habit of raising one eyebrow. It was interesting and subtle, and seemed to have nothing to do with what he was saying. When I asked him to amplify it, to feel it more directly and act it out, he turned into this debonair, slightly superior-sounding, but charming character. He was a rather shy man ordinarily, and this part of him was trying to express itself in the midst of the rest of his personality.

Another young woman had the habit of crossing and resting her right leg over her left knee and moving it repeatedly back and forth. When she examined that more carefully, she discovered that her right leg represented the part of her that wanted to run, to be free, to look for adventure. The left leg was the immovable one; it was the part that said, "Be still. Stay in one place. Conform." The leg controversy continued as she tried to resolve this dilemma in her life.

Some body gestures are universal and have been around a long time. For example, hands pressed together, palm to palm, fingers touching and pointing upward, is a familiar prayer pose recognized by many cultures all over the world. It also has a physiological component. Acupuncturists tell us that bringing the hands together, especially with the tips of the fingers touching, helps to balance the body's energy. I have seen people make this gesture unconsciously in the middle of a frustrating discussion in an attempt to calm down or state their case more clearly. This same gesture is also recognized as a pleading pose.

Questions and Considerations

1. Is there a body posture, gesture, or movement that you repeat unconsciously? Amplify it, and act it out. Guess what it might be trying to express to you. Look for the possibility that a subpersonality is trying to emerge from the gesture or the movement.

2. In the privacy of your home, begin this exercise standing. Think of a few gestures, body positions, or movements that you've experienced in your life. (Clap your hands together; put your hands on your hips; nod or shake your head; jump up and down; cross your arms over your chest; march, etc.)

Act out each one. What does it feel like as you do it, and what kinds of memories does it evoke for you? You can also express something out loud as you experience each one.

Illness and Accidents

When we have an illness or an accident, we can move the healing process along by exploring our symptoms. Symptoms can be thought of as subconscious processes that are taking place just beneath our awareness.

They often represent persistent emotional issues or traumatic events that need to be made conscious and resolved in some way.

A symptom gives us the opportunity to gather information about what's going on psychologically when we allow the process of the symptom to unfold. Let's say your neck feels tight, your shoulder really hurts, and you've got a headache. Focus on each of these symptoms and describe them so carefully that someone else could imagine what it feels like. Notice which symptom is more prominent. If possible, let an image come up from the sensation, and ask what message the symptom is trying to convey. Focus on the primary disturbance and imagine what you need to do to release yourself from the symptom.

> Example
> The side of my neck feels like there's no room to move. Everything is scrunched up and compressed. My shoulder joint feels enflamed, and the pain seems to radiate up to the side of my head. My neck is the most painful. It feels like someone's clutching me with his hands around my throat. I can't move, and I can't speak. I know what it is. I'm really stuck in this relationship. He's holding me down. I have to get strong and speak my mind and assert myself, or else I just have to end it.

Questions and Considerations

Sit comfortably with your eyes closed and begin the primary centering process: take a few deep, cleansing breaths, surround yourself with the violet bubble, and center the royal-blue dot on your forehead. Turn inward and ask what part of your body needs attention and help. It can be an organ, like the stomach or the gallbladder. It can be certain muscles or bones, or it can be the whole circulatory system. From an energetic point of view, each organ, each part of our physiological system has its own frequency. The body gets thrown out of balance with physical or emotional stress. The different parts of our internal physical world are not always functioning well together. Sometimes the liver is not speaking the same language as the kidneys. Sometimes certain muscles are not operating efficiently because nerve damage interrupts the coordination between one set of muscles and the other.

Think of different organs in your body (the brain, spleen, stomach, etc.), as well as the systems that keep us alive (the immune system, circulatory, neurological, skeletal, etc.). Have them communicate with each other in the same language. Imagine their different frequencies operating together in a compatible orchestration. Let your mind wander creatively, and explore this in your own way. When you are ready to complete the process, surround yourself with a band of the grounding brown earth color.

Remembering Somatic Pleasure

Before we are born, sometime toward the end of the twelfth week of intrauterine life, we change from making minute mechanical motions to movements that are graceful and fluid.[3] There is room enough until the ninth month to float and move about freely in the buoyant liquid, turning from side to side and sometimes head over heels, doing somersaults. We float our limbs around our bodies; we can make a fist, and we can kick out a leg.[4]

Dr. Stanislav Grof, one of the leading scientists and researchers of realms of human consciousness, described the undisturbed intrauterine experience. It is associated with a blissful, undifferentiated, oceanic state of consciousness, a feeling of cosmic unity.[5]

Even though there are individual differences, depending on the temperament and health of the mother and various external circumstances, the experience seems to be universal. The memory of this state and the gracefulness of the movements that accompany it exist somewhere in our consciousness.

Some of us can reactivate the memory of that experience with the physical body by actually floating and moving slowly in a calm ocean, lake, or swimming pool. Slow body exercises like Tai Chi can also evoke that state of floating peacefulness.

Our bodies contain about 70 percent water. We are water beings living out of water, moving in a manner that often takes us away from our biochemical nature. We live in a world of varying and exciting pulsating rhythms. We can also remember that slow, elegant womb rhythm because when we do, we connect to our deepest and most complete peaceful reality before the time when the muddle of life began.

The following exercise helps our body remember. It was inspired by the work of Emilie Conrad, founder of the Continuum movement, who teaches about the fluidity of the body and our biological resonance with this watery planet.[6]

Exercise

Begin this exercise by standing, sitting in a chair, or lying down on the floor. Take a few deep breaths and exhale. Then, with your eyes half closed, imagine that you are floating around in water. Notice how your body, your head, and your limbs want to move. Nothing may happen for a while; just wait. Then perhaps one of your shoulders starts leaning to the left or you find one of your ankles making circles. Go with one of those and see where it takes you. Try not to think about or analyze what is happening. Just move slowly and let your body explore the space around you. Try doing this for about ten minutes or longer. When you feel ready, come back slowly to a still position, surround yourself with the band of grounding brown-earth color, and notice how you feel.

The Emotional Heart

There are many books today that emphasize the importance of the mind and brain, and rightly so, but the heart needs to be remembered.

I believe that we are all born with a potential for self-love and a natural ability to expand that love to include other people. When we're infants and we experience obvious or subtle disruptions to these natural exchanges of love, our bodies react to the stopping of that flow. We may develop defensive or aggressive body postures or rigid movements. Later on, as we grow up, our mind intervenes, and we try to make some logic out of this unnatural occurrence. We try to find ways of dealing with it so that we can somehow survive. We often blame ourselves. The more fear we experience as infants, the more deeply our self-love is submerged in some hidden compartment, until for some of us, it doesn't seem to exist at all.

The underlying dynamic is not that we don't love ourselves, but rather that the love at the core of our being is so crowded with fear that we can't get to it.

The heart is intelligent, but it's also the home of the emotions. When negative emotions predominate, they block the heart from functioning normally. Traumatic memories crowd the heart, and the mind compartmentalizes them. We try to repress and dissociate from painful memories. But we're not always successful, and they live on within us in negative thought forms that seem so much a part of our normal personality that we hardly notice them. They float around, whispering familiar insults in our ears, just when we think we're feeling pretty good.

If there is more fear than love in our early life, and our mind tries to submerge our child fear, it often takes with it our natural capacity for self-love. Sometimes we experience the wounding so powerfully that the heart feels empty, or it closes up and freezes, or it breaks under the pressure. Instead of merging with the heart, the mind separates from it and creates emotional confusion.

Inside, the battling energies of the wounding and the loving continue, while outside, we look for love somewhere else, from someone else. We spend a lifetime perpetuating a false sense of self-love, especially when society encourages us to experience it through power and sex. When we look outside for love and don't fully understand the early pain and loss of love, then power and sex can become very addictive. The expansion of our consciousness moves very slowly, if at all. We are trapped below the heart, not living through it.

In Western culture, men are expected to control their emotions, and are then accused of being cut off from their feelings. Women are expected to express their emotions, and are then accused of being too much in their feelings. Often when we control emotions, that simply removes them from our consciousness and crowds the heart, causing psychic pain and physical illness. Experiencing and expressing negative emotions without resolution can put undue pressure on the heart, which can also lead to the same thing. Life dramas that are experienced with the mind or the body without the heart can only release and shift energies; they cannot refine them.

In order to encourage the heart to fulfill its role, we can acknowledge both the love that is our intrinsic birthright, and the shadow side of that love: the fear. We can embrace the duality of our emotions and let the heart become the vehicle for their transformation. In order to do this, we need to establish a conscious intercommunication with this most important part of our physical being.

Exercise

Find a comfortable sitting position, close your eyes, and after completing the primary centering process, place all of your attention on your heart area and notice what it feels like. Is it still, or can you sense some activity there? Does it feel heavy or light, crowded or empty? Can you hear or feel your heartbeat? Stay with this focused attention for few minutes. Then, imagine that you are breathing through the heart. Each time you inhale, feel your heart expanding and opening, and each time you exhale, feel your heart relaxing. Do this for at least five minutes. Imagine that with each inhalation, you are welcoming heart-opening experiences and that with each exhalation, you are removing unnecessary stresses. Complete the exercise, as always, with a band of the brown-earth color.

The Intelligent Heart

For thousands of years, in Eastern traditions, the heart has been thought of as the seat of consciousness. Of all the organs in the body, the heart is believed to contain the highest potential energy—the one that can be activated in the most powerful way. While the physiological heart is the propelling agent of life, pumping blood throughout the body, the energetic heart is thought to be the mediating organ of transformation.

As mentioned earlier, the chakras are energy vortices located along a central axis corresponding to the spinal column of the physical body. The heart chakra is in the chest area. It has three main chakras below it, in ascending order: the root, spleen, and solar plexus; and three above: the throat, brow, and crown. Balanced in the center of the seven chakras, and connected to the endocrine system, the heart chakra is thought to be the most important because it acts as an interconnection between the lower and higher dimensions of consciousness. In Eastern spiritual beliefs, the heart has the ability to integrate human physical, mental, and emotional energies with higher universal ones.[7]

Transmission of Heart Information

In physics and neurobiology, research both scientific and theoretical is giving us a view of the heart's importance with regard to transmitting information. Some of the research suggests that the heart may be the most powerful sender and receiver of electromagnetic energy in the human body. The heart's rhythmic field has a strong influence on processes throughout the body. The rhythmic beating patterns of the heart change significantly as we experience different emotions. Negative emotions, such as anger or frustration, are associated with an erratic, disordered, incoherent pattern in the heart's rhythms. In contrast, positive emotions, such as love or appreciation, are associated with a smooth, ordered, coherent pattern in the heart's rhythmic activity. In turn, these changes in the heart's beating patterns create corresponding changes in the structure of the electromagnetic field radiated by the heart, measurable by a technique called spectral analysis.[8]

Our cardiac field extends beyond us and can affect people within five feet from where we are. One person's heart signal can affect another's brain waves, and heart-brain synchronization can occur between two people when they interact. The research also suggested that the heart's field is an important carrier of information.[9]

Dr. Paul Pearsall was a psychoneuroimmunologist who presented these findings and other research on cellular memory. He promoted the idea that the heart has the ability to store memory, think and remember, help regulate immunity, and communicate with other hearts.

Dr. Pearsall offered remarkable stories by some heart transplant recipients who experienced changes in their food preferences, dreams, fantasies, and personality manifestations. He suggested that these may be related to the cellular memories of the donors.

In one dramatic story, a psychiatrist told about an eight-year-old girl who received the heart of a ten-year-old girl who had been murdered. She knew nothing about the situation, but began to have horrific nightmares about the man who had murdered her donor. The psychiatrist and the mother called the police, and using detailed descriptions from the little girl—the time, the weapon, the place, and the clothes he wore—they easily convicted the murderer. Everything the little girl had reported had been completely accurate.[10]

In another story, a thirty-five-year-old female heart transplant recipient, who had no idea who her donor was, spoke to her psychiatrist about some rather shocking changes in her personality. She had never really been interested in sex that much or thought about it before her surgery. Now she wanted sex every night with her husband, enjoyed talking about it more, and sometimes masturbated two or three times a day. For the first time, she developed a taste for X-rated videos and even performed a strip for her husband now and then. Her psychiatrist thought that these things might be reactions to the medications and her healthier body, until they found out that her donor was a young college girl who had worked as a topless dancer and prostitute. She and her husband happily agreed that she must have gotten the young donor's sex drive and sexual inclinations.[11]

These are dramatic and unusual examples that point to active cellular memories and communications of the heart. But what about our everyday heart interactions? What does it mean to communicate from the heart and to trust cardiac intelligence? We have been top-heavy with brain exchanges for so long. Negative thinking often plunges us back into the intense emotions that crowd the heart from functioning freely.

When our stressful emotions are known, expressed, and released or transformed, our heart has a clearer path to do its work. When we are in conflict with a person we care about, sometimes we need to shout, express hurt, or be indignant. We feel all kinds of terrible and familiar emotions. We try to think of what to say to change the atmosphere. If, at some point during the exchange, we can remember to give the heart the space and the opportunity to speak, beyond the negative emotions and the thoughts, then perhaps a shift can take place.

There are no set rules or ways to speak from the heart. One person might do it by saying, "Why are we doing this? We're killing each other." Someone else might interrupt the talking to embrace the other person. It might happen when someone expresses a heartfelt apology, or when someone demands meaningful respect from the other person.

Heart-to-heart conversations are often able to pierce through our ego defenses. They reveal the compassion and respect that's possible to be felt, both for ourselves and for the other person, even in the midst of what seems like an impossible situation. It happens when our thoughts and emotions are integrated and pass through the heart without contradiction.

Exercise

The following heart-awareness exercise can be practiced on a daily basis. Sit in a comfortable position, and complete the primary centering process. With eyes still closed and using gentle pressure, place both hands, open palms down, on your heart, with the left hand first and then the right one over it. Inhale and exhale deeply several times, and then relax and breathe normally. Place all of your attention on feeling and hearing the rhythm of your heart. If emotions come up, let them be there, but concentrate on the energy exchange between your hands and your heart. Do this for a minute or more at any time during the day or night. End with a band of the brown-earth color, as always.

Each time you do this, you are reuniting with the intelligence of the heart. Listen to it. Heart palpitations tell you that something may be off-kilter. The heart feels relaxed with music that matches its rhythm, which is about seventy to eighty beats a minute, and the heart rate more than doubles during sexual orgasm. Learn its language. What is your heartbeat like, how does it change, and what is it saying?

One of my clients notices that her heart and body energy become more activated a day or two before and after a full moon. When confronted with a sudden external fear, another client feels as if a huge invisible hand is clutching his heart. When she is deeply moved by something beautiful, another one of my clients says that her heart feels like a radiating sun. High-Velocity Consciousness includes being in love with your own heart, unconditionally, with respect and gratefulness for keeping you alive. Practice being with your heart so that even in the midst of conflict or anguish, this interaction will feel familiar and comforting.

Heart-to-heart conversations between ourselves and the people close to us can become the more usual mode of interaction. Sometimes just taking a few deep breaths, exhaling, and focusing on your own heart puts you into a more receptive place to communicate with the other person.

Our Bodies and Societal Mind Conditioning

Societal mind conditioning affects the choices we make to keep ourselves healthy. Advertisements surround us with pharmaceutical quick-fix solutions so that we can function better physically and emotionally. We have long-term medical aids that can save lives in ways that were not possible a hundred years ago. However, the dark side of the medical community—especially with regard to advertising and propaganda— should be looked at carefully. We need to be smart, discerning consumers and not dopey, entranced victims of slick, beautiful, or funny advertising.

Direct-to-consumer advertising, known as DTCA, refers to medical advertising that is directed to the patient or consumer, as opposed to the medical practitioner or pharmacist. As of this writing, New Zealand and the United States are the only industrialized countries that allow DTCA. However, many other countries are grappling with the issue of whether to permit DTCA. At this writing, legislation pending in New Zealand presented examples of the dangers of DTCA to consumers:

- Misleading advertisements containing partial, incorrect, or unbalanced information

- Overstatement of medicine efficacy and failure to detail success rates
- Minimization of potential adverse effects
- Inappropriate use of emotional persuasion[12]

Those opposed to DTCA argued that a ban is justified under the New Zealand Bill of Rights Act of 1990. Arguments for justifying a ban on DTCA and on purported infringements made by DTCA to the Bill of Rights Act included the following:

- DTCA is misleading and can lead to inappropriate prescribing, resulting in medical misadventure and harm to consumers.
- DTCA encourages increased uptake of new prescription medicines that do not have established safety profiles.
- DTCA targets consumers, who cannot access prescription medicines without a health professional—any advertising should be aimed at these professionals, who are able to understand and evaluate it.
- Legislative controls over the sale and advertising of tobacco products, liquor, and firearms provide a precedent for DTCA in the context of protecting the interests of consumers. The nature of the risks associated with prescription medicines warrant a restricted approach to advertising.
- Commercial expression is on the fringe of the freedom of expression protected by section 14 of the Bill of Rights Act: "Advertising is a profit-driven type of expression, far from the 'core' of freedom of expression."
- A rational connection exists between a prohibition on DTCA and the objective of reducing the risks associated with such advertising.[13]

The legislation pointed out that direct-to-consumer advertisements rarely discuss the range of available treatments or costs to the patient of treatment. It is not appropriate for drug information to be delivered by individual pharmaceutical companies, because they have a commercially driven interest in promoting increased sales of prescription medicines. This conflicts with the right of the patient to have easy access to high-quality, independent, comparative information on the risks and benefits of available pharmacological and nonpharmacological treatments. There is a clear need for independent information to aid informed consumer choice, and should be addressed by the establishment of an independent health information service.[14]

In 1995, French Canadian medical doctor Guylaine Lanctot wrote a controversial book called *The Medical Mafia.* After its publication, she lost her medical license and was not allowed to practice again. In the book, she described how we have "a medicine of sickness." Instead of the health system being at the service of the patient, as it claims, in practice it is at the service of an industry that pulls the strings and maintains a system of sickness for its own profit. She wrote that patients are exploited by doctors, health service providers, and pharmaceutical and technological industries that make people sick and keep them dependent. Dr. Lanctot did not target individuals, but looked at the whole system of orthodox medicine and society in general. She urged patients to take back their power to change the system and promote "self-health" so that the medical system is at the service of the patient, not the other way around.[15]

Since that time, there have been other books that have questioned the medical industry with respect to pharmaceuticals. Recently, Dr. Peter R. Breggin, an American psychiatrist and expert in clinical psychopharmacology, wrote a book called *Medication Madness.* Dr. Breggin has served as a medical expert in many criminal and civil cases, including product-liability suits against the manufacturers of such psychiatric drugs as Prozac, Paxil, Zoloft, Xanax, Ritalin, Risperdal, and Zyprexa. His position is that these and other psychiatric medications may spellbind patients into believing they are improved when too often they are becoming worse. Psychiatric drugs drive some people into psychosis, mania, depression, suicide, agitation, compulsive violence, and loss of self-control without the individuals realizing that their medications have deformed their way of thinking and feeling.[16]

Over the past twenty-five years, many of Dr. Breggin's initially controversial observations on the harmfulness of some psychiatric drugs to the brain and mind have been confirmed by the FDA and by other scientists. In the book, he documents how the FDA, the medical establishment, and the pharmaceutical industry have oversold the value of psychiatric drugs.[17]

In today's quick-fix world, the bombardment of advertisements for pharmaceuticals is everywhere. Please carefully collect as much medical information as you can from various sources before taking one of these drugs yourself. Look at opposing or contradictory opinions about the drug. Know about the risks and side effects. Even when a prescription drug "works," always remember to ask, *what else is happening at the same time?* In other words, how is this going to affect my immune system, my brain functioning, or my emotional state of mind?

Pfizer, the manufacturer of Chantix, a prescription drug for smoking cessation, now has to include a warning for suicide among the possible side effects in their commercials. This requirement was issued by the FDA in February of 2008 even though it had been on the market with FDA approval since 2006. Chantix carries a real risk for suicide ideation. Some people have come close to suicide, some have actually made the attempt, and some have unfortunately been successful.[18] Though reactions vary with each person, check other people's personal experiences before you make a decision to take something for a long period of time. A friend of mine stopped taking Chantix after just three days because he had sudden nightmares that stopped as soon as he discontinued the drug.

Sometimes drugs are put on the market without a long enough period of research to guarantee their safety. Merck, the manufacturer of Vioxx, a popular anti-inflammatory drug for arthritis, agreed in late 2007 to settle lawsuits brought by roughly fifty thousand people. The consumers alleged that their use of the former pain drug caused heart attacks and other injuries, and that Merck failed to properly warn of such risks. Merck withdrew the drug from the market in 2004 after it was linked to increased risk for heart attacks and strokes.[19]

There is such a proliferation of drugs today that there is not much known about the effects of combining medications. We are usually reminded about the danger of mixing drugs when it involves a celebrity. New York's medical examiner revealed that actor Heath Ledger died from an accidental overdose from combining six different prescription drugs: two strong painkillers, two anti-anxiety medications, and two sleeping aids.[20] This unfortunate tragedy was not an isolated case. A statistical study of hospital deaths in the United States revealed that prescription drugs kill more people every year than are killed in traffic accidents. Adverse drug reactions are now the fourth leading cause of death in the United States after heart disease, cancer, and stroke. Generally, 51 percent of FDA-approved drugs have serious adverse effects not detected prior to approval. The biggest offenders are painkillers and drugs that modify the immune system to treat arthritis.[21]

In 2007, Dr. Leonard J. Paulozzi, medical epidemiologist with the Centers for Disease Control and Prevention, offered his testimony before the United States House of Representatives. The topic was "Trends in Unintentional Drug Poisoning Deaths." The number of deaths involving prescription opioid analgesics increased from roughly 2,900 in 1999 to 7,500 in 2004, an increase of 160 percent in just five years.[22] Prescription drug abuse is the fastest-growing drug problem in the United States, and results in one death every nineteen minutes, federal health officials say.[23]

Do not be seduced by joyful or humorous TV and Internet commercials that promise relief through pharmaceuticals. The claims in these presentations do not mean that the success and safety of the products is guaranteed, even with FDA approval. Pharmaceutical companies spend billions of dollars to get your attention. Be careful about combining medications. Do explore alternative methods using vitamins and supplements when you want to take care of your body. They may take longer to get results, but they are less dangerous and can be more effective than some pharmaceutical solutions. Do not automatically succumb to the expanding pharma world. Get into the habit of communicating with your body about your health. Especially do this before you make a decision to ingest anything, whether it's food, herbal supplements, or medication. Close your eyes and ask your body to give you an indication about whether what you are going to take is good for you. If you decide to take it, close your eyes, tune in to your body, and tell it to utilize the food or medicine in the best way possible for your health.

Somatic Exercises

Thymus Thumping

According to Dr. John Diamond, author of *Life Energy*, the thymus gland monitors and regulates the body's energy flow. It plays a vital role in the body's immune system. The first response to emotional or physical stress is shrinkage of the thymus gland and a reduction of life energy. Imbalances in the body can be resolved by stimulating the thymus gland.[24]

The thymus acupressure points are just under the clavicle, or collarbone. To find them, place your index fingertips on the U-shaped notch at the top of the breastbone Then move your fingers down over the collarbone, out to each side about an inch, into the soft tissue under the clavicle, to the left and right of the sternum. Most people have small depressions there. With both hands, thump or tap the points with the fingertips of your index and middle fingers while taking several deep breaths, in through the nose and out through the mouth, for about fifteen seconds. You can do this once or twice a day or whenever you need an energy boost, just not before going to sleep.

Cross Crawling

The cross crawl is a simple and powerful right-left brain balancing technique developed by educational kinesiologists Paul and Gail Dennison. Humans are contralateral beings in reference to their neurological organization. The left hemisphere of the brain sends information to the right side of your body, and the right hemisphere sends information to the left side. This crossing of energy helps you feel more balanced, think more clearly, and also improves your coordination.[25]

While standing, lift the opposite arm and leg at the same time in a sort of slow march. An alternative to this march is to touch your right hand or your right elbow to your left knee, and then your left hand or your left elbow to your right knee, as you step. Repeat either technique for at least a minute while breathing in deeply through the nose and exhaling through the mouth. In addition to resulting in better body coordination, it gives you more energy and increases your metabolic rate.

Cross crawling results in large areas of both brain hemispheres being activated at the same time. It facilitates balanced nerve activation across the corpus callosum (the part in your brain that connects the right half to the left half). When done on a regular basis, more nerve networks form and more connections are made in the corpus callosum. This makes communication between the two hemispheres faster and more integrated for high-level reasoning. If you are able, you can also try this lying flat on your back and touching your right elbow to your left knee and then your left elbow to your right knee.[26]

If you can, get on the floor and actually crawl on your hands and knees. This can be quite wonderful because you are also activating and remembering the determination, struggle, and excitement that you felt as a baby when you first discovered that you could actually move this way.

Observations and Declarations

Several times during the day, tune in to your body sensations and briefly describe the experience.

> Examples
> - "My head feels like it's being pulled by strings in different directions, like when I was in school."
> - "My stomach won't stop gurgling. It's interrupting me, and I'm not even hungry."
> - "I feel lighter every time she walks into the room."

Noticing your somatic experiences opens up the doorway to longer and more informative exchanges between you and your body. Make this declaration: *I honor and respect my body, with its multileveled functions and unique characteristics. Every day I include some kind of physical action that promotes my well-being and balances my body, mind, and soul.*

FIFTEEN

OBSERVING EXTERNAL FIELDS

What is needed is a relativistic theory, to give up altogether the notion that the world is constituted of basic objects or building blocks. Rather one has to view the world in terms of universal flux of events and processes.

—David Bohm

Step 4. Observing External Fields

Become aware of the surrounding atmosphere and its effect on you.

An external field can be thought of as the prevailing atmosphere that surrounds us in a given place. A room or a building in which an activity is repeated builds up an atmosphere that can be felt when we enter it. A church or a temple has a different feel to it than a hospital or a classroom. The field is created because of the tangible physical components: the architecture, the objects, colors and furniture, and the activities that occur there. It also reflects the general personality or mood of the people in it. All classrooms are not the same.

A field can also exist beyond the boundaries of a room or a building. The music of a marching band moving down the street can change the silent field of the crowd into a celebratory one. An explosion in the middle of a city can create an atmosphere of terror and anguish in minutes.

These are dramatic examples, but there are more subtle ones as well. We can be affected by a field and not even realize it. Earlier we saw how a charismatic speaker could influence a large group of people to cross their legs without their conscious awareness.

The arena of family dynamics can pull us into an atmosphere that can affect our mood rather quickly. One of my clients described what it was like whenever she visited her parents during large family gatherings. She said that everyone was generally friendly enough with each other, but she often found herself hurrying to finish her thoughts before the person she was talking to interrupted her or was distracted by something else. This was a familiar atmosphere for her. It was like walking into a professional ADD group and automatically becoming part of the crowd. It provoked her own difficulty with focusing and attention.

We can also be so absorbed in our own process that we're oblivious to the field around us. For example, we can get caught up in our own pleasure with such self-gratification that after speaking for a while in front of a group, we don't notice that the field with the people in it has changed from being attentive and adoring to being restless and bored.

Why Is It Important?

Awareness of external fields—how they change, how we relate to them, and how we create them—helps us to be more in tune with the tangible and subtle energies that affect our well-being. It reminds us of our ongoing communication with the collective.

To use our free will successfully, we need to be mindful about how we're interacting with and being affected by the environment around us. We want to move to a place in our process where as independent thinkers we have more effect on our surroundings than the environment has on us. This is important with regard to our emotions that can be easily triggered by the mood of the collective.

We can sense the world around us with more open curiosity and adventure, and also with caution. Being aware of external fields means developing a sensitivity to the subtle, as well as the dramatic, energy changes that happen every day so that we orchestrate ourselves within them as we wish.

The Changing Personality of Groups

I have been part of many conflict resolution groups over the years, especially through the innovative research of Jungian analyst and author Dr. Arnold Mindell. I have witnessed angry exchanges in a group of a hundred people go on for an hour or more where the energy feels scattered and hopeless. I've watched that atmosphere change in a few minutes by one person standing up in the center and expressing some truth that is so moving that the very air seems to settle and become calm.

The emotional power of groups is profound. They can move us to hate or to love. We are drawn and fascinated by groups, and we are also afraid of them. Every gathering, whether it consists of three people or three hundred, has its own personality or atmosphere, which can shift and change as it is influenced by different things.

In ordinary waking reality, we have a blocking mechanism that protects us from reacting to every stimulus and thought that's presented to us. We selectively perceive some sounds and ignore others. We can forget painful memories, ignore bodily discomfort, and suppress emotions and thoughts. Without this blocking mechanism, our nervous systems would be overloaded with too much internal information and external stimulation from the outside. As we saw earlier, in today's world, this blocking mechanism is becoming more difficult to operate as the external fields that surround us become more intrusive.

What is it that happens when certain thoughts, emotions, and images seem to travel almost telepathically from one person to another, especially in groups? No one really knows. There are some clues, however. Nothing is solid, not the table we see or the physical body that we feel. Matter is not solid, and it is not still. Even the tallest mountains are moving on a time level and time frame that we cannot perceive.

As we saw before, everything is moving and interacting with everything all the time. This means that information in the form of vibrations, energy, thoughts, emotions, and images travels beyond the confines of one human mind, and can affect other minds.

How does this happen? Resonance may have something to do with it. A state of resonance occurs when the vibrations of one object reach out and set off vibrations in another object. For example, if you have two tuning forks in front of you that have the same pitch (frequency), activating one will set up a vibration in the other and create a sound.

With people, some invisible transmission, like a primary vibration in the form of a thought, emotion, or image, may travel over long distances, sometimes instantaneously, and create a resonance in another person of like frequency. Similar genetic makeup in a mother and child or in identical twins might increase the possibility of telepathic communication. Mothers often sense danger when their children are in trouble. Similar emotional states seem to facilitate such transmissions, as in the intuitive connections between lovers. Meditative states of relaxed attention, where extraneous thoughts are eliminated or reduced, also open receptivity.

In my private work with clients over the years, I've noticed a particular kind of emotion/thought transmission. Under certain circumstances, what happens in a private session seems to be projected into the external field and can affect another person. It's almost as if the other person is an invisible but potent presence in the room and can somehow sense what's happening.

Here is a general example. Let's say my client Freda has a specific issue with someone she is very close to, like her partner, and the conflict is still "in the air." Freda talks about it during the session. She expresses her feelings and reaches some understanding about what her part in it was, how it all came about, and how to deal with it with her partner. Then a day or two later, I'll get a report that even before Freda began the conversation, her partner was open and responsive. The emotional anguish that was in the air had diminished significantly, perhaps totally. They were able to communicate and work through the initial problem rather quickly.

Now this doesn't always happen, but when it does, there are components to it that seem to make it more possible. The sooner I see the client, the more likely it is to work. It's as if the problem is still fresh, and so the troublesome emotional energy is still around and they are both resonating with it. And the sooner they talk about it, the better chance there is of a reconciliation. Freda's willingness to look at the whole issue and recognize her part in it was important. If the session just involved being angry at the other person, it wouldn't have worked as well. There had to be some ability on Freda's part to be sensitive and self-reflective even if her partner was not so clear about the situation at that moment.

The prominent London biologist Dr. Rupert Sheldrake speaks of "fields of morphic resonance" created between or among people and events that make possible such subtle transfers of information. They are invisible, like the gravitational and electromagnetic fields around us that we take for granted, but which still have a profound effect on us. Sheldrake believes that these morphic fields contain within them a kind of inherent memory, and that the strength and carrying effects of this memory depend on the influence of like upon like across time and space.[1]

Sheldrake suggests that the continued improvement of task performance in successive generations of laboratory animals may be due to accumulated information. So the great-grandson of an Olympic maze-runner rat already has a blueprint for success that exists in the morphic field.[2]

Sheldrake believes that there are behavioral, mental, and social fields that underlie human behavior and mental life. For example, the longer a pattern of learned behavior has existed, the more quickly it can be learned. So, it should be easier for a five-year-old to learn how to use a computer today than it was ten years ago, and it will be even less difficult ten years from now.[3] He also suggests that it would be easier for someone to complete the Sunday *New York Times* crossword puzzle on the Monday or Tuesday after rather than Sunday, because by that time, hundreds of people would have completed it and the answers would already exist in the morphic field.[4] Sheldrake has written about many fascinating ideas and experiments that advance his theory.

External Fields and Contagious Emotions

Emotions are contagious, especially in groups. Many years ago, my husband, Bob, and I were invited to a party given by a neighbor in our small summer community. We were both in a good mood as we joined the group of about twenty-five people—some old friends, some new ones.

A couple we knew walked in and grumbled their greetings. It was obvious to us that they had been fighting with each other even though they pretended that everything was fine. The unexpressed anger was there, and this was noticed by some people and ignored by others. Bob and I moved away and started to mingle. Soon, we noticed that another couple standing near the first couple started bickering. In the other corner, two friends who usually got along started a political argument and ended up walking away from each other.

A few minutes later, Bob and I looked around. The unexpressed anger of the original couple seemed to be affecting some people in the group. It was spreading like a virus throughout the party and began to change the atmosphere. We watched with fascination.

Any repressed emotion, especially a strong one such as anger, can affect a group, especially a small one. It tends to get diluted when you have a larger number of people. We can think of it as a potent energy looking for a place to be expressed and released. What seemed to happen at the party was that the angry energy moved toward those people who were most vulnerable to it—the people who were most likely to be in conflict anyway. We can say that the repressed emotions of the original couple resonated with other existing conflicts and caused them to erupt.

Bob and I continued to watch as pockets of discomfort became more apparent. The really interesting thing was that after fifteen minutes or so, the original couple seemed fine. They were laughing and joking with each other. What had happened? When their anger was picked up and expressed by others, it may have been a relief for them. They didn't have to own their anger anymore. It had spread out through the crowd.

When the music and dancing began, more of the anger energy dissipated. The room felt lighter—not completely so, but the emotional atmosphere was decidedly different than when we had walked in.

Questions and Considerations

1. Describe one or more situations where you became aware of a change in the surrounding atmosphere. Describe the emotional feeling of the field before and after, and how you were affected by it.

2. Begin to notice the emotional atmosphere (personality) of different fields in your life.

Contagious Happiness in Social Groups

The example above showed how anger between two people can spread and be experienced by others in a small group. It also suggests that the positive atmosphere of the party—the music and dancing, good food and drinks, and close friends— influenced the group as well. Happiness is also contagious. So, what is it that makes some of us feel good most of the time? Though there are many reasons that determine a happy disposition, one of them seems to be the social groups that we belong to.

This is what Harvard internist and social scientist Dr. Nicholas Christakis and political scientist Dr. James Fowler discovered. They published their research in the *British Medical Journal*. It was a twenty-year longitudinal study, from 1983 to 2003, of almost five thousand people and the more than fifty thousand social ties they shared.[5]

Clusters of happy and unhappy people are shown in the social groups, and the relationship between people's happiness extends up to three degrees of separation (for example, to the friends of one's friends'

friends). People who are surrounded by many happy people, and those who are central in the network, are more likely to become happy in the future.[6] The authors postulated that people who are in closer, more frequent contact with each other are more susceptible to catching each other's moods. The researchers stress that personal factors such as jobs or marriages also affect happiness and that although happiness may fluctuate, people tend to return to a personal happiness "set point" through time. It is this relatively stable emotional condition they examine in the paper, not the fleeting moods people experience day-to-day.[7]

Their conclusions were that people's happiness depends on the happy disposition of others with whom they are connected. This provides further justification for seeing happiness, like health, as a collective phenomenon. In other words, happiness is not merely a function of individual experience or individual choice but is also a property of groups of people. The researchers said that evolution may have encouraged infectious happiness if it helped early humans enhance their social bonds so they could form successful groups.[8]

Emotional happiness is an ongoing process. The triggers for this subjective experience are not the same for everyone. If it snows heavily, one of my clients feels happy for the whole week. Another client loves going to noisy, crowded piano bars. There is something for everyone. We have a spirit within us that wants us to feel good. Some people have the ability to evoke that more readily within themselves. They seem to find more things that can elicit a positive reaction even in the midst of difficult times. There will be more about this pleasure experience in a later chapter. Your social network (which now includes digital social networking) can have an effect on how good you feel. Take a moment to explore your experience with groups from early on, beginning with your family, friends, and extended relationships, continuing on to the present day. Have these communications remained the same, or have they changed over the years? Examine your early and current networks and the general emotional disposition of the people in them with regard to degrees of happiness or unhappiness. Notice how you feel after being with some of the people you know. Do you feel better afterward? Are you energized, bored, or drained? If you don't have a satisfying social network, think of ways of creating one now.

Digital Social Networking

Digital social networking grows as more people use the Internet to expand their external fields. Most social network services are web based and provide a variety of ways to interact. Users can create profiles with photos and list personal interests, contact information, and other personal data. They can communicate with friends and other users through private or public messages. Facebook is the most widely used digital social network in the world these days. As of May 2012, it had reached over nine hundred million active users.[9]

While social networking use has grown dramatically across all age groups, older users have been especially enthusiastic. As of February 2012, 34 percent of American Internet users age sixty-five and older were using social networking sites such as Facebook.[10]

The website Twitter lets you keep in touch with people through the exchange of quick, frequent messages limited to 140 characters. People follow the sources most relevant to them and access information via Twitter as it happens—from breaking world news to updates from friends.[11]

Social scientists name this continuous online contact "ambient awareness," and the personal social networking "ambient intimacy." Clive Thompson wrote about this in a *New York Times Magazine* article. One of his friends who uses Twitter noted that the brief and frequent messages seem rather mundane and insignificant at first. Samples may include a friend who posts about starting to feel sick. Another one describes what kind of sandwich she's making. Sometimes people post random thoughts like "I really hate it when people clip their nails on a bus." But Thompson observes that, taken together, over time, the little snippets coalesce into a surprisingly sophisticated portrait of your friends' and family members' lives. This was never before possible, because in the real world, no friend would bother to call you up and detail the sandwiches she was eating.[12]

I visualize digital social networking as many expanding circular fields of energy intersecting and overlapping with other expanding fields. Ambient intimacy can lead to actual face-to-face socializing, but doesn't always. In these fast-moving, busy times, people are traveling away from home more, college students have less time to socialize as much as they would like, and more people are self-employed and working in isolation at home. Online communication helps a lot of people feel less lonely. Thompson asks, what sort of relationships are these? What does it mean to have hundreds of "friends" on Facebook? People who use these services differentiate between close friend and family relationships and more peripheral acquaintances. The close relationships become richer through constant communication, but not necessarily larger. However, the number of acquaintances increases tremendously. This means having immediate access to a large number of people with a wide range of backgrounds, experience, and information. One woman who had a tax problem with her accountant noted it on Twitter, and within ten minutes, her large online audience had provided leads to lawyers and better accountants. That's an example of information gathering that results from expressive exchanges.[13]

In the early '90s, the Internet was thought of as a place where you could present yourself in some new way. There was a certain aspect of privacy and anonymity. But what has happened with the popularity and growth of online exchanges is the opposite. Who you are is more public and revealing to more people. There are also privacy concerns, such as dealing with someone who posts an objectionable photo of you on their website without your permission.

Thompson suggests that this incessant updating is creating a culture of people who know much more about themselves. The constant self-disclosure encourages stopping several times during the day to reflect on what you're doing and also how you're feeling.[14] This is a good thing if it promotes mindfulness. We need to see how ambient intimacy evolves, but its popularity feeds our need to be interconnected.

External Fields and Societal Mind Conditioning in Groups

It is our natural inclination to form and join groups. Our very survival depends on interacting with others from babyhood to elderhood. We like to be part of a defined external field with people who share our interests and beliefs, so we join gay Republican organizations, motorcycle clubs, church choirs, or Kabbalah classes.

Being in a group often represents the idea of a family on a larger scale. This is especially true when there is a leader who serves as a kind of parental figure. When we are deeply involved, we feel inspired and loyal to the group, and we may respond harshly to outsiders who question our commitment.

Some people resist the conformity of a large social group, so they form their own unique in-group. Sometimes this in-group expands its boundaries and has an influence on the larger social group. The psychedelic era of the '60s began as a small counterculture group of social protest, drug experimentation, and insistence on the expression of individuality. In time, the movement gradually spread its influence through music, art, pacifism, and a free-loving lifestyle to larger groups in society and the rest of the world.

When an external field organizes itself into a dramatic cohesive group, it's good to look at the general atmosphere of society at the time and ask, *what else is happening?*

In the beginning, the psychedelic "hippie" era embraced alternate lifestyles and promoted altered states. The slogan was "Turn on, drop out, tune in." Many turbulent things were happening in the '60s and early '70s, including civil rights turmoil, moon walks, assassinations, and Vietnam. If you were in some position of military or government power in those days, you might have publicly denounced, while secretly promoting, the psychedelic movement. A "love and flowers" group might have been distracted from other things, namely, the unpopular Vietnam War. If that was the plan, it didn't quite work. Soon hippies became politically vocal, and others joined them in strongly opposing the war. On November 15 of 1969, over five hundred thousand people marched in Washington, DC, for peace. It was the largest antiwar rally in United States history.[15]

There is a small but potent early example of how the existing atmosphere of the times was used to direct and influence women to smoke. In 1920 in the United States, women were finally able to vote, and the women's rights movement was growing more vocal in the external field.

At that same time, Edward Bernays, Freud's nephew, mentioned earlier, was doing public relations work for the American Tobacco Company. He hired a group of young models and sent them to march in the New York City Easter Sunday Parade. He then told the press that a group of participants would light "Torches of Freedom." On his signal, the models lit Lucky Strike cigarettes in front of the eager photographers. The *New York Times* from April 1, 1928, printed "Group of Girls Puff at Cigarettes as a Gesture of 'Freedom.'" This helped break the taboo against women smoking in public.[16]

That happened over eighty years ago. Imagine what public relations through cybernetic propaganda and technological mind manipulation can do now.

The power of groups is enormous. They can create trends, change laws, and advance civilization. They can also be used by powerful people to dazzle us and coerce us into directions that sound good, but are ultimately more for their benefit than ours. Large numbers of people gathered together for an emotional cause are easier to manipulate.

Select your groups carefully. Don't be so drawn in that you stop asking questions about the workings and intentions and effects of the organization or movement. Be open to opposing views, and feel free to examine them. Cognitive dissonance can be a step toward keener knowledge and clarity.

Because conditioning is everywhere these days, look at how you are involved with groups and how they are involved with you. A group can offer you something that is satisfying, and at the same time, it can be flawed in ways that are not obvious at first. When she was nineteen, one of my clients found protection from her dysfunctional and sometimes violent family through a religious group. She was grateful for that, but in time, the group became more controlling and punitive and demanded total allegiance from her. It was difficult to leave, but she was finally able to break away and continue her journey on her own terms.

It's a challenge to be unified with others in a common experience and at the same time keep our individuality intact. Sometimes we put aside our personal feelings in order to conform to the requirements of the group. We develop a kind of mythology about groups just as we do about the well-run family unit. Groups can be just as dysfunctional as some families or have hidden agendas that we're not always aware of. We want to believe that we belong to a group that we can trust, one that represents our true beliefs and also functions responsibly. Think of organizations and groups that you've been connected to in your life. What was the emotional atmosphere, and what were the expectations for each member? How important was the experience, and how did it affect you?

Projecting Intentions and Goals into External Fields

So far we've concentrated on observing the personality of external fields, and how we are affected by them. We can also affect changes in the atmosphere around us by projecting our intentions into it and manifesting what we want.

In order to achieve a goal, our minds must become like laser beams of directed power. Most often, when we want something, we dream about it in the old linear way. The goal is usually directed only one way. We see ourselves reaching it and having it. We do not always imagine that the lover, the house, or the business opportunity is looking for us as well.

Imagine two electrons resonating in the same way though they are separated out and at a distance from each other. They are still somehow interconnected because they have the same spin or characteristic. We need to create a far-reaching resonance in our wish that matches an equal resonance in our goal. This matching of resonances naturally attracts one to the other.

There are several guidelines to effective laser-beam intentions:

1. The goal must be clear and specific. "I want to make more money" is too general. "I want to find an interesting position as a web designer that offers me at least X amount of money so that I can pay off my debts" is better.

2. Eliminate any creeping negative mumblings and anxiety intrusions like "Do I know enough about the latest technology? Can I really handle it?" or "They want a twenty-five-year-old guy. What chance do I have as a forty-five-year-old woman?"

3. Be clear about deserving it. Harboring self-judgments, or insecurities about achieving the goal, creates side trips of procrastination that prolong the trip and can even negate the intention. "I deserve it because I've been a victim all my life" doesn't cut it. "I want to meet someone because I'm really lonely" isn't an attractive presentation. "I am at my best with a partner, and I want to interact and grow with someone on a daily basis" is better because it's stated in a more positive way. While anger and fear can help propel us toward the goal by mobilizing our efforts, persistent dark emotions can have the effect of scattering and diffusing energy. They must be transformed in the service of direction and laser-beam clarity.

Take some action every day, no matter how small, that in some way relates to your goal. This can be as simple as talking about it with a friend, cutting out a newspaper article, getting a new haircut, etc.

Take as much time and energy visualizing the goal in the external field from that vantage point, as well as from your personal intention. For example, imagine an opening in a business situation that is looking for someone exactly like you and is willing to offer you what you want in terms of position and salary. In this way, you visualize the energy moving both ways, and you maximize the line of laser-beam transmission.

Disappointments along the path should not be looked at as failures, but as information about redirecting, restating, or reexamining some aspect of the intention.

State your intention in a strong but calm meditative state once or twice a day, especially before you go to sleep at night. When you can do that consciously with total focus, everything is possible.

Focused Expectation Without Fixation

When we project our intentions into the external fields of the future, it is also important to develop an alert system that tells us when uncomfortable emotions creep in and give us trouble about what we want. When we become fixated on a negative personal outcome, it's not a realistic vision. When we become fixated on a positive outcome, that is also a narrow view. Both obsessive positions, usually tinged with fear, perpetuate duality: *I will succeed. I will fail. It will be wonderful. It will be terrible.* In reality, the future contains not just negative and positive outcomes, but possibilities of every kind, and many reasons why something "works" or doesn't "work."

One of my clients had an interview for a position that she felt was the perfect dream job for her. She projected her intentions into the field and felt quite confident. The interview went exceptionally well, and everything looked very promising, but ultimately they decided not to hire her. She was confused and rather devastated. Two months later, she was hired by another, smaller firm. Four months after that, the first company went out of business.

While High-Velocity Consciousness teaches us how to focus without fear on a desired outcome, the most important mind pattern to develop is the belief in our ability to handle whatever happens. A personal statement that reflects that might be: *I have the clarity and the power to react creatively to unexpected events, and I have within me all the practical, emotional, and spiritual tools to manifest what I want.*

Observations and Declarations

Everything around us is rich with information and filled with various kinds of dynamic energy. Notice the personality of the atmosphere around you and your relationship to it—whether it's a family gathering, a business meeting, or a cyberspace exchange.

Say the following to yourself from time to time: *I use my emotional, physical, and intuitive sensibilities to notice how I am interacting with the external field around me. I can choose to be part of the atmosphere, remove myself from the scene, experiment with changing the field, or just have fun with it.*

SIXTEEN

OBSERVING NIGHT DREAMING

All that we see or seem, is but a dream within a dream.
—Edgar Allan Poe

Step 5. Observing Night Dreaming
Remember and record your dreams as often as you can.

Dreaming is universal, and as infants, we dream before we can speak. We never actually begin a dream—it's already happening as we enter it. It's an ongoing film that may include information from all the dimensions of consciousness. Unfortunately, dreams are also subject to societal mind conditioning and programming.

Why Is It Important?

Dreams are valuable arenas of knowledge—a wider range of information than we have available to us in everyday reality. When we dream, we travel along familiar roads or we wander off onto strange side trips. The journey may be filled with odd characters, uncomfortable revelations, or bone-chilling scenarios. Dreams can present us with ancient or modern heroes. They can offer us sensual, sexual, or spiritual exhilarations. Dreams can also be mundane and boring.

Tonight, about ninety minutes after you fall asleep, you will find yourself in the middle of a story. You may be in the Sahara desert arguing with an obscure classmate from twenty years ago about who has the right change for the bus fare to Paris. In the distance, a tiger wearing a baseball cap is floating in a small pond, and you suddenly realize Paris is out of the question because you're late for work. There will be an intermission, perhaps, and then there will be more scenes and more stories. You will spend about an hour and a half during the night dreaming in and out of the drama. You will spend approximately five years of your life in some kind of dream activity.

When we allow more conscious and continuous interaction between the dream state and the waking state, we find out more about who we are and what we can be.

Remembering Dreams

The following are general guidelines for remembering dreams. They have been compiled from my own experiences, accumulated client information, and from working with various dream researchers over the years.

- Have writing equipment near your bed, within easy reach. Some people prefer using a tape recorder. I find that writing down dreams in a journal allows for easier examination, especially if one is viewing or comparing dreams over a period of time.

- Alarms and clock radios can be jarring and disruptive to the dreaming process, although some people find that a sudden awakening works better for them than a gradual one. If you can program yourself before you go to sleep to wake up at a particular time, that works very well.

- As you lie in bed at night, just before dozing off, tell yourself, *I want to remember my dreams when I wake up in the morning.* Continue repeating this gently to yourself. If random thoughts or feelings interfere, imagine putting them in a bubble. Watch the bubble float far away from you, and go back to repeating the phrase.

- When you wake up in the morning, keep your eyes closed and don't move your body right away. See if you can catch the dream story. If nothing comes through, then very slowly shift to another position in bed. Sometimes moving to the position in which you had the dream (e.g., on your right side) will cause it to come flooding back into your consciousness. If after a few minutes of slowly shifting around, nothing happens, then, with your eyes still closed, ask, *How am I feeling?* Are you peaceful and calm, strangely apprehensive, curious and puzzled, sexually aroused? Take a moment then and quickly make up a short story that goes with the feeling you woke up with. What you invent in a limited period of time will often be close to what you actually dreamt.

- Dreams are like wisps of clouds that leave our consciousness very quickly. Procrastination is the thief of dreams, so write down your dream or story immediately before doing other things and before you start thinking about what it means. Date the page and record the dream without judging its importance or logic.

- If you have time after you've finished, read it over and reexperience it with the following questions in mind:

    - How were you experiencing the dream emotionally? While the koala bear was chopping up the dollhouse, were you feeling frightened, amused, or curious? Did the whole dream retain the same emotional atmosphere throughout, or did it change?

    - Where were you in the dream action? How involved were you in the scene? Were you watching the parading clowns from the platform as they marched on top of the train, or were you one of the clowns banging the drum?

    - What kind of movement was happening in your dream (either your own or the movement of other people or objects in the story)? Were you running in different directions or plodding slowly down an endless road? What movement was predominant: the rolling of the waves or the fast-approaching car?

    - Is there a repeated theme? Is this the fifth time you've dreamt about being late? Is this the third time you've dreamt about dirty sneakers or lost chickens?

- Who were the main figures in your dreams? Picasso and the moving pyramid? And who were the secondary figures? The two shadowy people in the distance who giggled and quietly disappeared?

- Record the date and give the dream a title that represents the basic theme. (e.g., "Endless Trail without Boundaries...")

- If possible, tell your dream to someone else. Do not let them interpret your dream. Instead, have them ask you questions about the figures and objects in your dream, the movements and the actions. Dialogue with some of the figures in your story, either with a friend or by yourself. Take on the different roles and see what happens. Don't push an explanation onto the dream. Let yourself feel it and move with it. Hold the meaning of it lightly and wait for further dreams to see how your story unfolds. Remember, dreams are not intellectual answers—they are unfolding processes of direction, presentations of conflict, wishes, warnings, spiritual guidance, or programming from outside sources.

- Try not to focus just on the images or content in a dream, but also notice the emotions, the movement, and the energy behind the story.

If you want to dream about a particular subject, and your intention is strong, and you follow some simple directions, you will be successful. It may take a week or more, but with patience, it will happen.

Choose a topic and be specific. Just before you go to sleep, think about it, feel it, write a short sentence about it, and even put the paper somewhere near your bed. If other thoughts interfere as you try to focus on the topic, take these thoughts, put them in a bubble, and watch them float away and disappear through a window or out the door. Then go back to the topic at hand. It's helpful to visualize the situation before you go to sleep, whether it is about resolving an argument or making a decision. See it as a photograph or a symbol that represents the issue. Dreams are primarily images. You are helping to translate thinking about the subject into a visual modality ahead of time. Remember that a dream is a continuation of consciousness translated into a different language.

One of the most exciting dream-inducement experiences that I was privileged to be a part of was with a client. He was a pianist and wanted to play and compose music in his dreams. His idol was Cole Porter, so he planned to have dreams with Porter as his guide. Nothing happened for a number of weeks, but then Porter started appearing in his dreams. Later, my client was able to compose and play original compositions in his dreams and program himself to wake up and write them down. That's how exciting dreams can be when you learn how to merge your everyday experiences with your dream night life.

Activating a Dream

Dreams pass into the reality of action. From the actions stems the dream again; and this interdependence produces the highest form of living.[1]
—Anaïs Nin

One night in a dream, I was taken aback to discover that I had a brownish-gray slug in my pocket. I had to go about my daily activities, but this slug in my pocket could be squashed by mistake or harmed in some way. I had to pay careful attention to it throughout the day. This was rather uncomfortable, but I did it. Then all of a sudden, the slug turned into this beautiful blue hummingbird suspended in the air in front of me. It filled the whole room with a brilliant royal-blue light. This vivid dream affected me deeply. Later that day, I went to a store to see if I could find some mobile or painting that matched the beautiful image in my dream. I didn't even have a chance to look around because my eyes immediately spied a magnet on the wall display: a brownish-gray slug. I had never seen a slug magnet before and haven't since. I bought it, of course. I understood. My conscious self wanted to skip to my transformed hummingbird self, but the magnet was telling me that I had to protect and take care of my slow-moving slug self first.

By activating the dream in my waking reality, I was able to discover it more fully without analyzing it out of its magical significance. We don't need to go out and buy a toy to activate a dream. But a continued awareness about our dreams can tell us many things.

A dream can have more than one level of meaning. It can be personal; it may also represent a collective fear. It can be a prediction, an intrusion from another source, or even a fragment from someone else's dream that we're close to.

One dream may not always be clear, but if we keep in touch with our dreams over a period of time, we can begin to see patterns that make sense. A wonderful, peaceful dream about making love to your sister could obviously be interpreted as a terrible, incestuous act. It needn't be that at all. It may have a strictly symbolic meaning, especially if the emotion in the dream is a positive one. It may mean that you are merging with the part of yourself that your sister represents. It may be a wish fulfillment to find someone like her to love.

How we feel emotionally in a dream is usually more significant than analyzing the details of the dream. Dreams are not always to be taken literally. If you dream about murdering someone and you feel triumphant, it doesn't necessarily mean that you enjoy hurting people. You could have anger that needs to be expressed. It may mean that you have to get rid of some aspect of yourself that's destructive. What it refers to may not be obvious at the time, but the emotional issue will probably reappear in later dreams.

Questions and Considerations

1. Choose a dream that particularly interests you. Once you've written it down, read it out loud. Act out parts of the story as if you are performing in front of an audience. Insights can come when you convert the dream from an imaginary process into the verbal and physical modalities.

2. Whenever something like an insect or an animal is prominent in a dream, ask yourself what it means to you personally and how you perceive it. An owl appearing in a dream can be experienced as wise and knowing and associated with Athena, the Greek goddess. To someone else, its appearance may represent spooky surveillance with eyes that are watching you wherever you go.

3. When a person appears in your dream, an old friend you haven't seen in twenty years, a public figure, a celebrity, or anyone, what do you see as the main characteristic of this person? Is there anything about who they are and what they represent that relates to you in some personal way?

4. Notice if any aspects of the dream present themselves to you during the next day or so. Look for any symbols, synchronicities, or situations

that may be associated with the dream.

Dreams and Dimensions of Consciousness

Our dreams reflect the different dimensions of consciousness. When we dream about everyday events, this generally relates to middle consciousness. When we experience emotional issues and anxiety in our dreams, this usually involves the lower unconscious. When we have informative and satisfying dreams, these seem to come from the superconscious arena. We probably experience all of these dimensions in one form or another every night, or possibly even in one dream story.

The content in most dreams tends to depict ordinary events and the general concerns we have when we're awake. If anxiety is the most common emotion we experience in dreams, this suggests that middle consciousness combined with the lower unconscious dominates our dream process. We have the wisdom of the higher self and the knowledge of the superconscious ready to break through to help us, but it doesn't happen often enough. Our own personal issues and external programming perpetuates our anxiety level and keeps us sequestered in the lower dream states.

Dreams Help Us Explore and Resolve Conflicts

Dreams help us look at conflicts that upset us. They draw attention to the fragmented and dissociated parts of our personalities and offer us information about how to deal with our problems. Sometimes a dream can also be quite literal. If you have a dream about losing your keys, it may be telling you that you need to be careful so that you don't lose your keys. Or the dream may have a deeper symbolic meaning, where the keys represent access to inner security.

Activating the dream process helps to interpret what the conflict is. One of my clients had a dream that she was in a battle with another person. Virginia had no martial arts experience in her waking life, but her dream told another story. In it, she was a karate expert who warded off her female opponent successfully and surprisingly with swift blows to the neck area. All was going well, until at one point, her opponent's head fell off. Virginia was not horrified—just flabbergasted. She tried to put it back on, but it didn't quite fit. That made her uncomfortable, and she woke up. When she played out the dream scene using actual movement, she was delighted to be able to use her body in this freeing way. When she acted out the last part, where the opponent's head fell off, the meaning of the dream began to unfold. The opponent was her thinking self—overanalyzing, top-heavy. The dream was showing her that she needed to prevent the intellectual part of herself from becoming so powerful that it stopped her freedom of expression. However, she had to learn how to do it without losing her head (her intellectual self) completely. That would be presented in other dreams.

Most often, the characters in our dreams represent parts of us. The ones that have negative qualities to them are what Mindell calls the "edge dream figures." They hover around the edges of our identity and disturb us, especially when we want to move beyond the boundaries of our self-imposed limitations.[2] In Virginia's dream, she was battling to free herself from her analytical thinking self into a new identity. She was going over her edge and feeling freer until her intellectual self (the edge figure) warned her that she had to do this carefully and not totally eliminate the thinking part of her personality.

Questions and Considerations

1. Select a dream you had that presented an issue or a conflict. How did you experience it in the dream?

2. If there were other people in the scene, what aspect of you might they represent? Any guesses about what they were trying to convey to you?

3. Using elements from the dream, create another story or another ending that successfully resolves the conflict.

Physical Symptoms and Medical Information in Dreams

The physical symptoms in our dreams are trying to unfold into our conscious awareness. Mindell has worked with hundreds of physically ill people and many thousands of dreams. He states that he has never come across one case in which the process of a body symptom was not reflected in a dream. Just as psychological issues are projected literally or symbolically, so are physical symptoms mirrored in our dreams.[3] They are usually presented as we experience them. One person may dream about her cancer as an angry dog that chews up and demolishes her lawn. Another person may dream about his cancer as a toxic, slow-moving, muddy river.

For example, when a dream that urges someone to express his or her anger is ignored, the result can manifest in a physical symptom such as asthma. In a waking state, when we focus on a physical symptom and explore it, we may find a direction that moves us toward some kind of understanding. In the dream state, we can also be aware of physical symptoms. They may be depicted realistically or symbolically, and we can glean from them helpful information that's not always available to us in the waking state.

Dreams may play a role in diagnosing an illness, determining a prognosis, and sometimes even formulating a treatment plan. Here is an account of a dream from a client that illustrates this:

> I'm in a hospital. There are lots of people milling around. There's a baby boy, with a round face, lying on one of the desks. He looks calm. He's less than a year old, but he can talk. He's waiting for a doctor or nurse. He's in a precarious position on the desk. I move him to a basket on the floor. I'm quite concerned about his condition and look around for help. He seems very calm, however, and says, "It's just the nodules or points, or something in my body, that's blocked and needs better circulation—nothing serious," and he smiles.

The client then said to me:

> In my waking reality, I had been feeling ill. I was worried that there was something wrong. My higher self, in the form of that baby, was reassuring me that it was not serious and that I just needed better circulation. It was an accurate diagnosis that was corroborated medically the following week. After that, I began to pay closer attention to my diet and began to exercise more.

This was a fairly direct presentation of a symptom. Most dreams are not as clear. Often our symptoms persist because we don't understand what they're trying to tell us. Dream messages can be mildly suggestive or dramatically dogmatic: "Try this, and you'll feel better" or "Do this, or you'll die."

Dreams about cancer, AIDS, or heart attacks are not always prophetic statements. They're often presented to us dramatically in order to scare us into attention, so that we change some existing pattern or way of being. One of my clients dreamt that he died of a heart attack and was buried in a coffin. When he realized that he was still alive and buried underground, he began to yell. Finally, someone opened the casket and said, "You jerk. Get up and deliver these flowers."

In his waking life, he was healthy, but overstressed and overworked, and hadn't had a vacation in years. During our session, when he acted out his dream and played dead in the casket, he felt so calm and relaxed that he almost fell asleep. In the middle of this dead time, he remembered his sister yelling at him several months before to "wake up and smell the flowers." Though in reality he had no heart problems, the dream was a warning that was telling him to relax more. The figure in the dream, which represented his sister, was his inner diagnostician/psychologist urging him to enjoy life more.

Figures of illness appear frequently in dreams because illness is one of our main concerns. The figures may represent us or someone else. We need to ask who they are. How is each one of these figures behaving emotionally? What is the nature of the disease, and what part of the body is ill?

Mindell states that children's early dreams often realistically or symbolically depict later adult chronic symptoms.[4] These kinds of dreams are especially prevalent in childhood because the child's conscious self is less developed and less separated from unconscious material. For example, I worked with a forty-two-year-old woman who had an uncomfortable skin condition that had manifested in her late thirties; she remembered a vivid early childhood dream about being at a picnic with bugs and insects crawling all over her. The early dream was symbolically forecasting her body's predisposition to skin problems.

Begin to pay attention to physical symptoms, bodily sensations, and medical information in dreams. Also, before you go to sleep, select a health issue that concerns you and present it into your night dreaming process for clarification and help.

Questions and Considerations

1. What is the earliest childhood dream that you remember? Does the dream represent a physical symptom, some recurring theme in your life,

or a health challenge to be examined?

2. Have you ever had a physiological condition represented in a current dream either in yourself or in some other dream figure?

3. What was the emotional atmosphere in the dream? What might be the diagnosis, prognosis, or advice represented in the dream?

Nightmares

A nightmare is a dream that is often long, quite vivid, and frightening enough to wake us up. It is usually so real that the feelings persist even after waking. Though the figures are not exact, it is estimated that 30 to 50 percent of the adult population remembers at least an occasional nightmare, perhaps one a year. Children before the age of five have more frequent nightmares, and on average, adults tend to have fewer nightmares as they get older. However, as one would guess, people with post-traumatic stress syndrome have more frequent nightmares, as do people suffering from various forms of mental illness. Increased drug use and medication, especially in the elderly, may also result in more incidents of frightening dreams.[5]

Nightmares are different from night terrors, which result in waking up suddenly in utter terror, but with no dream recollection. It is believed that there is some internal biological disturbance that creates an abnormal arousal that causes the terror.[6]

When nightmares are explored over a period of time, they most often lead back to childhood fears of abandonment, loss of sustenance, physical harm, mutilation, suffocation, destruction, or dissolving of the self. All children have such fears, and these may be reactivated in adulthood when people feel helpless or out of control, or when they feel guilty about their hostile impulses.[7]

The following is a nightmare recorded by one of my clients:

It was the middle of the night. I heard something in the dark that had a metallic sound—something moving back and forth. It wasn't loud, but it was continuous. I realized with horror that it was the sound of a doorknob being turned, first one way, and then the other. It was coming from the front door of my apartment. Someone was trying to get in. Had I forgotten to secure the lock?

I quickly ran out in the darkness and locked it. But whoever was outside continued to turn the knob and was now pushing against the door so hard that it began to shake and move with the pressure. Whoever it was, he was determined to get in and hurt me. The sounds stopped for a moment, and there was dead silence. My eyes and my heart froze. Whatever he or it was had become a thick white vapor that was now seeping in around the edges of the door and slithering toward me. Then I woke up.

A nightmare is a dramatic wake-up call. It is often an ally disguised as an evil entity whose intention is to scare the hell out of us and take us into the deeper shadows of our psyche. If we try to forget it or deny it, it will come back to bother us in another way.

Dream monsters are expressions that challenge us to open up to another awareness. Ignore them, and they might reappear as sudden anger, persistent anxiety, illness, or accidents. It may take time to consciously uncover and face what we dare not look at, and often we may need professional help. It is useful, however, to try on dreams, even nightmares, to wear them for a while and become the characters in them. It's another way of objectifying our fears.

At one of my workshops, we built a small, dark tent in the center of the room. We crawled into it and sat close together. We took turns telling our worst nightmare stories. Then we went outside the tent, drew the nightmare images on paper, and acted out the stories with each other. We became the monsters and looked to see what redeeming quality, if any, could be discerned from acting out the characters' movements. Some were slithering beings; others were fast, stomping animals; grabbing witches; or killer machines. There were some insights, a few transformations, heroic confrontations, and a lot of laughing. At the very least, we paved a path into the nightmare realm; we looked around and felt less alone. Courage often becomes a natural side effect of acting out this dream process. Creatively confronting that which is trying to kill us curiously makes us feel more alive and present.

Questions and Considerations

1. Select a dream that frightened you. What was the dream monster or figure in the dream? If there were no figures, what was the dominant frightening aspect of the dream? Give it a name, draw it on a sheet of

paper, and describe it to someone.

2. Become that figure. Walk, crawl, or stomp around, and imagine what it would say to you and how it would say it, if it could speak. What does it represent that needs attention or awareness from you?

3. If needed, call upon a superhero (Wonder Woman, Superman, Spider-Man) to help you confront the fearful elements in the dream.

Telepathic Dreams

In telepathic dreaming, the dreamer links with another person's thoughts or emotions, or with events that occurred in the past or the immediate present.

Freud thought that telepathy, especially during sleep, "may be the original archaic method by which individuals understood one another, and which has been pushed into the background...But such older methods may have persisted in the background, and may still manifest under certain conditions."[8]

Telepathic activity during dreams is promoted particularly during emotion-laden situations. One of my clients was enjoying a pleasant dream when it was suddenly interrupted by a scene of her sister, looking confused and running around in a burning building. She woke up startled. The next morning she called her sister, who lived alone in another state. The night of the dream, her sister had developed a dangerously high burning fever.

Some dreams are not clearly telepathic. They are what Dr. Jon Tolaas calls "fine cueing." We unconsciously pick up cues in our daily lives such as sounds, vocal inflections, or subtle body language. The brain registers these cues without our conscious knowledge and organizes them in a dream.[9]

Let's say you meet someone you care about for lunch and you have an argument. That night you have a romantic dream about him, and you find out the next day that he also had a similar dream. The day before, during lunch, while both of you were exchanging angry words, other things were happening as well. His body language, perhaps a slight touch, or a look toward you, conveyed caring. You matched his gestures without realizing it, even in the midst of the argument. The positive body language was incongruous with the angry feelings expressed. In the dream state, both of you ignored the argument, picked up the body cues, and created a positive dream. Romantic resonance between partners often promotes telepathic communication.

Research on dream telepathy continues and substantiates Freud's view that it is an "incontestable fact that sleep creates favorable conditions for telepathy."[10]

Questions and Considerations

1. Have you ever had a telepathic dream? If so, what were the circumstances? What did you learn from it?

2. Choose someone you are close to and plan to communicate something to them in a dream. You can send them a very simple message or a simple symbol. After you complete the primary centering process, program this intention just before you go to sleep every night for a week and see what happens.

Precognitive Dreams

Precognitive dreams are ones that present the dreamer with a vision of a future event, and they are more common than telepathic dreams, according to Dr. Montague Ullman's profound early dream research.[11] I have found this to be true with regard to my own experiences. These dreams can be depictions of some positive, negative, or neutral future event. They can be of great personal or global significance, or just mildly important and interesting.

The dream is not always an exact duplication of the event, but has enough elements within it to constitute what dream researchers call a "hit." In my experience, I find that in addition to seeing the visual event, sometimes with slight variations, two other variables occur in the dream that seem to match the actual event quite accurately. The first is the emotion I experience in the dream. The second is the spatial placement of myself in the dream, with respect to where the event is taking place.

One time I dreamt that the oceans were overflowing (this was years before the flooding in New Orleans or the tsunami in Japan). In my dream, the Hudson River was rising, and the lower part of Manhattan was going to be flooded. I looked outside my living room window and saw about a foot of water rushing through the streets. I called my friend to warn her about it, and she told me not to worry. I became less anxious, but was still dumbfounded. I thought I heard someone laughing in the distance—then I woke up.

A few months later, I was working at home, in my apartment on the sixteenth floor of my building, when I heard some commotion outside. I looked outside the window, and the street, as far as I could see, from east to west, was flooded with rushing water. Soon the streets, gutter, and sidewalks disappeared under a fast-moving river. The water was slipping into some of the stores on either side of the street. It was, for the moment, unnerving, until I discovered that it was a water main break. The impromptu river ran for several hours. People constructed makeshift bridges in order to be able to step in and out of the buildings. There was some minimal water damage. Then I heard someone laughing. I looked out the window again. It was a woman who had rolled up her dress, taken off her shoes, and was wading across the street.

I hoped that the dream was not predicting a more calamitous event. But for the moment, that was the outcome of my dream.

The most important and exciting thing for me about that incident, so many years ago, was that an experience was presented to me in a dream that manifested in a real life situation. It strengthened my belief in precognitive dreaming. What also happened is that it raised my awareness about the possibility of flooding in New York City. After that dream, I remember going downtown near Battery Park and looking at how close the water level was to the walkway and thinking, "One powerful storm could easily cause an overflow here." Unfortunately, that's what happened with Hurricane Sandy. Many suffered water damage in my neighborhood in lower Manhattan though my building was spared. Was that dream connected in any way to this event? Perhaps.

Questions and Considerations

1. Have you ever had a precognitive dream? If so, what were the circumstances, and how long after the dream did it manifest?

2. For a week, just before sleeping, ask for a dream that describes something positive to you about a future event.

Lucid Dreams

In most dreams, our conscious volition is not operating. We are not aware that we're dreaming; we think we're awake. In lucid dreaming, we become conscious in the middle of a dream and recognize that we are asleep and dreaming while the story is still going on. Lucid dreams tend to be more vivid than ordinary dreams or waking reality. There is usually a heightened awareness of three-dimensionality with more brilliant colors, kinesthetic feelings, exhilaration, and most importantly, the ability to direct the action.

Lucid dreaming was already known in fourth-century Athens. Aristotle wrote, "When one is asleep, there is something in consciousness which declares that what then presents itself is but a dream." Tibetan Buddhists have practiced lucid dreaming since at least the eighth century.[12]

Since the mid-eighties, psychophysiologist Dr. Stephen LaBerge has brought lucid dreaming to the forefront of research and exploration. How the conscious mind is able to have awareness and control while asleep and dreaming, and why it happens, is still a mystery. However, though it's not a common occurrence, it can be taught. [13]

I've had a few dreams that had lucid components to them. In one, I found myself running to catch a train, carrying the heaviest suitcase in the world. It was a struggle. I was breathing hard and running as fast as I could, but I was still in slow motion, and the suitcase was dragging me down. All of a sudden, I thought, *Wait a minute. This is a dream. There's no train, and I don't have to carry this stupid suitcase.* So I stopped and kicked the suitcase, which suddenly became lighter and flew away. Then I thought, *I have to go to the bathroom. I think I'll wake up.* And I did.

Questions and Considerations

1. Have you ever had a lucid dream, or a situation in a dream, where you realize that you're dreaming? Were you able to alter the dream event?

2. Before you fall asleep, relax, remove all other thoughts, and tell yourself that sometime during the next week, you would like to have a lucid dream: an awareness during a dream that you are dreaming.

The Global Dream Dimension

As we grow emotionally and chronologically, our dreams tend to be less personal and more involved with universal issues. As we transform and clear the residue of our personal past, we begin to dream more about our relationship to the larger field: the global dimension.

One of my clients had a vivid dream that she was flying high over the earth and could see beautiful areas of land flourishing with magnificent trees, flowers, and grass, but there were also other parts that were dark and lifeless. It so moved her that she became interested in global ecological issues and began working for land preservation.

Many years ago, at a dream workshop I attended, there was a woman who'd had a dream when she was young that shocked her. In her dream, she saw silver machinelike monsters with no faces, moving slowly across a dark and barren place. They made no sound as they moved. She also remembered seeing a small flag somewhere in the background. Twenty years later, as she watched the moon landing on television, she realized with astonishment that it was exactly like the scene in her dream. This seemed to be a precognitive global dream. It inspired her to study the dreaming process in depth, something she had not thought of doing before.

Questions and Considerations

1. Have you ever had a dream that had universal elements to it? How did you experience the event in the dream? Did it change your feelings or beliefs in any way?

2. What is your interest and or concern about universal matters? State this in a simple phrase, and for a week before you go to sleep, ask for a dream that presents you with some information on this topic.

Night Dreaming and Societal Mind Conditioning

Most of our night dreams reflect what we experience in everyday life. I always believed that, in general, the way colors appeared to us in most dreams was similar to how we experienced them in waking reality. We live in a world of colors, but we're not always attending to them in a conscious, deliberate way. Subliminally, we may have registered the deep purple coat on the woman walking by, and the bright green leaves on a tree, but if we're busy with other thoughts, we don't consciously remember those color details. Similarly, in a dream, the story, the action, and the emotions that are going on probably take precedence over noticing all the color details, unless they are important to the dream event, like "He was a spiritual being. His skin was blue like the Hindu god Krishna." Or, "I pushed away the red roses because they looked prickly and dangerous, and I chose the pink orchids instead."

However, some research suggests that the type of television you watched as a child actually has an effect on the color of your dreams. The study showed that while almost all people under twenty-five dream in color, people over fifty-five, all of whom were brought up with black-and-white television, often dream in monochrome—even now. Earlier research, from 1915 through to the 1950s, suggested that the vast majority of dreams that people remembered were in black and white, but the tide turned in the sixties, and later results suggested that up to 83 percent of dreams contain some color. Since this period also marked the transition between black-and-white film and TV and widespread Technicolor, an obvious explanation was that the media had been priming the subjects' dreams.[14] It's an interesting hypothesis that needs further research.

Can societal mind conditioning affect our private dreaming? Yes. I believe it can and does. We incorporate all kinds of external stimuli in our night dream stories, especially what we've experienced the day before or during the pevious week. Remember, the brain can perceive subliminal messages at a subconscious level without realizing it, like the flash of the McDonald's logo that appeared in the middle of a Food Network program on TV.[15] But even if it's not subliminal, our constant exposure to TV and the Internet places us in a kind of perpetual hypnotic state—open to receiving images, ideas, and emotions right into our subconscious. These can become incorporated into our dream stories.

One of my clients fell asleep in front of the TV one evening (not a good thing to do), and had a dream later that was puzzling, somewhat disturbing, and didn't make any sense to her on a personal level. She realized the next day that even though she fell asleep during the first ten minutes of the show, she had incorporated most of the plotline of that *Law & Order* episode into her dream.

External auditory stimulation can become incorporated into a dream state, especially music. I have found that when I go to a music performance, especially when it includes singing, I usually hear some kind of replay of the concert in my dreams that night, whether the musical experience was good or bad.

The infiltration into our dreams from outside sources happens because our subconscious picks up everything. Mind manipulation through various advertising and propaganda techniques has been going on for decades. While it may not matter to you if a McDonald's hamburger appears in your dream, we always need to ask, *what else is happening?*

The most common recorded emotion experienced in dreams is anxiety.[16] How much of that is personal, and what part does technological intrusion play in creating that stress or adding to it? Television and the Internet have a stake in keeping us somewhat unhappy and dissatisfied with what we have so that we can continue to be perpetual consumers in search of fulfillment. Every day we are confronted with troubling local and world news that makes us look for relief and solutions. How much anxiety programming are we subjected to that convinces us to accept solutions like bailouts, tax readjustments, and unexamined Constitutional amendments? There's no conclusive answer to these questions, but there are steps we can take to process our night dreaming so that we diminish some of the anxiety that follows us into our subconscious dream state.

1. The first step is to monitor how you approach the sleeping experience. Try not to watch the nightly news on TV or on the Internet just before you go to sleep. The anxiety-provoking programming can affect your dreams even when you're not watching with full attention.

2. Sometime before you go to sleep, take one or two seconds to mentally collect all extraneous TV, video, or Internet material that you've been exposed to during the day. Don't think of each one; just gather them all together. Then compress and compact them into a ball, toss it away into the air, and watch it disintegrate and disappear in the atmosphere high above and far away from you. Or, you can imagine placing all the extraneous material from the day into a special deprogramming file on your computer; then put all the contents of that file into the trash and empty it.

3. If your mind is too active, try the following exercise to induce sleep: Lie flat on your back on the bed, and raise both your straightened arms up to the ceiling, at right angles to your body. Then just let them fall and drop onto the bed beside your body. Next, raise both straightened legs up to the ceiling, almost at right angles to your body, and let them fall and drop down onto the bed. Do this exercise five or more times, alternating between arms and legs. If this does not appeal to you (or the person sleeping next to you), try gently massaging the area around your anklebones on both feet for a few minutes. This stimulates the sleep response.

4. As you lie in bed with your eyes closed, go through the primary centering process. After you complete the cleansing breaths and surround yourself with the violet protective bubble, think about something you would like to work on in your dream state. Direct the issue upward, beyond the lower dimensions and middle consciousness, into the arena of the superconscious, and ask for a dream from your higher self. And as always, tell yourself to remember the dream when you wake up the next morning.

Observations and Declarations

The night-dreaming process can affect us when we're awake even when we don't remember our dreams. Conflict resolutions, health diagnoses, telepathic communications, and precognitive flashes can appear during the day. They may be crossover projections from a dream. The everyday sensory world and the creative night-dreaming world are interfacing with each other all the time. Look at what happens to you every day like a waking dream. Notice what stories you get involved with during the day, what affect they have on you, and where you are in the action. Acknowledge and value your night-dreaming reality and its continuation in your everyday waking life.

Declaration: *I open myself to the richness of my dreams and live my dreams both awake and asleep to the best of my ability with help and orchestration from the highest spiritual source.*

SEVENTEEN

ACTIVATING KÉFI: PLEASURE EXPERIENCE

Life is not measured by the number of breaths we take, but by the moments that take our breath away.

—George Carlin

Step 6. Activating Kéfi: Pleasure Experience

Once or twice during the day, close your eyes and remember a moment from the past that was pleasurable.

Kéfi is a Greek word that represents a spirit of goodwill and exuberance that moves through us. When we feel it and our heart expands, it cannot be contained. It needs to be expressed. I think of it as an avalanche of the soul that fills us with the ecstasy of life. We all have it. It's closer to the surface with some people, less prevalent with others. When Greeks feel it…we dance! It's part of our tradition.

When Kazantzakis's great fictional character Zorba the Greek was asked what came over him to make him dance so wildly and exuberantly, Zorba answered, "What could I do, boss? My joy was choking me. I had to find some outlet. And what sort of outlet? Words? Pff!"[1]

When I was about three, I remember being on the beach with my parents. I was fascinated by the water and the wet sand at the edge of the ocean. I watched the frothy bubbles move up toward me and then recede over and over again. I stamped and splashed with my bare feet, and felt the wet sand between my toes. I giggled and laughed with pure pleasure. I was feeling and expressing kéfi through my feet.

Kéfi is not just the absence of stress. It's not just the relaxation we feel after eating a good meal and drinking a glass of wine. It's not a passive state. It's an active pleasure experience between you and someone or something.

On a biochemical level, it's often related to the release of endorphins in the brain that spill over and affect every cell in the body. We can think of it as the "runner's high" that athletes experience. It may be felt in a moment of profound intimacy with someone you love. It may be joyful tears as you watch an inspirational scene in a movie. It can happen when you have deep eye-to-eye contact with an animal or when you find yourself laughing uncontrollably with a close friend.

Why Is It Important?

Even without watching the latest disturbing events on the news, stress-producing fly-by thoughts predominate our lives. When we remember good times and activate kéfi in our lives, the positive neuronal pathways that expand consciousness begin to deepen. Spending a moment or two every day remembering and experiencing pleasure is no longer a luxury; it is a necessity to counteract all the other stuff that is going on.

Activating kéfi is not just an escape from anxiety and stress. It is a reminder of our ability to experience pleasure. When we tap more frequently and easily into pleasure without artificial stimulants, we can use this power to become less anxious and more in control of our bodies and our minds.

As we go through life, most of us are caught in a conflict of emotions. We are excited by the prospect of moving toward all that we can be. At the same time, we have within us the fear of being. We worry that becoming fully who we are might bring with it unfamiliar experiences that could make us uncomfortable. Sometimes we'll decide to stay with the familiar discomfort because we're afraid of the unknown.

However, when we have a kéfi moment, we know who we are in our essential being. It feels true, and we can say, "Yes! This is who I am and what I love," even if it's brief. We want to incorporate this into our daily life so that we can be more of who we are more of the time. And we must encourage and evoke the experience of love as an integral part of any process. Without it, our efforts would only be exercises of the mind.

During my childhood kéfi experience on the beach, I was in love with something. It may have been the feel of the watery sand, or my power to splash with my baby steps, or with the ocean's magic—probably all of that. We forget so much of who we really are and what we're in love with. If it's difficult for you to remember a memory filled with kéfi, you need to create one now.

Begin to notice where you sense love and excitement in your life. Remembering experiences of pleasure expands the doorway between you and higher consciousness.

Questions and Considerations

Once or twice a day, close your eyes and remember a kéfi moment. Place yourself in the scene. Visualize it and experience it as clearly as possible with all your five senses. Let it be a pure memory without negative thought attachments like, *Well, we broke up after that,* or *I'll never feel that again.* Experience the event in the immediacy of the pure pleasure moment without any extraneous interference. You can activate the same scene or different ones every day.

Encouraging Kéfi Through Play and Humor

Life must be lived as play.[2]

—Plato

I was on the Canadian side of Niagara Falls. The atmosphere was electric with the bright sun and the sight and sound of magnificent crashing waters. I breathed in the majesty of it all. And then I noticed them—a group of about ten seagulls. They were floating on the flat river as it moved to the top edge of the falls. Then, they abruptly flew off just before they got caught in the crescendo of the vertical drop. In a few seconds, they came back again, sat on the water, let it coast them along, and flew off again just in time. Many of the same birds kept coming back for more. It made me laugh. They were playing! It was a free water-world bird ride.

Play is natural to animals and humans. Fred Donaldson is an internationally respected play specialist recognized for his many years of research and use of play with children and animals. I remember a play-training weekend with him many years ago, and it was one of the most moving and heart-opening experiences I ever had. Donaldson points out that sages from many of the world's traditions, including Jesus, Lao-tzu, and others, remind us that in order to reclaim the wisdom and love we yearn for, we must again become as children. This does not mean a return to a second childhood, but recovering as a sage the lost characteristics of childhood.[3]

Play is feeling the enchantment of life, the pleasure of discovery, and the bravery of spontaneous expression. When we play, we remember the curiosity, simplicity, and natural spirit we had as children.

One day, while I was in the hospital recovering from my car accident, I found myself in the elevator with three other people. One was a patient who began humming and kidding around with his nurse, who then started singing the old jazz standard "Sweet Georgia Brown." He was joined by another nurse, who tapped the rhythm out on the metal part of an empty IV stand. I joined in the singing and started swiveling and dancing in my wheelchair. The impromptu musical number probably lasted less than a minute until the doors opened up again, but what a great kéfi moment that was!

One time I was in the middle of a marriage-counseling session. The couple had brought their two-and-a-half-year-old daughter along because they had not been able to get a babysitter. The husband and wife sat on the floor and faced each other with some distance between them. The little girl sat quietly in the corner and played with some toys. The atmosphere was tense with anger. The couple argued with each other for what seemed like a long time.

Then the little girl got up and, walking very slowly, went and stood in front of her father, who was still talking. With no words, she pulled her mouth sideways with her fingers and stuck out her tongue at him. Then she turned around slowly and went and stood in front of her mother. She opened her eyes wide, placed her open hands near her head, and wiggled her fingers. They both tried to ignore her, but it was impossible. She continued silently and slowly, moving back and forth between them, making those wonderful ugly faces.

The parents finally cracked up together, and it broke the angry atmosphere. Those two people, as angry as they were, could always laugh together. It was something they had always shared. And their little girl was reminding them about that in her own ingenious way.

Laughter often lurks in the background of our psyches and is more likely to erupt in the presence of others. Laughter is contagious. It can ripple through a crowd and change the atmosphere in minutes.

Physiological and Psychological Benefits of Humor and Laughter

Laughter is an instant vacation.[4]

—Milton Berle

While our emotional responses appear to be confined to specific areas of the brain, laughter seems to be produced via a circuit that runs through many regions of the brain. Subsequently, when we find something funny and laugh about it, this kéfi experience affects us in many ways.

On a physiological level, laughter appears to strengthen the immune system by heightening the activity of antibodies. Robust laughter increases blood circulation, works abdominal muscles, raises the heart rate, and gets the stale air out of the lungs. After a hearty laugh, blood pressure drops to a lower, healthier level than before.[5]

Laughing can be a total-body aerobic workout. Researchers estimate that laughing a hundred times is equal to ten minutes on the rowing machine or fifteen minutes on an exercise bike. Laughter provides a safety valve that shuts off the flow of stress hormones and the fight-or-flight compounds that swing into action in our bodies when we experience stress.[6]

The psychological benefits of humor are quite amazing, according to doctors and nurses who are members of the American Association for Therapeutic Humor. People often store negative emotions, such as anger, sadness, and fear, rather than expressing them. Laughter provides a way for these emotions to be harmlessly released.[7]

Humor puts us in touch with the wonderful absurdity of the world, with its endless possibilities, interesting combinations, and surprises. Just when we think we're going one way humor pulls us in another direction.

If God dwells inside of us like some people say, I sure hope he likes enchiladas, because that's what he's getting.[8]

—Jack Handey

We have a cosmic trickster hiding in the corners of our lives, waiting for us to *get it*—waiting for us to laugh at our own seriousness. Laughter is the spirit of the deeper reality trying to find a way to manifest itself. It wants us to take time now and then to relish the paradoxes of life instead of being anxious about the outcomes. Play and humor and laughter liberate us from viewing things in only one way. The unconscious likes to be seduced through novelty. Imagine thinking the same old boring thoughts day after day. Some new experience comes up through an action or an unusual thought, and the brain lights up with excitement. New neuronal pathways are created.

Humor in its best form usually accompanies play and encourages the mind to experience new things. These unexpected relationships are the basis of all creative activity. We see this in humor, science, and art. Humor creates surprising dualities and combinations. Science tries to examine dualities (e.g., how can light be both a particle and a wave?). Art presents new combinations and images of reality, for example by simplifying a tree into geometric patterns or creating a woman's torso from old bicycle parts.

Questions and Considerations

1. Close your eyes, take a few deep breaths, exhale, and think of some funny moments in your life. Reexperience one or two of them in your mind, and remember how you felt.

2. Choose an argument or a conflict that you had with another person. Let it be something that was troublesome but not too serious. Close your eyes, complete the primary centering process, and quickly remember the scene as it happened. Then choose a favorite comic actor, funny TV personality, or humorous literary figure. Imagine this person describing the situation that you just remembered, using his or her own comedic style. If you like, you can put the humorist in the actual scene. It doesn't matter how you do it as long as you have fun with it. If it doesn't work, choose another conflict, another comic, or try it on another day.

3. Choose two objects that you have around the house that are not usually associated with each other, like a begonia plant and a pot holder, or a chair and a toothbrush. Imagine a funny conversation they might have with each other about who they are, how they feel, and what they know.

4. Look for absurd combinations of things, funny incongruities, silly images, humorous conversations. Watch for them as you go to the

market, sit on the train, or walk through the park. They're waiting to be discovered to make you laugh.

Encouraging Kéfi Through Visual Experience

Of all our senses, the one we use most frequently is the visual. We move through life seeing a variety of colors, shapes, textures, and spatial arrangements.

When we have an aesthetic experience with our eyes, we are suddenly attracted to something. Whether it's a silver car, a beautiful face, or an explosive painting, we separate that thing from everything else around it. We become engaged with it in a very immediate way. We are suspended in time and space. A few minutes later...it's gone. The mind interrupts us with thoughts or someone bumps into us, or we need to leave and catch the bus.

The possibilities for visual experiences that induce kéfi moments are all around us. In nature, tiger lilies, turquoise stones, and sand crabs are artistic products of the creative life force—visible expressions of the invisible cosmos. Human-made artistic products represent channeled aspects of the deeper reality combined with our personal creative stamp.

Colors, shapes, and spatial arrangements around us reflect who we are and what we're made of. We ourselves are also filled with color. The electromagnetic field around our bodies and the energy centers of our chakras shimmer with the different colors of the spectrum. We are walking rainbows. Geometric designs and shapes are contained in our physiological and energetic consciousness. Every spatial arrangement, every spiral movement of the tiniest cell in our bodies mirrors the spiral movements in the universe.

Questions and Considerations

1. Think back to a kéfi moment that involved an exciting visual experience, like the first time you saw fireworks or fireflies. Close your eyes, and re-create the scene.

2. Feast your eyes often on a brilliant painting, a strange flower or fruit, or a small passing dog.

3. For one day, choose a color. Let's say blue. Let yourself notice things

that you see around you that contain shades of blue: a book cover, a computer screen, someone's jacket, parts of a billboard, etc. Experiment on another day with other colors. Also, choose another day to notice designs like plaids or stripes, or shapes like circles or triangles.

The Creative Encounter

One of the early kéfi moments that most of us experience is the creative encounter. When we're about two years old, we discover something that fills us with amazement. We discover scribbling. What only a moment ago had been a blank piece of paper is now filled with something we alone have created, something that did not exist in the world before. Scribbling is spontaneous. When we're about three, we grasp our crayon firmly, and with a single line, we begin to draw forms and shapes like circles, triangles, squares, and crosses. Almost as soon as we can outline forms, we begin to combine these basic geometric forms into designs. Soon after, we begin to create pictures and stories. For most of us, in a few years this spontaneous pleasure diminishes with the rules of education, judgments of the ego, and the critics of the culture.[9]

Look at your hands for a moment. Turn them over and view them tenderly. They are functional, sensual, emotional, and filled with personality and energy. They carry the line pattern of our lives in their palms. They are also extension sorcerers. Their fingertips can reach out into the vast space of form and color, gather what they want, add some personal touch, and produce something visually unique, if given half a chance. They're capable of discovering new combinations and rearranging old ones.

We can reawaken the natural creative process that we had as children and let our hands do the talking spontaneously, without critical judgments, just for fun. We are all artists, capable of getting caught in the mystery and the kéfi of the creative encounter.

Questions and Considerations

1. Give your hands a creative adventure. Scribble, paint, draw, work with clay, or make collages.

2. Carry a small pad and a pen or pencil with you. Draw something every day or so that comes up in your mind or catches your eye on the

street or while waiting for the laundry to be done. It can be anything: a spontaneous scribble, a shape, a design, an object, or a person. Forget about the sketches for a week or two, and then look at them together and see what you see. Spend no more than ten minutes doing any of this.

Encouraging Kéfi Through Music

I AM HERE TO LIVE OUT LOUD.[10]

—Émile Zola

The human ear is the first sensory organ to develop in the fetus. It is fully functional about five months before we are born. When we hear music in the womb, we seem to prefer Mozart and Vivaldi to Beethoven or Brahms. Plants seem to respond most positively to Bach, Indian classical music, and jazz.[11] Cats seem to prefer Mozart, and so do birds. And in fact, Mozart himself was inspired by birdsong. He even composed music for his companion starling.[12]

Some people believe that the singing of birds sets up a particular sound vibration that promotes the growth of the young leaves of trees, plants, and flowers. That may be the reason why birdsong is fairly constant all day long in the spring, while the new growth is occurring, and less so in the summer months.[13]

The winds are tuned to certain rhythms, the waves crash to a certain beat, and the leaves of trees whisper to each other—everything is alive with sound.

Long before we can see clearly as infants, we respond to music by moving our bodies. I have watched infants listen attentively to certain music, and I have sung duets with many babies who are less than a year old.

Music is miraculous. Its rhythm causes us to move our bodies, tap our feet, clap our hands, march in a parade, or go into a hypnotic trance. Its melodies touch and evoke the sadness of a memory or the thrill of a romance.

Jung wrote, "Music expresses in sounds what fantasies and visions express in visual images…Music represents the movement, development, and transformation of motifs of the collective unconscious."[14]

Theoretical physicist Dr. David Bohm wrote about listening to music, "At a given moment a certain note is played, but a number of the previous notes are still reverberating in consciousness. It is the simultaneous presence and activity of all these reverberations that is responsible for the direct and immediately felt sense of movement, flow, and continuity."[15]

We do not listen to music by taking the previously heard notes, remembering them, comparing them to the present notes, and predicting future ones. It's not a thought process. Rather, we are directly and immediately involved in what we're hearing. Listening to music evokes various emotional responses, bodily sensations, muscle movements, and a wide range of personal meanings.

Some of these responses to music occur below our level of consciousness. We are not always aware that our breathing slows down, or our heartbeat quickens with the rhythm of a particular piece of music, or that a certain melody pattern triggers an emotional feeling.

We are influenced by the sounds and rhythms all around us. When we are near the ocean or a mountain, away from the sounds of the city, our bodies begin to resonate with the earth's pulse. Our heart rate and our brain waves slow down. Our endorphin levels rise, and we feel better. This rhythm stays in our system for hours.

Please include more music in your life. Hum, chant, sing, play an instrument, tap out a rhythm, join a choral group, listen more acutely to the sounds of life around you. Let music pour into your soul often, for healing, for fun, for sadness, for passion.

> The moment in and out of time…
> Music heard so deeply
> That it is not heard at all, but you are the music
> While the music lasts.[16]
>
> —T. S. Eliot

Questions and Considerations

1. Think of a kéfi moment in your life when you were particularly affected by a piece of music, a song, or a rhythm so much that you lost yourself in it. Close your eyes, and hear it playing in your mind.

2. Choose a piece of instrumental music. Turn the volume up a bit. Lie down somewhere and imagine that you can hear the sounds through every pore of your skin. Listen to it with your whole body. Then experiment

listening to it with just the top of your head, or with your heart, your feet, etc.

3. Listen to people speaking, but don't concentrate on the words. Simply notice the pitch, timbre, and rhythm of their voices. If possible, record yourself speaking with one or more other people, and without judgment, listen to the sound personality of each voice.

Encouraging Kéfi Through Dancing

I would only believe in a god that knows how to dance.[17]
— Friedrich Nietzsche

Today we are moving faster and farther than we have ever moved before. We drive cars, take trains, fly planes, but we're functioning with a reduced repertoire of active body movement. We are increasingly replacing our own body movement with propulsion of the immobilized body; we are replacing motion with frozen speed.

The exercise and fitness movement is a valiant attempt to counteract the rigidification of the body, but it is not enough. We also need to dance!

As you read this, there are dances going on inside your body. Subatomic particles are spinning and dancing together. In the air around you, everything is moving, like the rainbow dust dancing in a shaft of light. And higher still, the whole universe is engaged in endless motion and activity in a cosmic dance of energy.

Dancing is an intimate participation between our body and music, rhythm, and vibration. It's a natural physical response to a pulsing beat or a sparkling song. One- and two-year-old children automatically move to a bouncy tune, even before they are fully steady on their feet.

Dancing can take us into the sensual depths of the earth, where we can feel our humanity and sexuality, and higher, into the ecstatic whirling of the universe, where we can know our divinity. It can take us into ourselves and out of ourselves. When we engage in dancing fully, without ego or judgment, we remember our relationship to everything around us, our unity with nature, our similarity to the movements of animals, our duplication of the microscopic and macroscopic rhythms of life. It is that important.

Socrates was thought to have begun dancing lessons later in life. One report claims that at a dinner party, he talked about dancing to the amusement of his guests. He declared, "But what is it you keep on laughing at—the wish on my part to reduce to moderate size a paunch a trifle too rotund? Is that the source of merriment? Perhaps you are not aware, my friends, that Charmides—yes! he there—caught me only the other morning in the act of dancing?"[18]

I love imagining the most famous of all Western philosophers moving around and dancing as he developed his brilliant ideas.

Questions and Considerations

1. Begin walking around the room or in some open space. Do this for a few minutes, until you feel ready to improvise a step. It can be a small toe tap, a little leg lift, a swivel or shuffle to one side, anything that feels interesting. Whatever you choose to do, repeat the movement several times in a row. Keep doing it until a patterned rhythm is produced, and then just improvise.

2. Stand comfortably, and close your eyes. Think of a dance experience from your life. If you can't think of one, remember a dance performance that you enjoyed. With your eyes still closed, reexperience the movements of that dance. Now, with eyes open, move around the room and actually do some dance steps from it.

3. Play a favorite piece of music and let your right arm lead the dance. That is, focus on your right arm, begin to move it and let the rest of your body follow. Repeat this exercise by doing the same thing with other parts of your body, like your left hip, or one knee, or your head, and let them lead.

4. Do you remember skipping as a child? If you have a large enough space, try skipping, with or without music, for a few minutes, and remember the freedom of that action. Or else, just walk around and skip a step or two now and then.

Kéfi and Societal Mind Conditioning

We humans are innately pleasure-seeking beings, but we can be just too busy or anxious to have fun. For some of you reading this, activating kéfi by deliberately playing, laughing, drawing, being with music, and dancing may seem slightly silly. Or, the ideas may be interesting, but difficult for you to do. If this is so, then please find something that personally appeals to you. Understand that activating kéfi and including pleasure in your life is important for your survival. It's that serious, especially today, when our lives are being mediated, monitored, and programmed more and more. Become aware of the societal conditioning around you that directs *how* you should experience pleasure in your life. Differentiate between the actual personal experience of kéfi and manufactured virtual-reality kéfi, especially through TV, the Internet, and film. Of course, some of those experiences can be wonderful and stimulating. The question is, where do they take us in real life?

I had been pretty isolated for a while during the time I was completing this book. One night I was working late, and my mind was too alert to sleep. I tried some meditation and exercises. That helped, but it wasn't enough. Then I realized that it was late enough to watch one of my favorite talk show hosts, Craig Ferguson. He can be smart and funny, especially in the opening monologues. That night, with his wonderful Scottish accent, he was talking about "filthy feathered chickens strutting around with their big breasts like they own everything. You know," he said, looking straight at the camera and almost whispering, "they're the Vegas strippers of the animal kingdom." I found myself laughing out loud. I realized that I missed laughing with some of my friends and having funny face-to-face exchanges. I looked forward to getting that back in my life. That night, at that moment, however, this worked quite well.

Notice how commercials promise you fun, pleasure, and happiness. The assumption is you don't have these things, or you should have more of them, and they have the kéfi solution for you. Years ago, the "Coca-Cola Happiness Factory" TV commercial became the highest-rated global spot the Coca-Cola Company had ever tested. It won several awards. The commercial takes you on a journey through a Coca-Cola vending machine into a fantasyland full of wondrous characters and spectacular landscapes. It's quite engaging, and you feel good watching it.[19]

Coke was a standard refreshment when I was growing up, but I hardly drink it now after reading the research on the high-fructose corn syrup (HFCS) found in so many foods and beverages, including Coca-

Cola Classic. The studies detected mercury, which is toxic, in about one out of every three common foods or beverages, especially when HFCS is the first or second labeled ingredient. This results from long-term use of outdated mercury-cell technology for making caustic soda—a key ingredient in HFCS. There are safer, readily available alternatives, and the researchers urged the FDA to take steps to better protect our food and beverages from this unnecessary contaminant.[20]

I think it's important to rebel now and then and not be addicted to a structured regimen. So once in a great while, I'll drink a Coke. We are all free to choose or reject the end product of a pleasure-promoting commercial, TV program, or movie trailer. At the same time, we can, and should, also have an eye open to *what else is happening,* and notice when and how we choose to activate kéfi, or whether it's chosen for us. Use the other arenas of consciousness to help you decide where your personal pleasure-seeking takes you.

Kéfi: Then and Now

In *The Greek Way,* Edith Hamilton wrote that the ancient Greeks "played on a great scale...To rejoice in life, to find the world beautiful and delightful to live in, was a mark of the Greek spirit...The Greeks knew to the full how bitter life is as well as how sweet...But never, not in their darkest moments, do they lose their taste for life. It is always a wonder and delight, the world a place of beauty, and they themselves rejoicing to be alive in it."[21]

Observations and Declarations

Every day, find something to laugh about; look with new curiosity at some remarkable product of nature; scribble; play with an animal; listen to music with full attention, and make music; dance like Zorba or Fred Astaire.

At least once a day, close your eyes and remember a personal kéfi moment, and feel the pleasure of that in every cell of your body.

A continuing experience of kéfi frees the mind to be in a state of love, and this freedom gives us the energy to tackle problems and fears with greater resilience and wisdom.

Make this declaration often: *I invite the natural ecstasy of my soul to be present in my life, to fill me with the infinite power of love, the deepest reality.*

EIGHTEEN

ACCESSING THE HIGHER DIMENSIONS

Reality is merely an illusion, albeit a very persistent one.

—Abert Einstein

You knock at the door of Reality,
You shake your thought-wings,
loosen your shoulders, and open.

—Rumi

Step 7. Accessing the Higher Dimensions

At least once during the day, close your eyes, place yourself in a meditative state, and move into higher dimensions of consciousness.

Twenty-five hundred years ago, the brilliant Greek philosopher Pythagoras said that everything in the cosmos, including us, is made up of different vibrations, and that matter can be thought of as frozen music. The idea is that the universe existed in some kind of harmonic order that was then translated into our physical world.[1]

In the 1930s, Swiss researcher Hans Jenny discovered that sound could affect and shape physical matter. When sand, oil, or metal filings were placed on a thin metal plate and vibrated at certain frequencies of sustained musical tones, they formed themselves into shapes similar to patterns in nature, such as honeycombs or nautilus shells. These beautiful, dramatic images vividly showed how inanimate matter can be brought to life through sound. These experiments are repeatable and will produce the same patterns each time. Dr. Jenny concluded that sound is primordial, and that it is the creative principle in all life. He called the sound-form phenomena "cymatics," after the Greek word for "wave."[2]

Dr. David Bohm, mentioned before, suggested that what we perceive through our senses as everyday reality is only a small fragment of a larger matrix that he called the "implicate order." Our everyday sensory reality is like a holographic projection of this larger matrix.[3] The reality we experience is valid, but it is a myopic view, a smaller field of a larger panorama.

The Higher Dimensions and Sensory Reality

There is a deeper world than this that you don't understand.
There is a deeper world than this tugging at your hand.[4]

—Sting

These ideas, and others like them, remind us of the existence of the higher dimensions of consciousness within our everyday sensory reality. Our challenge is to develop greater awareness about this relationship and discover the realms of freedom that exist within what appears to us as a limited three-dimensional world.

Everything we have created and manufactured on this planet has its origins in the higher dimensions. Every thought we have can manifest in the material world. Since our very distant past, we have wanted to fly. Somewhere deep in our consciousness, we know, and have always known, the experience of flying. We are all space travelers in our dreams. What a persistent longing it had been to fly, going against all logic and knowledge of gravity! Yet, we knew it and dreamed it for thousands of years, and then we finally saw it happen a little over a hundred years ago.

There are phenomena that take place every day, like miraculous health recoveries through prayer and meditation, that challenge somber medical predictions. A thought travels hundreds of miles in an instant, and its power effects a change in the person receiving it. The flash of a dangerous event appears to someone before it happens, and a disaster is avoided.

The universe is filled with other planets, other physical beings, and other dimensions that are within reach of our conscious exploration. Our minds have imagined these things for some time. They have taken shape in our myths, in our dreams, in our science-fiction stories and films, and in our religions. The truths of the universe are all available, and the manifestation of these truths is just at our fingertips, waiting to be revealed.

Sensory reality is a point of view. It depends on where you look and how you see. The circle of your life moves around you, and you are also part of a boundless universe. You can choose to look straight ahead, or you can expand your vision to include a multitude of views and possibilities.

Why Is It Important?

When we access the higher dimensions, we are in the arena of the superconscious, where we receive our highest artistic, philosophical, spiritual, and scientific inspirations. Our intuitive sensibilities and psychic functions are strengthened and activated, and we can experience the purest forms of love, compassion, and joy. Through the superconscious, we receive the wisdom of the collective unconscious. Who wouldn't want to go there?

Harnessing all of these potentials more deliberately and integrating them into our everyday sensory reality is the driving force of our human existence. We've done well with producing magnificent creative structures and amazing technological achievements throughout history, but we haven't done so well in promoting altruistic love and compassion. These exist, of course, but they are usually overshadowed and eclipsed by fear, self-righteous power, and greed.

We can diligently follow a spiritual or religious path far away from the crowd and learn how to be in the higher dimensions most of the time. That's a choice that some people make. The challenge for the rest of us is to utilize superconscious knowledge within the context of everyday living. It's a multileveled process: immensely gratifying, exciting, and in my opinion, absolutely necessary in order to deal with the issues that we are confronted with in today's world.

Accessing the higher dimensions is our natural birthright. When we live in this expanded state of consciousness more deliberately, it fulfills us personally and enhances the vast energy field around us.

How Do We Experience the Higher Dimensions?

Prominent research psychologist Dr. Lawrence LeShan, with whom I trained many years ago, described what a person's experience is like when they are in an altered state of consciousness. He called this state the clairvoyant reality and compared it with the sensory reality.[5] The following are some of Dr. LeShan's definitions and observations. I add to them examples of what I have learned over the years:

1. In the clairvoyant reality, time and space are perceived differently from sensory reality. Time is not linear, and space is not compartmentalized.[6]

For example, our perception of time often slows down in near-fatal accidents. Also, the feeling of space changes in near-death phenomena. Some people report seeing their whole lives flash before them as they move through tunnels toward a bright light. In these events, the past, present, and future are experienced in a millisecond. Precognitive dreams can manifest into actual events. Telepathic transmissions can occur where the mind travels beyond the confines of linear time and space to communicate instantly with other minds and also receive information from distant sources.

When we are in a deep meditative state, we are usually less aware, and sometimes totally unaware, of the passage of time because we are so fully immersed in the immediate process.

2. Information seems to be available other than through the five senses.[7] During meditation, sitting still with our eyes closed, we can sometimes hear sounds, see images, or experience things moving without consciously thinking of them. They just appear.

Clairvoyance can occur. This is the ability to view a scene or an event that is currently happening in another location. It is usually experienced as a visual sensation, but sometimes it has a visceral or emotional component to it. For example, a mother's sudden sense of concern over the safety of a daughter who lives a thousand miles away is corroborated later by finding out that her daughter had an accident at the exact time that she experienced the anxiety.

Clairvoyance is also called remote viewing, a technique that has been used for many years by the United States military to gather important information from specific geographical locations.[8]

3. The deeper we find ourselves in a meditative state, the more we experience positive and negative events and actions differently. We have a sense that what is, is, and is neither good nor evil, but part of the eternal universal plan beyond polarities.[9]

In other words, the judgments we usually make in everyday reality are suspended. For example, in a beginning meditation, you might feel angry and even violent toward someone, and then without willing it, you may find your emotions slowly shifting into a kind of compassion and empathy for that person. Or in a more generalized example, you may have the realization that an erupting volcano is an inevitable expression of nature rather than an evil, destructive force.

It doesn't eliminate the necessary opinions and judgments we have to make every day. However, it allows us to move away from the details of life that block us from knowing our intrinsic connection to the larger and wider scheme of things.

4. When we are in the clairvoyant reality, instead of separateness and individuality, we have a sense of unity and universality.[10] We become more aware of our relationship to the collective. There is an experience of being one with all of humanity, nature, the universe, or God. It's the state some of the astronauts described as they viewed Earth from space for the first time. We can sense it in the middle of a spiritual or religious revelation. Sometimes it can happen when there is a transcendent merging during love and sexual union in its highest form. We can feel it in the middle of an illness or a near-death experience.

Someone I know had been in the hospital with such excruciating physical pain that she was ready to give up, but was afraid of dying. She described what came to her in a half-dream state. She was suddenly surrounded by millions of people who were all suffering. It was as if everyone in the world who had ever experienced pain like hers was there. She felt comforted and calmed by this universal sharing of pain. She knew that when she decided to let go, these multitudes of people would be there for her. She died peacefully some time later.

The clairvoyant reality, as LeShan describes it, has relevance when we look at how we experience the higher dimensions. Accessing the higher dimensions and the arena of the superconscious can result in a variety of experiences that contain some or all of the various states and sensibilities mentioned above.

I also believe that uncomfortable emotions, especially fear, are experienced primarily in our everyday sensory reality and in the dimensions that are nearest to us, like the lower unconscious. This arena reflects to us the conflicts of daily life so that we can learn to release the ego's fears and frustrations. We can also travel to the higher dimensions during sleep, but we don't always recall what happens there because our emotional conflicts, when not attended to, predominate.

I believe that beyond a certain boundary in the higher dimensions, fear does not exist, because we are in the absolute present moment without the apprehensive thought mumblings of the past or the future. We are just *being*.

An example of experiencing the immediate present can be illustrated with certain types of music. If we listen for the first time to a classical music selection, it may evoke emotions and memories for us, but these tend to be temporary because we're attending to the music that is changing. Unless we're professional musicians analyzing the piece, we do not have the time to dwell on the musical notes that were just played or have apprehension about what notes are to come in the next passage. Being in the here and now is crucial to expanding our minds.

I remember someone speaking at a conference about his experience of jumping out of an airplane and finding out that his parachute wasn't opening. Somehow, on the way down, he managed through many maneuvers to cause it to finally open just in time. A person in the audience remarked what a terrifying experience that must have been for him.

The speaker said, "No. There was no fear. I was too busy figuring everything out to be scared."

So, practicing being in the moment, with or without danger, has the accumulated result of building up our courage so that we can experience fearful situations with more clarity and mindspeed integration. Accessing the higher dimensions by traveling from the sensory reality to the superconscious and back again helps us do that.

Physiological Expressions of States of Consciousness

How does our physical brain react during everyday thinking activities and when we are in higher dimensional levels? Different states of consciousness and attention can be monitored through EEG machines that display the electrical activity emanating from the brain in the form of brain waves, categorized as follows:

- **Beta waves** are associated with waking awareness, logical thinking, and with performing various activities in a conscious manner. It is our everyday thinking state when we have awareness of our body, our environment, and time.

- **Alpha waves** relate to relaxation, when the brain slows down and one feels a sense of calm. It is a common state for the brain and occurs when a person is alert but not actively processing information. It happens when we close our eyes and meditate and find ourselves less conscious of the external world.

- **Theta waves** are associated with total relaxation, promoting creativity, and enhancing our problem-solving ability. Although it is almost a sleep process, the brain opens up to a deeper alert state where it is receptive. It relates to the process of dreaming, deep meditation, paranormal phenomena, and telepathic experiences.

- **Delta waves** represent a period of deep, dreamless sleep where there is very little activity in the cerebral cortex.[11]

- **Gamma waves** are impulses that are typically present when the brain is making new circuits. It is the only frequency group found in every part of the brain. It's hypothesized that when the brain needs to simultaneously process information from different areas, the gamma activity consolidates the required areas for simultaneous processing. It is believed that usually only experienced meditators can accomplish this.[12]

Generally speaking, we all have the ability to access and become aware of these various states. Then why are most of us still operating predominantly in the lower dimensions when these rich arenas of consciousness exist within us? We might guess that societal mind conditioning over thousands of years has resulted in suppressing the idea that each one of us can reach these higher states naturally. Did ancient people believe that these realms were open only to the Sumerian gods, the high priests of Egypt and Greece, or the specially anointed persons of certain religious and spiritual traditions? There are hints throughout ancient history that more was known about the pathway to higher consciousness than was revealed to the ordinary person. This is a complicated topic, and I will briefly touch on it here.

The Pineal Gland and the Higher Dimensions

As I mentioned in an earlier chapter, in some Eastern and Western spiritual traditions, the heart chakra is thought of as the mediator between the mind and the body. Also, the brow chakra, known as the third eye, located in the center of the forehead, between the eyebrows, has long been considered the gateway into higher consciousness. We focus on the royal-blue dot of the pineal in the primary centering process. In anatomical terms, it is associated with the pineal gland.

The first description of the pineal gland, and speculation about its functions, were found in the writings of Galen (130–210 AD), a famous Greek medical doctor and philosopher. He explained that its Latin name, *glandula pinealis*, referred to its resemblance to the shape of a pinecone. He believed that the pineal regulated the flow of thoughts out of storage in the brain. Many of his ideas dominated medical thinking until the seventeenth century.[13]

During that time, French mathematician and philosopher René Descartes paid special attention to the pineal gland and described it as "the seat of the soul." Most of the parts of the brain exist in duplicate, while the pineal gland is singular. This suggested to Descartes that it is through this place that the soul can influence the body and is where information from the body can enter the soul as perceptions, emotions, and knowledge.[14]

Today, information about the pineal gland is still incomplete. We know that it is a tiny endocrine gland about the size of a pea, situated deep within the center of the brain. Research has shown that the pineal chemically regulates our cycles of sleep and wakefulness. It contains a number of important neurotransmitters, including serotonin, whose secretion prepares the brain to be awake during the hours of daylight. Melatonin, the major pineal hormone, is secreted during darkness and prepares the body to experience sleep during the night hours. In addition, the pineal gland also seems to infuence hormonal changes that usher in sexual maturity during adolescence. It is most active early in life and begins to calcify and diminish in its activity sometime after about twelve years of age.[15]

A five-year research project completed in 1995 by medical doctor and psychiatrist Rick Strassman pointed to some additional ideas about the pineal gland. It contains high levels of the enzymes and building blocks for making dimethyltriptamine, or DMT. This naturally produced human psychedelic is found in trace amounts in the body. Strassman suggests that the pineal gland is most likely the source of this DMT molecule.[16]

According to Strassman, it is particularly stimulated in the extraordinary conditions of birth, sexual ecstasy, childbirth, extreme physical stress, near death, psychosis, and physical death, as well as in deep meditation and mystical states. It may also play a significant role in dream consciousness. In addition to being found in the human body, DMT is also found in many animals and plants around the world..[17] Dr. Strassman's study was the first federally approved psychedelic research in the United States in nearly a generation. Strassman administered the drug DMT to sixty volunteers who found themselves going through both positive and negative explorations into personal emotions and thoughts. They viewed brilliantly colored mystical scenes and experienced various forms of profound spiritual enlightenment and cosmic consciousness. What was also commonly reported were unexpected encounters with strange and sometimes disturbing forms of alien beings that tried to communicate with them.[18]

Strassman's study presents the need for further research. He emphasizes the evolutionary significance of endogenous (naturally existing) human DMT. He concludes that DMT exists in our brains in order to provide consciousness a necessary mechanism: as a spirit molecule allowing us to gain access to nonmaterial realms.[19]

Some earlier research suggests that DMT in the form of the *Amanita muscaria* mushroom has probably been used in sacred rituals for thousands of years to induce altered states of consciousness. The *Amanita muscaria* mushroom contains a high concentration of DMT. The image of this mushroom can be found in religious and spiritual iconography throughout many ancient civilizations.[20]

There appears to be a relationship between the mushroom and the pinecone. The *Amanita muscaria* mushroom is most commonly found growing under evergreen trees, especially pine trees. Being of Greek origin, I was especially drawn to explore some of the threads of ancient Greek mythology and altered states of consciousness.

The Greek god Dionysus (called Bacchus in Roman mythology) was known as the god of wine. He symbolized fertility and wild revelry. He was also known as god of the trees, and the pine tree was particularly sacred to him.[21]

Dionysus is usually depicted carrying a staff called a thyrsus, which is made of a long stalk of fennel, sometimes encircled with ivy vines, and always topped with a pinecone. This staff is thought to represent fertility, but might it also be connected to the dramatic and frenzied altered states of consciousness for which Dionysus is noted for? According to Robert Graves, world-famous translator of the Greek myths, the *Amanita muscaria* was sacred to Dionysus and was his main intoxicant, as well as his followers'—the centaurs, satyrs, and maenads (the wild women). This gave them enormous muscular strength, erotic power, delirious visions, and the gift of prophecy.[22]

The impact of psychedelic mushrooms on human consciousness is a fascinating and controversial area of study that may be researched elsewhere. However, the pinecone and its symbolic connection to the pineal gland and alternate states of consciousness that often result in spiritual and divine experiences is hardly addressed today.

Did the ancients know about the natural psychedelic molecule found in the pineal gland symbolized by the pinecone? In stone reliefs from at least five thousand years ago, Assyrian gods are shown holding pinecones as if offering them to others. And today, pinecones are common in Roman Catholic architecture and sacred decorations. The largest pinecone sculpture in the world is found in the Court of the Pinecone at the Vatican in Rome. And like Dionysus, the pope carries a pinecone on his staff.[23] In general, the pinecone is associated with eternal life and regeneration in the same way as is the evergreen tree, which seems to continue to survive in ways that other trees do not. But are pinecones also symbols of the pineal gland and the gateway to higher divine consciousness? I present these observations not to encourage mushroom gathering and ingesting (dangerous), or pinecone collecting (optional), but to suggest that suppressing individual access to the higher dimensions began a long time ago. And foremost, to emphasize the importance of focusing on and reactivating the pineal gland during meditation.

Encouraging Pineal Activation

1. Make certain that the room where you sleep is absolutely dark, without shadows. The absence of light stimulates melatonin secretion, which helps you sleep, and it may also have an effect on stimulating dreaming.

2. Try to eliminate fluoride from your drinking water, toothpaste, etc.

Continuing research presents mounting evidence that long-term use of fluoride can have a variety of toxic effects on the body. The highest accumulation of fluoride was found to be in the pineal gland. [24]

3. Begin to pay gentle attention to your pineal gland, that place in the center of your forehead, between the eyebrows. Imagine the small royal-blue dot in that area. At different times during the day, touch that spot gently with your finger, and even make a tiny circular motion on it.

4. Frankincense has always been associated with divinity, and used for thousands of years in sacred rituals. Ancient Egyptians burned frankincense. The aroma produces a calming effect.[25] Try this if incense appeals to you. A simpler method is to find a pure essential oil made of frankincense, or even a combination of frankincense and myrrh, and dab just a touch of the oil on your pineal gland before meditating. While the gifts of the Magi for the infant Jesus, including gold, had symbolic meaning, their medicinal qualities may also have been known in those ancient times.

Meditation

Meditation and mindful attention are the clearest ways to access the higher dimensions. Studies have shown the positive psychological and physiological effects of meditation on the body. Among other benefits, it can help reverse heart disease, the number-one killer in the United States. It can reduce pain and enhance the body's immune system, enabling it to better fight disease.[26]

A five-year review of the effects of various meditation techniques on the mind, the brain, the body, and behavior concluded that cultivating this method of awareness is associated with less emotional distress, more positive states of mind, and a better quality of life. In addition, mindfulness practice can influence the brain, the autonomic nervous system, stress hormones, and health behaviors in positive ways.[27]

A study published in *Psychosomatic Medicine* taught a randomized group of ninety cancer patients mindful meditation. After seven weeks, those who had meditated reported that they were significantly less depressed, anxious, angry, and confused than the control group, which hadn't practiced meditation. The meditators also had more energy and fewer heart and gastrointestinal problems than did the other group.[28]

These are only a few examples of what can happen through meditation and mindful attention. We were meant to utilize the full spectrum of our psyches. For so many years, this ability has been minimized due to emphasis on left-brain functioning, the encouraged separation between the left and right hemispheres, and external manipulation of right-brain functioning.

When we are immersed in the higher dimensions, we experience the present moment without the agitation or judgment of the ego. The previous seven steps help us to move easily from one state of awareness to another. With meditation, we bring together our fragmented selves to a state of "knowing and being" instead of "thinking and worrying." This is not an easy task in these mind-manipulated times, but it is attainable and immensely valuable. We are, and always have been, connected to the superconscious. We just need to practice being in it more easily and more frequently.

In my own personal experiences and in my work with clients over the years, I have found that when we practice different forms of meditation and mindful contemplation, something interesting happens. In the beginning, we're aware of the chatter: the ego-laden mutterings of confusion, impatience, distraction, or self-judgment. This can go on for a while as we try to relax and get centered. Then at some point, sooner or later, in the middle of some of the negative and irrelevant stuff that comes up, we may be interrupted by a curious symbol, a good memory, a sudden insight, or a funny image. These are sparse at first and not always understandable. Then, as we become familiar with the meditative process, they may appear more frequently, and like repetitive symbols in dreams, some of them begin to make sense after a while. It feels like the higher self is trying to crash through in the middle of our troubles to remind us that hope and wholeness exist no matter what is going on.

How Do We Get There?

There are many ways we can access the higher dimensions. Different forms of meditation can get us there. Try some of the following exercises, and find one that appeals to you. With practice, you can move into the superconscious more quickly as the mind gets used to traveling there.

Basic One-Point Concentration Meditation

The following exercise is an extension of the primary centering process. In the beginning, you want to spend at least twenty minutes practicing it. The more familiar you become with the exercise, the easier it will be to move into it.

1. Sit in a comfortable position with your back straight and hands open, with palms up or down, resting on your lap. Have your legs uncrossed with feet flat on the floor. Close your eyes and complete the primary centering process. Take at least three deep breaths through your nose and exhale deeply through your mouth. Imagine the small royal-blue dot on your pineal gland between your eyebrows. Surround yourself with the violet bubble. Now place all your awareness on your breath. Focused breathing helps our brain waves move from the ego-alert beta state, toward the slower alpha and theta states of relaxed attention. Then just breathe normally at your own pace. Allow your mind to unwind, and let your body relax with each breath you take.

2. If thoughts, images, or sensations come up, just let them be there without attending to them. Try not to judge or interpret anything that happens. The intention of this basic meditation is to clear and relax the mind. We are so easily distracted much of the time by so many things. After a while, thoughts, images, and emotions will become less intrusive and eventually disappear into the background.

3. Keep going back to your breathing. Become totally engaged with this process. Let it become a calm pleasure to just be with the phenomenon of this breathing process that keeps us alive. Try to sustain that deep attention. If you like, you can count from one to three as you inhale, and count again from one to three as you exhale. You can listen to the sound of your breathing, be aware of how your chest moves, or feel what the air is like as you breathe in and out. Create a gentle balance of internal attention. When you feel ready to complete the meditation, surround yourself with the band of brown-earth color, take a deep breath, exhale, come back slowly, and open your eyes.

The Infinity Symbol

The following exercises improve coordination between the left and right hemispheres of the brain and encourage access into the higher dimensions. You can complete them in less than a minute or take as long as you like. Choose one that appeals to you. Begin each meditation with the primary centering process: close your eyes, take a few cleansing breaths, visualize the royal-blue dot at the pineal, and place yourself in the violet bubble.

The infinity symbol is associated with the superconscious arena. It is represented as the figure eight lying sideways. It loops in and out of itself in a continuous, unbreakable line. You can visualize it in silver.[29]

1. Sit comfortably with your eyes closed. Begin the primary centering process, and then imagine the infinity symbol floating just above the top of your head in the crown chakra area. See it or think about it in silver surrounded by the violet bubble. Feel the calming effect of that floating symbol of higher consciousness. It is always there for you to connect with anytime you want. Imagine it there for as long as you like, and when you're ready to come back, take a deep, cleansing breath, let the visualization go, and surround yourself with a band of the brown-earth color.

2. Stand in a comfortable, relaxed position a few feet away from a blank wall. With your eyes closed, begin the primary centering process. Then open your eyes slightly and imagine that there is a large infinity symbol on the wall in front of you, just above eye level. Trace the figure on the blank wall with your eyes. This means that you move your eyes horizontally, continually looping in and out of the figure. Do this for several seconds or as long as you like. When you're ready to come back, take a deep, cleansing breath, let the visualization go, and surround yourself with the band of brown-earth color. (An alternative method can be to actually draw the infinity symbol on a large sheet of paper and place it on the wall in front of you, just above eye level.)

Humming and Toning

Humming is believed by many to be an archetypal sound. It is experienced first by the fetus as a background sound in the womb, and it is universally associated with comfort and well-being. The m sound is thought to have divine significance in many cultures. In the Eastern traditions, the sounds of *om* act as a link between the objective world of sensory reality and the higher dimensions. In Christianity, the *M* sound is contained in the word "amen," which when used in prayer, is an act of connecting with God.[30] When we hum, the vibrations are both energizing and soothing, and different sustained pitches can be experienced in different parts of the body. Humming for long periods can stimulate the emotional limbic area of the brain to reduce stress and give us a sense of balance.

A powerful form of humming is toning. Toning is the conscious elongation of a sound using the breath and the voice. *Ah, oo, ee, ay, oh,* and *om* are examples of toning sounds. Music scientist, artist, and extraordinary teacher Don Campbell always spoke with reverence about toning and how experiencing it can create a deep sense of being bonded within ourselves. The emotional part of the brain, when stimulated through toning, acts as a gatekeeper between the conscious and unconscious worlds. When we tone for long periods of time we can reach a state of contentment in a safe and fully aware state of mind.[31]

Brief Exercises With Sound

1. Sit in a comfortable position, close your eyes, and begin the primary centering process. Now place all of your awareness on your inner sensations. Listen to the sound and rhythm of your own body, your breathing, your heartbeat, the gurgling of your stomach, sudden twitches, or the subtle vibrations in your fingers or hands. At first, you may hear or feel nothing, but be patient and listen closely. Then after a few minutes, just imagine what kind of sound or rhythm or song your liver is making, or your head, or your feet. Be curious, and become engaged with the internal sounds of your body. If nothing comes, just make it up and guess what rhythms are there. When you're ready to complete the exercise surround yourself with a band of the brown-earth color.

2. Sit in a comfortable position, close your eyes, and do three cleansing breaths. Now *hum*. Make some sounds with your mouth closed. Try free-form humming (as opposed to humming a familiar song) several times. Experiment with different pitches, and notice where you feel the vibrations in your body. Also try humming a song or a musical piece or anything while you're at home doing the dishes, in the car, or walking down the street.

3. Sit or stand in a comfortable position, close your eyes, and do three cleansing breaths. Now, take a deep breath, and on the exhale, with your mouth open, make an audible sigh. Do this several times, and then prolong the sound to create a tone. Continue doing this, and experiment with different pitches. Notice where you feel the different tones in your body.

4. Stand in a comfortable position with your eyes open or closed and take a few cleansing breaths. Create a short, positive phrase like "Let's go for it" or "I'm looking good" or "Troubles rock and roll off my back." Repeat the phrase several times out loud, until a rhythm and then a song develops. Sing it, and if you like, try adding movements as well. Remember this phrase, or create another one, and practice repeating it to yourself silently at different times during the day.

5. A wonderful exercise for left- and right-hemispheric balancing is to choose a book, a magazine, or a play and read out loud for several minutes. Be as dramatic as you like—emphasize words, give a speech, read a poem. With a play, act out all the parts. Do this at least once a week with an audience or alone.

Left- and Right-Hemisphere Balancing

This is an abbreviated version of an exercise that was introduced to me many years ago in a training workshop by brilliant mind/body researchers Dr. Jean Houston and her husband Dr. Robert Masters. Its intention is to integrate different functions of the brain by bringing together words, images, senses, and emotions.

Sit in a comfortable position, close your eyes, complete the primary centering process, and then relax and breathe normally.

With your eyes still closed, move your awareness to your left eye. Keeping both eyes still closed, and your head still, look down with your left eye, then up, to the left, and then to the right. Now, keeping your awareness still on your left eye, allow the eye to circle around clockwise and then counterclockwise two or three times.

Now shift your attention to the right eye and, still keeping your eyes closed, repeat the same process. Look down, up, left, right, and then circle clockwise and counterclockwise.

Then relax your closed eyes, and take a deep, cleansing breath.

Still keeping your eyes closed, direct your attention to the left side of the brain, and now to the right. Shift back and forth easily a few times over the top of your head, going across the corpus callosum, the longitudinal pathway of nerve fibers that connects both hemispheres.

Now, still keeping your eyes closed and relaxed, you are going to imagine activating the senses: sight, touch, sound, smell, and taste, alternating back and forth in each side of the brain. Some senses will be stronger than others, and each person experiences them differently. The idea is to play with this without judgment. Below are some examples of this imagination process. You can then experiment and conjure up your own personal sense memories. Mix up the senses if you like. You can make an audio tape of the exercise and play it back. You can try this with a friend. There is no right and wrong in this process. The idea is to exercise the brain.

Examples
- On the left side of your brain, imagine seeing a birthday cake. On the right side of your brain, imagine seeing a sunset.
- On the left side, imagine touching silk. On the right side, feel the bark of a tree.
- On the left, hear a rooster crowing. On the right, hear somebody sneezing.
- On the left, smell coffee. On the right, smell gasoline.
- On the left, taste a lemon slice. On the right, taste ice cream.

Keeping your eyes closed, take a deep breath, exhale, and relax. Now, with both eyes, circle around your whole brain, from side to side, back to front. Make several small and large circles at different angles and overlapping inside your brain; then make large circles horizontally around the level of your eyes. Let them get smaller and smaller until they become a royal-blue dot in the middle of your forehead, just above your eyebrows, at the pineal gland.

Now inhale deeply, and as you do that, imagine sending the inhalation to your whole brain, expanding it as you do. When you exhale, imagine contracting the whole brain. Do this for a few minutes, and be aware of the whole brain breathing. Thank your brain for supporting you.[32]

Then surround yourself with the band of brown-earth color, and come back slowly.

Let Your Superconscious Do the Work

In the dream chapter, I suggested that if you are looking for an answer to a question, or if there is something you want to work on, you can direct it up to your superconscious and ask for help. You can do this anytime, especially during meditation. Complete the primary centering process and then imagine sending the issue to your crown chakra on top of your head. You can present it as a simple question or an image. State that you want the answer from the highest source. You may not get anything right away, but check back in a day or two during meditation. A response may appear to you in a dream. It may take place in some synchronous event, or you may just have a sudden insight as you're buying groceries.

Higher Dimensions and Societal Mind Conditioning

There are many people today who are teaching how to reach the higher dimensions. Inner attainment of wisdom is in the atmosphere much more so now than it was fifty years ago. In those early days, alternate states were initially associated with hippies and drug euphoria.

Interest in meditation was especially promoted by the Beatles because of their trip to India and their training with the Maharishi Mahesh Yogi.[33] The Beatles embraced meditation and the spiritual path, but ultimately left when they found that the guru was using them to promote himself. They felt that as a spiritual leader, his continued focus on money wasn't acceptable. They also felt he was not truthful about certain things. John Lennon came to believe that the Maharishi's claim to celibacy was a lie.

Years later, John said, "There is no guru. You have to believe in yourself. You've got to get down to your own god in your own temple. It's all down to you, mate."[34]

Choose your teachers carefully, and cross-check your impressions about them with High-Velocity Consciousness. Evaluate the leaders' personality and integrity. What the people are teaching may or may not be valuable, but also pay attention to who they are as human beings. Many spiritual groups fall apart after a while because the discrepancy between the teaching and the actions of the leaders is too wide. Be wary of the hypocrisy and obsession for power that may lurk behind charismatic figures.

Do not be overly impressed with leaders and teachers who claim that their words come directly from this ascended master or that benevolent alien from the planet Puglio. This channeling may be deliberate programming from some group that wants you to believe in what they say because a higher being than you has spoken. Much of the wisdom of channeled information is probably coming from our own higher self. We are so used to experiencing spirituality in a hierarchical way, beyond our ordinary capabilities, that it's easier to credit a higher master than to acknowledge our own divinity.

Earlier we talked about developing awareness about the power and personality of external fields. This is especially necessary when we find ourselves in large groups where meditation, Yoga practice, and chanting take place. These are all chakra-opening experiences and can feel quite wonderful because we're sharing an experience with other people, and that reminds us how we are all interconnected. However, that opening in our spirit and energy can also make us vulnerable to subliminal programming. What can also happen sometimes is that we pick up and take on someone else's depression or anxiety from the group without realizing it.

Surround yourself with the violet protection bubble before you join any large group, and then at the end, before you leave, ground yourself with the brown-earth color. This way you can feel connected and still maintain your spiritual and energetic boundaries of protection.

Remember that societal mind conditioning can intrude into our everyday consciousness, into our meditations, and into our dreams. This is especially true nowadays when we are surrounded by technology and well-trained spiritual "influence technicians." Learn to distinguish between programmed entrancement and self-induced higher-dimension traveling during meditation. Begin to notice the difference between a comfortable half-asleep state in front of the TV or Internet, and a relaxed no-thinking state during meditation.

Be suspicious when respected religious or spiritual figures suddenly appear in the middle of a peaceful meditation and act inappropriately, out of character, or relate to you in a punitive fashion. That may be external programming or an interruption from your lower unconscious.

During meditation, do not stop to analyze every thought or image. You have time to think about it later. When questionable things come up, take a deep breath, exhale, and think to yourself, *I am connecting to the highest spiritual source, always.*

Observations and Declarations

Our personal will, that deep, energetic intention that moves us to do certain things, needs to be activated and maintained so that accessing the higher dimensions becomes a part of our daily routine. Relive moments in your life when the strength of your will sustained you through a particular challenge or a complicated scenario. Think about a time when you persevered in something that eventually paid off. Remember the excitement of crawling and how we used the power of our will against all odds to stand up and walk. We were able to do this because somewhere embedded in our DNA we knew that it was possible. It was a natural human achievement to walk upright. This walking accomplishment freed us to live more fully in the world.

Using the full scope of our psyches, especially the higher dimensions, is also a natural human achievement that frees us. Let the power of your own will lead you to keep the channel of communication clear and open between your conscious self and your higher self.

Declaration: *Each time I access the higher dimensions, I am freeing myself to experience who I am in my essential being.*

NINETEEN

REVIEWING THE SEVEN STEPS

Success is a welcomed gift from the uninhibited mind.

—Adlin Sinclair

Each of the previous chapters presented information for you to think about and questions and exercises to explore. Experiment with what appeals to you, and also feel free to create your own exercises. Become familiar with the seven steps so that it becomes natural for you to include them in your everyday awareness. When you do that, mindspeed integration will take less time. Remember that the seven steps of cross-referencing do not need to be used in succession.

Some issues are more complicated than others and require patient exploration, especially when dealing with lifelong mind patterns that need changing. Let's review the seven steps and begin with a simple situation, then move on to a more complicated one that took a longer time to be processed.

Vera and Lois

Vera met Lois at a gallery opening. They were both artists and became friends. They had a lot to talk about, especially in the creative field, and the conversations were stimulating for Vera. Both were married, though Lois was having difficulties with her husband. They met about once a week for lunch or dinner and talked fairly frequently over the phone. However, Vera began to get busy with work and felt that she was not able to spend as much time with Lois as before. She started to think about how she was feeling about the friendship.

Step 1. Noticing Emotions and Moods

Vera began to feel uncomfortable when Lois talked about her problems at home. They both exchanged personal stories about whatever they were going through, but Vera began to be drawn in and affected by her friend's difficulties.

Step 2. Noticing Personalities

More and more, Vera found herself being in a therapist role with Lois. She tried to help her by listening carefully and sometimes offering advice. This was not an unfamiliar part of her personality. She was like that with some other people as well.

Step 3. Tuning In to Somatic Experiences

One day Vera woke up and her eyes were irritated and sensitive. Sometimes she experienced an allergic reaction to some of the art materials she used, but this hadn't happened in years, and she was not using anything new. She stopped painting for a while and for the next day or two needed to close her eyes and rest them frequently.

Step 4. Observing External Fields

She began to notice that she felt better being alone during the day or just spending some time with her husband at night rather than being with other people. She felt guilty about not meeting with Lois as often as before.

Step 5. Observing Night Dreaming

During this time, Vera's dreams were vague and unclear, and she couldn't remember them very well. One morning she woke up from a dream with her eyes still sensitive and asked herself, *What is irritating me? What do I not want to look at?*

Step 6. Activating Kéfi: Pleasure Experience

Some of the best times that Vera and Lois had were going to galleries and museums together and inspiring each other creatively. However, this was in contrast to most of the interaction that was now going on between them.

Step 7. Accessing the Higher Dimensions

During meditation, Vera realized that she was not looking at what was really going on with Lois. There was less time spent with Lois that was an equal interaction between them. Their time together had become predominantly Lois talking about her problems to Vera. Even when the focus of the conversation was on Vera, Lois would soon bring it back to herself again.

What Was Happening?

For Vera, what had begun as an interesting friendship based on creative exchanges turned into one that placed her in a familiar therapist role that made her feel uncomfortable and "irritable." What Vera didn't want to look at was the idea that Lois was using her as a sounding board and overstepping the boundaries of their friendship. Much of the interaction now was one-sided, with Lois taking center stage and Vera allowing it. Soon, Vera was able to back away from being the therapist and suggested that Lois needed professional help. Lois was hurt initially, but did eventually seek help. They saw each other less frequently, but remained friends in a more compatible way.

Ashley and George

Ashley and George had been living together for almost two years. They had some problems, and they were trying to work them out. Ashley had recently become attracted to a man in her office and had gone out to lunch with him several times. She thought of breaking up with George, but was afraid to talk to him about it. She was stuck in a state of fear, frustration, and immobility. Here's how she used the seven steps to help with her situation.

Step 1. Noticing Emotions and Moods

Ashley realized that the more attracted she was to the man at work, the less satisfied she was with George. Ashley was eight years older than George, and more successful financially. Also, it was her apartment that he had moved into. These and other things made her feel that she was entitled to be in charge of major decision making, but she wasn't happy about it.

Step 2. Noticing Personalities

Ashley's predominant personality with George was as a loving and caring partner. He was a reasonable guy most of the time, though they sometimes got into fights when she turned into the bossy, tyrannical critic—especially when she felt he was not being responsible about doing household chores. Their sex life was very satisfying, and here she felt like a wild teenager. In this arena, she liked to have him lead. It was a relief not to have to be in control.

Step 3. Tuning In to Somatic Experiences

Whenever Ashley thought about talking to George about possibly ending the relationship, her stomach always tightened up. George was very sensitive emotionally, and she couldn't bear to hurt him. She concentrated on the mind pattern underneath the stomach tightness. It was a familiar feeling: wanting to say what she felt, but not wanting to cause pain for the other person. She traced it to the conflict with her father when she was growing up. Her father's chronic illness made it almost impossible to disagree with him about anything, especially when he was unfairly critical of her. He would get visibly upset at her angry words, and she would end up feeling guilty for hurting him. Eventually she gave up saying anything.

Step 4. Observing External Fields

When Ashley and George were with other people socially, everybody liked him. He was funny and often held people's attention with his stories. He was getting less funny and less talkative when they were alone. She began to step back and realize that he was on guard with her most of the time. She felt terrible.

Step 5. Observing Night Dreaming

She found herself fantasizing about living with the man from her office and what it would be like. He was different from George. He was successful and assertive (a little too assertive?). One night she had a romantic dream about him, but in the middle of it, he got up and left abruptly because he had to go somewhere. She tried to chase after him, but he was gone, and she found herself totally lost and alone in a strange city. She tried to find her way back home by looking at some old maps, but the city had changed, and the maps were useless. She had to find new ones, but she was getting more and more frightened, and then she woke up.

Step 6. Activating Kéfi: Pleasure Experience

Ashley's kéfi moments were usually filled with other people. She was either at a party, or a concert, or in some situation that involved groups of people.

Step 7. Accessing the Higher Dimensions

Ashley meditated and asked her higher self about the meaning of the dream, and what she got was a statement: "all alone." Then she saw in her mind's eye a large book with empty pages. This made her sad, but she also felt it was important.

What Was Happening?

There was more information gathering and cross-referencing during the next few weeks. Ashley realized that her reluctance to upset George by telling him how she felt was similar to her reluctance to confront her father about anything because of his sensitivity and his illness. However, with George she was able to talk to him, and even get angry, in a way that she never could with her father. She felt guilty and had to admit that George was not like her father at all. In fact, *she* was more like her father when she got into her controlling critic role.

The romantic dream where the attractive man in her office just disappeared seemed to be telling her that he was not going to be around for long. She had to admit that he wasn't really her type anyway. She was using him as an excuse to get up the courage to leave George. The dream of being lost, and the words and images in her meditation, told her she had to face her fear of living alone, something she had never done.

She was using old maps (outdated mind patterns) to try to find her way home, and the book with empty pages that appeared in her meditation meant that she had to face her aloneness and begin to write a new, as yet unwritten story on the blank pages.

Ashley finally got up the courage to speak to George about separating. He reluctantly agreed and moved out. Instead of getting a roommate right away, Ashley challenged herself to be alone for a while. She wanted to use the time to turn inward and be more honest with herself before getting involved in a new relationship.

Results of Cross-Referencing

When you cross-reference with the seven steps, you are in training to better understand and integrate multidimensional pieces of information. Instead of being satisfied with a narrow band of consciousness, you learn to trust the expanded freedom of your own mind. You learn how to prevent fear and worry from lingering too long. You develop less tolerance for intense emotions that immobilize you or push you in destructive directions. You become more suspicious when you recycle old mind patterns that don't move or change anything. In time, you become less self-critical and more curious, alert, and self-satisfied.

PART IV

THE COLLECTIVE ARENA

TWENTY

COUNTERACTING SOCIETAL MIND CONDITIONING

May the forces of evil become confused on the way to your house.
—George Carlin

Practicing the seven steps helps us coordinate the experience of the outside world with the multidimensional reality of our inner world so that we can deprogram from fear, evaluate truth, and activate our natural creative powers. With this consciousness-raising backup, we will now review the mind-manipulation situations mentioned in the beginning of the book with some added suggestions about how to counteract their influence on us.

Overstimulation

To counteract overstimulation from the outside world, we need to divorce ourselves from it periodically, especially in large cities, where there are more sight and sound interruptions, and embrace silence in whatever way we can. Here are some suggestions.

- Turn off the light, and sit in a pitch-black room. Close your eyes and relax your body. Begin the primary centering process and then place all of your attention on your breathing. Slowly inhale through your nose and exhale through your mouth. Count to yourself on each inhale, beginning with one, until you reach ten breaths, and then start counting over again from one to ten. Continue to do this for several minutes. When you feel like stopping, take a long, deep breath, and on the exhale, let yourself make a full, deep, audible sigh. Surround yourself with a band of the brown-earth color and go on to other things.

- If you're at home, go into the bathroom, leave the door slightly open, turn off the light, and turn on a lukewarm shower (without getting into it). Sit or stand, close your eyes, breathe normally and just listen to the sound of the water for several minutes or as long as you like.

- Take a break from whatever you're doing, close your eyes, and visualize a relaxing scene or reactivate a kéfi memory.

- What is especially liberating is to declare a technological fast for one day (or more). Turn off and ignore computers, cell phones, TV, film, and music.

- Once in a while, deliberately pay attention to the silent spaces between the sounds of your everyday surroundings.

- Try not to watch TV or be on the Internet just before you go to bed.

- When you can, spend twenty minutes or more soaking in the bathtub in warmish hot water filled with a cup of sea salt. This is excellent for relaxing and very effective because it relieves tensions and removes accumulated toxins from the body. Rinse off in a warmish hot shower without soap. If bathtub soaking is not your style, try a footbath in a container filled with about a quarter of a cup of sea salt. Do this as often as you like.

Entrancement

Sometimes we become entranced *because* of overstimulation. As we mentioned earlier, places like theme parks, large movie theaters, and sports events are meant to put you into an excited but ultimately dopey trance state by presenting you with sensory experiences at every corner. Large department stores and malls are specifically designed to get you in and get you lost and entranced so that you wander around and buy more things. Altered states can be seductive, and you may *want* to get lost. But you can also instruct a part of you to check in now and then to snap you out of it if the entrancement goes on for too long. What works very well sometimes, though it may sound silly, is to actually snap your fingers three times in front of your forehead. Or you can tap the middle of your forehead a few times with your fingers. This can momentarily interrupt your state of mind and help you out of a daze.

Practice moving in and out of entrancement deliberately so that you can become aware of your changing consciousness states. Create your own personal entrancement exercise. Find something nontechnological that engages your attention fully. In addition to the exercises that we presented before, experiment with your senses for five or ten minutes. For example, choose a piece of fruit or vegetable or some food that appeals to you, even one that you've never tasted before. Eat it very slowly with the curiosity of an alien being, experiencing the sensations for the first time. Become totally involved with the color, taste, and texture, and become aware of the process of biting, chewing, swallowing, and digesting as this food becomes a part of you. And then snap out of it and do a math problem or read a page from a book out loud.

We can become entranced with admiration for a film or music celebrity, a writer, a sports hero, or a political leader. The person may be promoting sneakers or a political position. The product, the idea, the legislation becomes more interesting because we associate it with them. Some celebrities could probably raise the sale of toothpicks if they wanted to. Separate the person from the product, idea, or opinion. Especially in the political arena, do not accept a person's position because he's intelligent, attractive, charismatic, and seems sincere. Do not reject someone's idea or opinion because he or she belongs to the wrong political party, stutters a bit, and is somewhat overweight. Carefully explore the substance of what the person is saying. People in the mind-manipulation business know very well how to charm us with handsomeness and intelligent-sounding prepared speeches. Dare yourself to hear arguments from the other side with an open mind. People are too interesting and complicated to be right or wrong all the time.

Subliminal Conditioning

The techniques of embedding subliminal images and messages in film, TV, and elsewhere have become very sophisticated. Even Disney films have been accused of including erotic subliminals in some of their films.[1] Be attentive to what you see and hear. Look at magazine advertisements with a keener eye. Sometimes you can catch the hidden form or image in the dark, cloudy background or written upside down on the small jar in the corner. Many people dismiss subliminal advertising as an exaggerated or ineffective process. However, subliminal programming repeated over a period of time can, and does, influence our subconscious.

Say the following to yourself now and then: *My discriminating thinking process is operating all the time. I reject any and all subliminal messages in any form.*

Manipulation of Information and Propaganda

A lie gets halfway around the world before the truth has a chance to get its pants on.[2]

—Winston Churchill

Become familiar with the following techniques. They are used by everyone, not just the "bad guys."

The Straw Man Argument

Be attentive when someone makes a dramatic negative declaration against the other side, no matter who it is. The person summarizes the opposition's position inaccurately, so as to weaken it, and then refutes that inaccurate rendition. It can be an overly simplified, distorted, or misrepresented statement. In a November 2005 speech, President Bush responded to questions about pulling troops out of Iraq by saying, "We've heard some people say, pull them out right now. That's a huge mistake. It'd be terrible mistake. It sends a bad message to our troops, and it sends a bad message to our enemy, and it sends a bad message to the Iraqis."[3]

The statement that unnamed "people" are advocating a troop withdrawal from Iraq "right now" is a straw man argument because it exaggerates the opposing viewpoint. Not even the most stalwart Bush adversaries backed an immediate troop withdrawal. Most proposed that the soldiers be sent home over several months, a more reasonable and persuasive plan that Bush undercut with his straw man argument.[4]

The straw man is used in countless other contexts as well. In his acceptance speech at the 1996 Democratic Convention, Bill Clinton said, "With all respect [to Bob Dole], we do not need to build a bridge to the past. We need to build a bridge to the future." Dole did discuss restoring the values of an earlier America, but Clinton falsely implied that Dole was looking backward (where Clinton was looking forward).[5]

Divine Communication

Claiming a connection to divinity is a standard propaganda technique. Take notice of political leaders, celebrities, religious leaders, or gurus who emphasize their special relationship or communication with God or elevated mystical beings. This can be a deliberate device to convince you of their special ranking so that you will believe them and follow their path.

After the initial public exposure of former senator Mr. John Edwards's indiscretions, ABC correspondent Bob Woodruff suggested that his career was coming to a close.

"I don't think anything has ended," Edwards said firmly. "My lord and my wife have forgiven me. So I am going to move on."[6]

Whether you believe that a person's divine communication is sincere or not, ask yourself, what is his or her intention in making that statement, and how do you react emotionally when you hear it?

The song "With God on Our Side" was written by Bob Dylan in 1963. It addresses the notion that God or some other higher power (or powers) invariably sides with certain humans and opposes those with whom they disagree, and thus they don't question the morality of wars fought and atrocities committed by their country.[7] The message is especially meaningful today.

Euphemisms

The more syllables a euphemism has, the further divorced from reality it is.[8]

—George Carlin

Notice the kinds of words a speaker uses. Be aware of euphemisms. This is when people substitute an agreeable or inoffensive expression for one that may offend or suggest something negative or unpleasant. When heard often enough, we can become dissociated from the real meaning. This happens especially during times of conflict and war.

Examples
- "Enhanced interrogation techniques" = torture, including waterboarding
- "Inoperative" = false
- "Terminate with extreme prejudice" = assassinate
- "Police action" = military action without the formal declaration of war
- "Friendly fire" = a military situation that causes unintentional death or injury to one's own side
- "Collateral damage" = unintentional or incidental military damage where civilians are killed or facilities like hospitals are destroyed [9]

Black-and-White

Notice when someone presents an issue as having only two choices. If you don't like one choice, you must choose the other. The phrase "You're either with us or against us" is commonly used to polarize situations and force an audience to either become allies or to accept the consequences of being deemed an enemy. An example of this was George W. Bush's quote: "Either you are with us or you're with the terrorists."[10]

Bandwagon

This is when you're influenced to hop on the bandwagon. Everyone is doing it, so you should, too. This technique is contrived peer pressure— no one wants to be left out or behind. Most people want to belong. If you're not part of the Green Movement today, you're not part of this in-crowd, and may be made to feel uncomfortable about not joining in. Explore every movement carefully. Some have hidden agendas that you may not agree with. Be active with your beliefs, and be discriminating about the groups you choose to join.

Glittering Generalities

This is using words and images that generally carry a favorable meaning to everyone, including "liberty," "hope," "democracy," and "freedom." It tries to associate a person, idea, or group with a positive feeling, but with little or no direct evidence or explanation. The largest problem with this technique is that all of these words mean different things to different people.[11]

An example of this type of statement was the slogan "Support Our Troops." For many people on the political right, it also meant an acceptance of the United States' military involvement in Iraq. For others it meant "I support our troops, but not the war." Some people on the political left stated that they did not support the troops because they did not condone the continuation of the war. Others added to the slogan— "Support our troops. Bring them home."

Distraction by Scapegoat

Be aware of situations where the weakest opponent (or easiest to discredit) is considered the only important opponent.

For example, if many countries are opposed to our actions, but one of them (say, France) is obviously acting out of self-interest, mention mostly France. Bash the French. Talk about freedom fries instead of French fries. Complain about France's ingratitude from World War II. Forget about the 90 percent of all other countries who feel the same way.[12]

Distraction by Phenomena

A risky but effective strategy is summarized in the movie *Wag the Dog*. The public can be distracted for long periods of time from an important issue by one that occupies more news time. When the strategy works, you have a war or other media event taking attention away from the misbehavior of a crooked leader. When the strategy does not work, the leader's misbehavior remains in the press, and the war is derided as an attempted distraction.[13]

The distraction can also work in the opposite way. Exposure of sexual scandals by politicians or well-known celebrities are especially effective in pushing important issues into the background. They divert attention from the latest war atrocity or controversial legislation.

When some current event monopolizes the media for more than a day or so, it's important to ask, *what else is happening at the same time?* For example, during the time of President Clinton's sex scandal in 1998, one of the world events that was taking place was the bombing of Iraq, called Operation Desert Fox. Some critics of the Clinton administration expressed concern over the timing. The four-day bombing campaign occurred at the same time the US House of Representatives was conducting President Clinton's impeachment hearing. He was impeached on December 19, the last day of the bombing campaign. A few months earlier, similar criticism was leveled during Operation Infinite Reach, wherein missile strikes were ordered against suspected terrorist bases in Sudan and Afghanistan on August 20. The missile strikes began three days after Clinton was called to testify before a grand jury during the Lewinsky scandal and his subsequent nationally televised address later that evening in which Clinton admitted having an inappropriate relationship.[14]

The Operation Infinite Reach attacks became known as "Monica's War" among TV newspeople, due to the timing. ABC-TV announced to all stations that there would be a special report following Lewinsky's testimony before Congress. The special report then was preempted by the report of the missile attacks. The combination of the timing of that attack and Operation Desert Fox led to accusations of a *Wag the Dog* situation.[15]

Misdirecting or Distracting

Some of the most effective propaganda techniques work by misdirecting or distracting the public's attention away from important issues. It's important to read between the lines of the news and see what isn't being reported, or what is reported once, quietly, and then not followed up. One way to test for distraction is to look for items that appear repeatedly in foreign press (from neutral and hostile countries) and that don't appear in your own. But also beware of deliberately placed lies that are repeated with the hope that people will believe them if they are repeated often enough. Repetition as a technique fits into the category of "weapons of mass distraction."[16]

All active propaganda techniques can be tested by asking if they lead the target audience to act in the best interests of the distributor of the propaganda. Remember that propaganda presents one point of view as if it were the best or only way to look at a situation.

Desensitization

A controversial issue presented in the media over a period of time can generate interest and discussion that leads to new understanding and progress. Of course, this doesn't always happen. With continuous and often repetitive media coverage, we may eventually dissociate from it because it's too complicated or disturbing or both. We may also turn away if we feel that the particular issue doesn't affect us that directly. As an example, I offer the following pieces of information about a subject that has been presented in the media in a variety of ways over a long period of time.

The idea of military torture became an open topic after 9/11. It raised important questions as it continued to appear in the news. In November of 2001, in a commentary for the *Los Angeles Times*, longtime civil libertarian Alan Dershowitz discussed a proposal for a "torture warrant." He wrote that he believed the law should sanction torture so it may be applied in certain cases, such as terrorist acts. His surprising position resulted in commentary both pro and con from various sources.[17]

Unrelated to the article, but rushed onto the air a few months later, on January 13, 2002, to beat the premiere of the strikingly similar ABC series *The Chair*, the Fox Network introduced their "extreme" game show *The Chamber*.[18]

On this show, each of the players was strapped into a chair situated in the middle of a "simulated environment" chamber. The object of the game was to win money by answering general-knowledge questions while being subjected to environmental elements, including extreme heat, bitter cold, and winds of a hundred-mile-per-hour. There were also electronically induced muscle contractions due to elements placed on the chair the contestant was strapped into.[19]

Watching someone try to answer questions correctly during escalating physical pain and possible danger was thought to be exciting at the time. However, more reasonable minds prevailed, and this "torture" show was canceled after just three episodes.

The question of military use of torture surfaced most dramatically in April of 2004 when the abuse of the prisoners at Abu Ghraib in Iraq was exposed with shocking photographs that were seen around the world. The Bush administration sought to portray the reprehensible misconduct as the work of a few bad apples. The "bad apples" were apprehended and held responsible.[20]

In the meantime, the popular American TV drama *24* regularly showed terror suspects being tortured so that Jack Bauer, the federal agent hero, could elicit information from them in "ticking time bomb scenarios" and save the day. Some people in the US military stated that the show was sending inappropriate messages to the troops, condoning torture.[21]

US intelligence officials have said that torture is extremely ineffective. Lt. Gen. John Kimmons, the army deputy chief of staff for intelligence stated, "I am absolutely convinced...no good intelligence is going to come from abusive practices. I think history tells us that."[22]

One of these methods of torture, called waterboarding, became prominent in the news after 2006. The public was introduced to this "enhanced interrogation technique" that re-creates the experience of drowning. In March 2008, President Bush vetoed legislation passed by Congress that would have prohibited the CIA from using waterboarding and other controversial interrogation tactics.[23]

In the summer of 2008, a new sideshow was added to the attractions in Coney Island, the famous Brooklyn beach resort. For one dollar, you looked through a barred window and viewed a scene of robotic waterboarding using animatronic figures. On an outside wall, a cartoon painting of SpongeBob SquarePants (a popular American cartoon character) was depicted saying, "It don't Gitmo better than this."[24] "Gitmo" is the nickname for the naval prison facility at Guantánamo Bay in Cuba. The intention was to show people the reality of waterboarding. Humor attracts people to a subject that they might ordinarily ignore or not understand fully. Humor is used as propaganda to make a definitive statement, disagree with a position, or humiliate an opponent. Used over a period of time, it can also result in trivializing a subject such as torture.

In October of 2008, a reality television show in England called *Unbreakable* was accused of crossing the line between entertainment and sadism. In it, the contestants undergo various forms of torture, including being buried alive, wading through piranha-infested water, and waterboarding. One of the volunteers was so traumatized that he had convulsions. Another ran into the African bush and had to be found with tracker dogs.[25]

Some reality shows still put people in humiliating, devastating, sometimes life-threatening situations and reward them with money when they face those challenges and succeed. Overcoming obstacles is heroic, but presenting torture as entertainment is disturbing.

The topic of torture went underground for a while as other events predominated, especially the global economic crisis and the American presidential election.

Hopefully, sometime in the near future, the torture issue will remain in people's consciousness long enough to be examined properly. However, unless the subject affects us in some personal way, public information about it can still have the affect of desensitizing our reactions. This is especially true when the legal and the moral issues connected to a subject like torture are difficult to face. Cognitive dissonance comes into play. For some people, this means being confronted with two opposing beliefs: condemning the process of torture by our enemies (they do it because they are monsters), and condoning it when we use it (we do it reluctantly to save lives). And a few others may also claim that the ends justify the means because "God is on our side." Discomfort about the subject, plus overexposure without follow-through, moves us away from serious public discourse about a serious matter.

When a certain topic is in the news over a period of time, do not assume that it is being reasonably examined. Desensitizing the public may be the intention of some of the parties involved. Look for distraction by scapegoating. This happened when the "few bad apples" from Abu Ghraib were punished even though later reports revealed that CIA operatives were, in fact, implementing torture under the authorizations of persons in the Bush administration. Notice when black-and-white distractions are presented—it's not a Republican or Democratic difference of opinion, even though sometimes it seems to be. Military torture has been going on for a very long time. It goes beyond party lines. Also the black-and-white argument of whether torture is successful or not in saving lives detracts from the deeper moral and ethical concerns. Remember to examine ideas and opinions from other sources around the world.

If the issue of military torture seems remote to us, we need to ask how this might ultimately affect us on a personal basis. For example, the United Nations Committee against Torture has declared that Taser use can constitute a form of torture. Amnesty International USA calls for clearer restrictions when using Tasers. More than 330 people are reported to have died since 2001 after being struck by police Tasers in the United States. Amnesty International is concerned that Tasers and similar devices are potentially lethal, especially when used on vulnerable people, such as those with heart disease or those under the influence of stimulant drugs. However, apparently healthy people with no drugs in their system have also died after being shocked.[26]

A growing number of people are describing Tasers as instruments of torture. They feel that evidence of widespread police abuse of Tasers is more than enough to warrant concern and justify a congressional inquiry. There are petitions being formulated to ask for Congressional hearings as to whether US police, policing policies, and actions violate federal and international laws prohibiting human rights violators.[27]

Let's not become desensitized to the torture issue. The role it plays in our military at the top level will ultimately influence police enforcement and what persuasive tactics and dangerous methods are allowed to be used on suspicious, but often innocent private citizens.

Protect and Promote Mind Freedom and Creative Power

Whether the subject is torture and Tasers, the latest blockbuster movie, breakthrough anxiety medication, or fracking in your neighborhood, you will ultimately be affected by some of these things.

What I have presented here about societal mind conditioning is really only the tip of the iceberg, the upper layer of a darker continuing story that we have the power to rewrite. We can be curious, truth-seeking, passionate detectives, gathering facts and ideas from the outside world and evaluating them through the lens of our internal multileveled consciousness.

Choose something that concerns you and counteract societal mind conditioning in any way you can. Keep your X-ray eyes wide open. Relish and protect your mind freedom. Activate your creative powers so that you can manifest your highest dreams into actual reality. It's also important to forget everything periodically and go to a really funny movie.

Say the following to yourself often, and when you're alone, say it out loud: *I am intelligent, resilient, courageous, compassionate, and optimistic. I can handle whatever is going on. I feel calm, focused, strong, loving, and powerful as I step into the future every day.*

TWENTY-ONE

GLOBAL HIGH-VELOCITY CONSCIOUSNESS

You must be the change you wish to see in the world.

—Mahatma Gandhi

I recorded the following dream in my journal on August 3, 2001:

> I am looking at a bold newspaper headline that states that Mayor Rudy Giuliani is probably dead. The story has to do with some catastrophic event that has taken place. But I don't see anything. I go outside into the street, and I see a huge truck moving slowly and silently. It is piled high (it seems like twenty stories high) with what looks like compressed garbage made of metal, paper, and other things all covered with a light dust. There are many trucks like that, one following the other. I feel the presence of something ominous and terrible. This is the crisis. What does it mean?

Several weeks later, in mid-September, as I watched the endless trucks in lower Manhattan transport the debris from the wreckage at the World Trade Center, I realized that my dream had shown me the aftermath of this terrible event many weeks before it had actually happened. Mayor Giuliani, who had been in a building nearby, had narrowly escaped harm.

But I was not alone in my premonition. Two of my clients and several friends revealed to me that they had had dreams of the Twin Towers exploding several weeks before the tragedy. A former client called to remind me that she had had a nightmare of both towers collapsing that she had revealed to me in a session twenty years before.

What did all of this mean? Did the previous disaster at the World Trade Center in 1993 place the fearful vision of further bombings or explosions in people's minds? Why were these precognitive dreams presenting themselves to a few people and not to others? Did the secret plan about this terrible act somehow leak out into the collective atmosphere of the city? Were some of us psychically tuning in to the information?

I wondered what it would be like if we lived in a world where dream exploration and psychic development were part of the elementary school curriculum. I imagined a situation where hundreds of people with similar precognitive dreams about the Twin Towers reported them to authorities and were taken seriously enough to prevent this disaster.

One evening in late spring, my dear friend Beatriz and I walked to the small wooded swamp area near her house. We were going to meditate and pray for her young cousin in Venezuela who was in the hospital. He had been diagnosed with a brain tumor, and he had been in a coma for over a week.

It was a dark night, and we walked carefully so we wouldn't disturb the frogs in the distant swamp who were busy with their mating calls. But as we stepped on the grass, breaking twigs and moving closer, the frogs suddenly stopped singing. Beatriz and I sat on a log and began to meditate. Then, quietly at first, the frogs began to sing again. Soon, Beatriz and I were both slowly breathing in rhythm with them. Then it felt as if the sound was all around us, blending into a soft symphony of rising and falling waves. We moved together in heart-opening sound, Beatriz and me—and the frogs.

After about a half hour or so, we walked slowly back to the house. We hoped that her cousin had heard our healing chorus. The echo of the music stayed with us and moved into our dreams.

The next day Beatriz received a phone call from Venezuela. Her cousin had come out of the coma that very night, and the tumor seemed to have mysteriously disappeared. Rehabilitation moved swiftly, and within a week, he'd recovered enough to leave the hospital.

That happened many years ago, and was one of the most thrilling experiences I've ever had. Today, different forms of meditative healing practices are being included in the training procedures for nurses in some hospitals around the country.

It's a crazy world we live in. Things are not going smoothly. We are breaking down in order to break through into another form of reality and existence.

With High-Velocity Consciousness, we revitalize our courage, clarify our thinking, trust our intuition, and use our free will to determine the truth about ourselves and the world. We can communicate across time and space, talk directly to the cells of our bodies, download information from the collective unconscious, or manifest a passionate goal.

During all this, we must remember that love, the opposite of fear, is the eternal energy force of a divine matrix that interacts with every human soul, every possible species, light and dark forces, every piece of creation, visible or invisible, that exists in the many worlds within us and around us. When we feel this universal energy force, anything and everything is possible. We can look forward to a wide-awake world filled with masses of people who refuse to be talked into fear and victimization. We can resist the seduction of technologies that promise extraordinary powers while slowly enslaving and robotizing humanity.

Millions of superminds working together multidimensionally are more powerful than any small controlling group that has ruled for such a long time in our human history. We are all being challenged to claim our divine right to live a more dynamic, compassionate, rich, and deep reality. We can do it.

> *Ring the bells that still can ring.*
> *Forget your perfect offering.*
> *There is a crack in everything.*
> *That's how the light gets in.*[1]
>
> —Leonard Cohen

NOTES

Chapter One: Technology, Speed, and Quick Fixes

1. "The Amazing Pictures of a Robot Conducting a Symphony Orchestra," MailOnline, May 14, 2008, http://www.dailymail.co.uk/news/article-566342/The-amazing-pictures-robot-conducting-symphony-orchestra.html.

2. "'Pupils' Will Soon be able to Download Lessons Directly Into their Brains," MailOnline, May 30, 2008, http://www.dailymail.co.uk/sciencetech/article-1023153/Pupils-soon-able-download-lessons-directly-brains.html.

3. "Scientists Extract Images Directly from Brain," Pink Tentacle, December 12, 2008, http://pinktentacle.com/2008/12/scientists-extract-images-directly-from-brain/.

4. Todd Gitlin, *Media Unlimited: How the Torrent of Images and Sounds Overwhelms Our Lives* (New York: Henry Holt and Company, 2002), 75.

5. Ibid., 105.

6. Robin Marantz Henig, "The Quest to Forget," *New York Times*, April 4, 2004.

7. Ibid.

8. Erik Baard, "The Guilt-Free Soldier," *The Village Voice*, January 22–28, 2003.

9. Scott LaFee, "Blanks For the Memories: Someday You May be Able to Take a Pill to Forget Painful Recollections," *San Diego Union-Tribune*, February 11, 2004.

10. Ibid.

11. Terrence Rafferty, "The Last Word in Alienation: Just Don't Remember,"

New York Times, November 2, 2003.

12. Ibid.

Chapter Two: Mind Manipulation

1. Matt Richtel, "The Lure of Data. Is it Addictive?," *New York Times*, July 6, 2003.

2. Ibid.

3. Clive Thompson, "Rush Hour on the Information Superhighway," *Time Out*, April 8-15, 2004, 13-14.

4. David W. Orme-Johnson, "Preventing Crime Through the Maharishi Effect," Institute of Science,Technology and Public Policy, http://www.istpp.org/rehabilitation/12.html.

5. Jeffrey K. Zeig, ed., *A Teaching Seminar with Milton H. Erickson* (New York: Brunner/Mazel Inc.,1980).

6. Use of NLP technology by the CIA, "How CIA and Secret Agents Make Use of NLP?," March, 23, 2009, http://www.cianlp.com/How-CIA-and-secret-agents-make-use-of-NLP?/B14.htm.

7. Elizabeth Bumiller, "The Ventriloquist Jokes Don't Bug the White House," *New York Times*, May 2, 2004.

8. Marilyn Elias, "Frequent TV Watching Shortens Kids' Attention Spans," April 5, 2004, http://www.usatoday.com/news/health/2004-04-05-tv-kids-attention-usat_x.htm.

9. Robert Kubey and Mihaly Csikszentmihalyi, "Television Addiction is No Mere Metaphor,"*Scientific American*, January 27, 2004.

10. Wilson Bryan Key, *Subliminal Ad-Ventures in Erotic Art* (Boston: Branden Publishing Company Inc.,1992), 7.

11. Research on subliminal perception and its effects, "Subliminal

Stimuli," *Wikpedia*, July 8, 2012, http://en.wikipedia.org/wiki/Subliminal_stimuli.

12. Key, *Subliminal Ad-Ventures in Erotic Art*, 32.

13. Wilson Bryan Key, *The Age of Manipulation* (Lanham, Maryland: Madison Books,1993), 51.

14. Key, *Subliminal Ad-Ventures in Erotic Art*, 19.

15. Key, *The Age of Manipulation*, 70–71.

16. Key, *Subliminal Ad-Ventures in Erotic Art*, 96.

17. Ibid., 95.

18. Ibid., 156–165.

19. John Egan, "RATS Ad: Subliminal Conspiracy?," BBC News Online, September 13, 2000, http://news.bbc.co.uk/1/hi/ in_depth/americas/2000/us_elections/election_news/923335.stm.

20. McCain/Fox Network Subliminal, http://www.youtube.com/watch?v=9ntSWP25KD8.

21. Margaret Ellis, "I Hate You: Vancouver Family Finds Surprising Message in Baby's Toy," *The Columbian*, January 11, 2003.

22. Key, *Subliminal Ad-Ventures in Erotic Art*, 33–35.

23. Adam Curtis, dr. of BBC TV documentary series about the early psychological techniques in advertising ,"The Century of the Self,",2002, http://topdocumentaryfilms.com/the-century-of-the-self/.

24. President Bush's opening statement on Iraq conflict, April 13, 2004, http://www.msnbc.msn.com/id/4734018/.

25. Thom Hartmann, Cheney Speaks to the Reptile Brain," Common Dreams, August 17, 2004, http://www.commondreams.org/views04/0817-13.htm.

26. Ibid.

27. Ibid.

28. Ibid.

29. Steven Johnson, *Everything Bad is Good for You* (New York: Riverhead Books, 2005), 32-62.

30. Alison Motluk, "Do Games Prime Brain for Violence?," *New Scientist Magazine*, June 23, 2005,10.

Chapter Three: Mind Intrusion

1. "Vision Scientists Demonstrate Innovative Learning Method," research presented by National Science Foundation, December 8, 2011, http://www.nsf.gov/news/news_summ.jsp?cntn_id=122523.

2. Ibid.

3. Definition and history of transhumanism, *Wikpedia*, http:en.wikipedia.org/wiki/Transhumanism.

4. David Gelles, "Mortality 2.0: A Silicon Valley Insider Looks at California's Transhumanist Movement," *The Futurist*, January 1, 2009, http://www.geneticsandsociety.org/article.php?id=4790.

5. Ibid.

6. Ibid.

7. Ibid.

8. Description and history of radio frequency identification tag (RFID) and microchipping, *Wikpedia*, http://en.wikipedia.org/wiki/RFID.

9. Ibid.

10. "Send Benneton a Message: Don't Buy Clothing with Tracking Devices!," April 9, 2003, http://www.boycottbenetton.com/PR_030407.html.

11. Katherine Albrecht, "Macy's Using RFID Chips in Shoes and Clothing," (blog) letter to Macy's Inc. on AscensionSerenity. blogspot. com, and Jim Sluzewski's (blog) letter response from Macy's Inc., July 21, 2012, http://fengshuiserenity.blogspot.com/2012/07/macys-using-rfid-chips-in-shoes-and_21.html.

12. Katherine Albrecht and CASPIAN, http://www.spychips.com/katherine-albrecht.html.

13. Katherine Albrecht and Liz McIntyre, *Spychips: How Major Corporations and Government Plan to Track Your Every Move With RFID* (Nashville,Tennessee: Thomas Nelson, Inc., 2005).

14. Orr Shtuhl, "California Could Become Third State to Ban Forced Microchip Tag Implants (RFID)."January 12, 2008, http://www.globalresearch.ca/index.php?context=va&aid=7781.

15. Bob Unrah, "Rebellion Erupts Over School's Student-Chipping Plan," September 3, 2012, WND Education.com, http://www.wnd.com/2012/08/rebellion-erupts-over-schools-student-chipping-plan/.

16. Security concerns of RFIDs with regard to privacy and infiltration, *Wikpedia*, http://en.wikipedia.org/wiki/RFID.

17. Danger of implantable tracking chips in humans, "Microchip Maker 'Hid Ties to Cancer,' September 9, 2007, WND.com, http://www.wnd.com/news/article.asp?ARTICLE_ID=57557.

18. Katherine Albrecht, "Microchip-Induced Tumors in Laboratory Rodents and Dogs: A Review of the Literature 1990–2006," November19, 2007, http://www.antichips.com/cancer.

19. Ibid.

20. Rauni-Leena-Luukanen Kilde, "Microchip Implants, Mind Control and Cybernetics," ce399 Research Archive, Dec 2, 2007. Original article

in Finnish-Language Journal SPECULA (3rd Quarter,1999). http://ce399.typepad.com/weblog/2007/12/microchip-impla.html.

21. Ibid.

22. Ibid.

23. Ibid.

24. Orr Shtuhl, "California Could Become Third State to Ban Forced Microchip Tag Implants (RFID)." January 12, 2008, http://www.globalresearch.ca/index.php?context=va&aid=7781.

25. As of 2010 Georgia and Virginia have banned forced microchip implants,*Wikpedia*,http://en.wikipedia.org/wiki/Microchip_implant_%28human%29#cite_note-28.

Chapter Four: Degrees of Mind Dissociation

1. www.spuddie.net/carlin.htm.

2. Sandra Aamodt and Sam Wang, *Welcome to Your Brain* (New York: Bloomsbury, 2008), 6–7.

3. Corbett H. Thigpen and Hervey M. Cleckley, *The Three Faces of Eve* (New York: McGraw-Hill Book Co.,1957).

4. Flora Rheta Schreiber, *Sybil* (New York: Warner Books, Inc., 1973).

5. Ellen P. Lacter, "Mind Control: Simple to Complex," on Tripod, November 14,2004, http://truthbeknown2000.tripod.com/Truthbeknown2000/id17.html.

6. *A Clockwork Orange*, dir. Stanley Kubrick, Warner Brothers, 1971.

7. Dominic Streatfeild, *BrainWash* (New York: St. Martin's Press, 2007), 135–170.

8. Jim Keith, *Mind Control, World Control* (Kempton, Illinois: Adventures Unlimited Press,1997), 151–154.

9. "The Tuskegee Syphilis Experiment," http://www.infoplease.com/ipa/A0762136.html.

10. Secret government experiments on humans to study forms of mind control and behavior modification, "Project MKUltra," *Wikpedia*, http://en.wikipedia.org/wiki/Project_MKULTRA.

11. Recruiting Nazi scientists to help with experiments of mind manipulation in the US, Ibid.

12. Covert, illegal, human research mind control experiments run by the Central Intelligence Agency, Ibid.

13. Senator Ted Kennedy's statement on the senate floor about an "extensive testing and experimentation" program which included covert drug tests on unwitting citizens, Ibid.

14. CIA mind control research into sexual blackmail, surveillance technology, and the possible use of mind-altering drugs in field operations, *Wikpedia*, http://en.wikipedia.org/wiki/Operation_Midnight_Climax.

15. Extensive research into sexual blackmail, surveillance technology, and the possible use of mind-altering drugs in field operations, Wikpedia, http://en.wikipedia.org/wiki/Project_MKULTRA.

16. Research experiments manipulating human behavior through the use of various mind-altering drugs, Ibid.

Chapter Five: Fear

1. Martha Stout, *The Paranoia Switch* (New York: Sarah Crichton Books, 2007), 52–53.

2. "Fear of Public Speaking Statistics," Speech Topics Help, Advice and Ideas,http://www.speech-topics-help.com/fear-of-public-speaking-statistics.html.

3. John M. Hettema, "A Twin Study of the Genetics of Fear Conditioning,"

Archives of General Psychiatry 60, no. 7 (July 2003), 702–708.

Chapter Six: Free Will, Movement, and Change

1. http://en.wikiquote.org/wiki/Heraclitus.

Chapter Seven: Dimensions of Consciousness

1. Roberto Assagioli, *Psychosynthesis* (New York: Penguin Books, 1976), 17–19.

2. Ibid.

3. Ibid.

4. Ibid.

5. Ibid.

6. Jean Hardy, *A Psychology With a Soul* (New York: Routledge & Kegan Paul Inc.,1987), 25–26.

7. Ibid., 21–33.

Chapter Eight: High-Velocity Consciousness

1. Malcolm Gladwell, *Blink* (New York: Little, Brown and Company, 2005), 21–23.

2. James Vargiu, "Creativity," *Synthesis* 3–4 (1974): 17–25.

3. Kekule's snake dream and the structure of benzine, "Physics: Discovery and Intuition," *Connections Through Time Magazine*, Issue 19: April –June 2003, http://www.p-i-a.com/Magazine/Issue19/Physics_19. htm.

4. Stuart Wolpert, "Is Technology Producing a Decline in Critical

Thinking and Analysis?," UCLA newsroom, January 26, 2009, http://newsroom.ucla.edu/portal/ucla/is-technology-producing-a-decline-79127.aspx.

5. Hiranmay Karlekar, "Tsunami: The Robots Next Time?," *The Pioneer*, January 7, 2005.

6. Daniel J. Siegel, *The Mindful Brain* (New York: W. W. Norton & Company, 2007), 113–115.

7. Joe Dispenza, DC, *Evolve Your Brain* (Deerfield Beach, Florida: Health Communications, Inc., 2007), 103–143.

8. Michael W. Clark, "Jung and Synchronicity," 2007, http://www.bibliotecapleyades.net/ciencia/ciencia_synchronicity02.htm.

9. John Shirley, " The Matrix:Know Thyself," in *Exploring the Matrix*, ed. Karen Haber (New York: St. Martin's Press, 2003), 62.

Chapter Nine: The Primary Centering Process

1. Richard Gerber,*Vibrational Medicine* (Santa Fe, New Mexico: Bear & Company, 1988), 128–135.

2. Stewart Swerdlow, *The Healer's Handbook: A Journey Into Hyperspace* (Westbury, New York: Skybooks,1999), 25–27.

3. Ibid.

Chapter Eleven: Stimulating Imagination: Mind Orchestration Tools

1. The Lozanov Method introduced by Sheila Ostrander and Lynn Schroeder with Nancy Ostrander in *Super-Learning* (New York: Delacorte Press and the Confucian Press, Inc.,1979), 15-37.

Chapter Twelve: Noticing Emotions and Moods

1. Kathleen Taylor, *Brainwashing: The Science of Thought Control* (New York: Oxford University Press, 2004), 213–214.

2. Ibid.

3. Jerome Pelofsky, "McCain, Obama Fight Over Soldiers' Bracelets," September 27, 2008, Reuters, Edition US, http://blogs.reut.com/frontrow/2008/09/26/mccain-obama-fight-over-soldiers-bracelets/.

4. Leon Festinger and cognitive dissonance, *Wikpedia*, http://en.wikipedia.org/wiki/Leon Festinger.

5. Overview of a case of cognitive dissonance written by Leon Festinger, Henry Riecker and Stanley Schachter in the book *When Prophesy Fails* (New York: Harper-Torchbooks,1956) http://www.answers.com/topic/when-prophecy-fails.

6. Taylor, 129.

7. History and controversy related to the Patriot Act, *Wikpedia*, http://en.wikipedia.org/wiki/Patriot_Act.

8. David Icke,*The David Icke Guide to the Global Conspiracy (and How to End It)* (Ryde, Isle of Wight, United Kingdom: David Icke Books Ltd., 2007), 255–263.

9. George Orwell, *1984* (New York: Signet Classics,1977).

10. Ibid.

11. "Libertarian Party UK '1984' campaign," November 6, 2008, http://www.911truth.org/article.php?story=20081106141654749.

Chapter Thirteen: Noticing Personalities

1. Kathleen P. Lacey, "Introduction to Psychosynthesis and its Application in Psychotherapy," on VISTAS 2006 Online, http://counselingoutfitters. com/Lacey.htm.

2. https://www.goodreads.com/author/quotes/229.Abraham_Lincoln.

Chapter Fourteen: Tuning In To Somatic Experiences

1. Peter A. Levine with Ann Frederick, *Walking the Tiger: Healing Trauma* (Berkley, California: North Atlantic Books, 1997), 15–21.

2. Ibid., 19.

3. Geraldine Lux Flanagan, *The First Nine Months Of Life* (New York: Simon and Schuster, 1962), 55.

4. Ibid., 69.

5. Stanislav Grof, *Realms of the Human Unconscious* (New York: E.P. Dutton & Co., Inc.,1976), 105.

6. Emilie Conrad, "Welcome to Continuum," http://www continuummovement. com/.

7. Richard Gerber, *Vibrational Medicine* (Santa Fe, New Mexico: Bear & Company, 1988), 128–135.

8. "Heart Rhythm and Heart Rate Variability (HRV)," Angelfire.com, http://www.angelfire.com/journal/ldps/HeartRhythmsandHRV.htm.

9. Paul Pearsall, *The Heart's Code* (New York: Broadway Books,1997), 169–170.

10. Ibid., 7.

11. Ibid., 89.

12. Alex Wellington,"To Ban or not to Ban: Direct-to-Consumer Advertising and Human Rights Analysis," ReadPeriodicals.com, October 14, 2010, http://www.readperiodicals.com/201010/2252086561.html.

13. Ibid.

14. Ibid.

15. Guylaine Lanctot, *The Medical Mafia: How to Get Out Of It Alive and Get Back Our Health and Wealth* (Bridge of Love Publications,1995).

16. Peter R. Breggin, *Medication Madness: A Psychiatrist Exposes the Dangers of Mood-Altering Medications* (New York: St. Martin's Press, 2008).

17. Ibid.

18. FDA ruling on side effects of Chantix in article by Gordon Gibb, "Pfizer Finds a Loophole in Advertising Chantix," Lawyers and Settlements.com, October 20, 2008, http://www.lawyersandsettlements.com/features/chantix-suicide-side-effects-3.html.

19. Merck withdraws Vioxx from market due to dangerous side effects, "Rofecoxib," *Wikpedia*, August 27, 2012, http://en.wikipedia.org/wiki/Rofecoxib.

20. "Heath Ledger Died of Accidental Overdose," NBC News.com, February 6, 2008, http://www.msnbc.msn.com/id/23029566/.

21. Shelly Narula, "The Dangers of Prescription Drugs," SteadyHealth.com, January 16, 2009, http://www.steadyhealth.com/articles/The_Dangers_Of_Prescription_Drugs_a807_f0.html.

22. *Testimony about Trends in Unintentional Poisoning Deaths Given before the Subcommittee on Oversight and Investigations*, United States House of Representatives (October 24, 2007) (statement of Leonard J. Paulozzi, medical epidemiologist), http://www.hhs.gov/asl/testify/2007/10/

t20071024a.html.

23. "U.S. Death Every 19 Minutes from Overdose," UPI.com, January 13, 2012, http://www.upi.com/Health_News /2012/01/13/US-death-every-19-minutes-from-overdose/UPI-28581326514265/.

24. "Boosting the Immune System by Tapping your Thymus Gland," http://www.shinyhealth.com/boosting-the-immune-system-by-tapping-your-thymus-gland/.

25. Gwenn Bonnell, "Feel Alive! Thrive with the Cross Crawl," SelfGrowth. com, http://www.selfgrowth.com/articles/Feel_Alive_Thrive_With_The_Cross_Crawl. html.

26. Ibid.

Chapter Fifteen: Observing External Fields

1. Rupert Sheldrake, *The Presence of the Past* (Rochester, Vermont: Park Street Press,1988), 112–116.

2. Rupert Sheldrake, "Seven Experiments That Could Change the World" (lecture and workshop at New York Open Center, New York, Oct. 6–7,1995).

3. Rupert Sheldrake, *Seven Experiments That Could Change the World* (New York: Riverhead Books,1995.).

4. "Tarrytown Ceremony Awards $16,511 to Winners of Sheldrake Competition," *Brain/Mind Bulletin* 2, no. 12 (June 7,1986), 2.

5. James H. Fowler and Nicholas A. Christakis, research paper, Dynamic pread of Happiness in Large Social Network: Longitudinal Analysis Over 20 years in the Framingham Heart Study, BMJ, December 4, 2008, http://www.bmj.com/cgi/content/full/337/dec04_2/a2338.

6. Ibid.

7. Ibid.

8. Ibid.

9. Information about Facebook, *Wikpedia*, http://en.wikipedia.org/wiki/Facebook.

10. Gary Price, "New Statistics: Older Adults and Internet Use, 53% of US Seniors now Using Net or Email," InfoDocket, June 6, 2012, http://www.infodocket.com /2012/06/06/new-statistics-older-adults-and-internet-use-53-of-u-s-seniors-now-online/.

11. Clive Thompson, "I'm So Totally, Digitally Close To You," *New York Times Magazine*, September 7, 2008, 44.

12. Ibid., 44–45.

13. Ibid., 46.

14. Ibid., 4.

15. "Opposition to the U.S. Involvement in the Vietnam War," *Wikpedia*, September 12, 2012, http://en.wikipedia.org/wiki/Opposition_to_the_Vietnam_War.

16. Edward Bernays and the American Tobacco Company Campaign, *Wikpedia*, http://en.wikipedia.org/wiki/Edward_Bernays.

Chapter Sixteen: Observing Night Dreaming

1. http://www.brainyquote.com/quotes/authors/a/anais_nin.html.

2. Arnold and Amy Mindell, *Riding the Horse Backwards* (New York, New York: Penguin Books, 1992), 48–49.

3. Arnold Mindell, *Working With the Dreaming Body* (Boston, Massachusetts: Routledge & Kegan Paul,1985), 2–9.

4. Ibid., 67.

5. Ernest Hartmann, *The Nightmare* (New York: Basic Books Inc., 1985), 25–48.

6. Ibid., 231–232.

7. Ibid., 173–175.

8. Montague Ullman and Stanley Krippner with Alan Vaughan, *Dream Telepathy* (Baltimore, Maryland: Penguin Books Inc., 1973), 28.

9. Jon Tolaas *Dreamtime & Dreamwork*, Ed. Stanley Krippner (New York: G.P. Putnam's Sons, 1990), 267.

10. Ullman, Krippner, and Vaughn, *Dream Telepathy*, 28.

11. Fred Alan Wolf, *The Dreaming Universe* (New York: Simon & Schuster, 1994), 176.

12. Stephen LaBerge, *Lucid Dreaming* (Los Angeles, California: Jeremy P. Tarcher, Inc., 1985), 19–21.

13. Stephen LaBerge and Howard Rheingold, *Exploring the World of Lucid Dreaming* (New York: Ballantine Publishing Group,1990).

14. Richard Alleyne, "Black and White TV Generation has Monochrome Dreams," article in *The Telegraph*, October 17, 2008, http://www.telegraph.co.uk/science/science-news/3353504/Black-and-white-TV-generation-have-monochrome-dreams.html.

15. "Subliminal McDonald's ad on Food Network," January 21, 2007, www.youtube.com/watch?v=amnZX-jjBD8.

16. Most common emotion in dreams is anxiety, Kendra Cherry, "10 Facts About Dreams." About.com Psychology, http://psychology.about.com/od/statesofconsciousness/tp/facts-about-dreams.htm.

Chapter Seventeen: Activating Kéfi: Pleasure Experience

1. Nikos Kazanztakis, *Zorba the Greek*, Trans. Carl Wilman (New York: Simon & Schuster, 1952), 71.

2. http://answers.yahoo.com/question index?qid=20100616210342AA2SlW5.

3. O. Fred Donaldson, PhD, *Playing By Heart* (Deerfield Beach, Florida: Health Communications, Inc., 1993), 131.

4. http://www.goodreads.com/author/quotes/79896.Milton_Berle.

5. Marshall Brain, "How Laughter Works," article on How Stuff Works, http://science.howstuffworks.com/environmental/life/human-biology/laughter7.htm.

6. Ibid.

7. Ibid.

8. Example of humor with a statement beginning in one direction and switching unexpectedly to another, http://www.thequotefactory.com/quote-by/jack-handey/if-god-dwells-inside-us-like/73295/.

9. Rhoda Kellogg with Scott O'Dell, *The Psychology of Children's Art* (New York: CRM Inc., Random House Publication,1967), 9–21.

10. Peter Tompkins and Christopher Bird, *The Secret Life of Plants* (New York: Avon Books, 1973), 171.

11. http://www.goodreads.com/author/quotes/4750._mile_Zola.

12. Bill Belcher, "Is Your Cat Purrrfectly Happy?," *Animal Times*, June/July 1994, 5.

13. Linda Goodman, *Linda Goodman's Star Signs* (New York: St. Martin's Press, 1987), 339.

14. Gerhard Adler, Ed., *C.G. Jung Letters 1: 1906-1950* (Princeton, New Jersey: Princeton University Press, 1973), 542.

15. David Bohm, *Wholeness and the Implicate Order* (London, Boston, and Henley: Routledge & Kegan Paul,1980), 198–199.

16. T. S. Eliot, *Four Quartets* (New York: Harcourt Brace & Company, 1943), 44.

17. http://www.quotegarden.com/dancing.html.

18. Socrates declaring that he dances, Xenophon: The Symposium, Section ll, {31}-{39}, Trans. H.G. Dakyns, Ancient History Sourcebook, Fordham University, http://www.fordham.edu/halsall/ancient/xenophon-sym.html.

19. Beautiful Coca Cola Commercial Full Version, January 7,2007, http://www.youtube.com/watch?v=R1NnyE6DDnQ.

20. Mike Adams, "High Fructose Corn Syrup Contaminated with Toxic Mercury says Research (Opinion)," January 27, 2009, http://www.naturalnews.com/025442_mercury_HFCS_corn.html.

21. Edith Hamilton,*The Greek Way* (New York: W.W.Norton & Company, Inc., 1983), 22–24.

Chapter Eighteen: Accessing the Higher Dimensions

1. Stephanie Merritt, *Mind, Music and Imagery* (New York: Penguin Books USA Inc.,1990), 87.

2. Peter Pettersson, Trans. Yarrow Cleaves, "Cymatics-the Science of the Future?," World-Mysteries.com, http://www.world-mysteries.com/sci_cymatics.htm.

3. David Bohm, *Wholeness and the Implicate Order* (London, Boston, and Henley: Routledge & Kegan Paul,1980), 207–213.

4. http://lyrics-a-plenty.com/l/love_is_the_seventh_wave.lyrics.php.

5. Lawrence LeShan, *The Medium, The Mystic, and the Physicist* (New York: The Viking Press Inc.,1974), 86–87.

6. Ibid.

7. Ibid.

8. US Military and intelligence agencies use of Remote Viewing, "Project Star Gate," http://www.remoteviewed.com/remote_viewing_history_military.htm.

9. LeShan, *The Medium, The Mystic, and the Physicist*, 86-87.

10. Ibid.

11. Joe Dispenza, *Evolve Your Brain* (Deerfield Beach, Florida: Health Communications Inc., 2007), 463–465.

12. Ibid., 64–65.

13. "Descartes and the Pineal Gland," Stanford Encyclopedia of Philosophy, November 5, 2008, http://plato.stanford.edu/entries/pineal-gland/#1.1.

14. Joseph Ledoux, *Synaptic Self* (New York: Penguin Books, 2002), 16-17.

15. Gary Farr, "The Endocrine System/The Pineal Gland," December 12, 2011, http://www.becomehealthynow.com/article/bodyendocrine/737/.

16. Rick Strassman, *DMT: The Spirit Molecule* (Rochester, Vermont: Park Street Press, 2001), 43-85.

17. Ibid.

18. Ibid., 185-201.

19. Ibid., 310-328.

20. A description and history of entheogens, psychoactive substances used in religious, shamanic, or spiritual contexts, "Entheogen," *Wikipedia*, http://en.wikipedia.org/wiki/Entheogen.

21. James G. Frazer, *The Golden Bough* (New York: Avenel Press, 1981), 320–322.

22. Robert Graves, *The Greek Myths: 1* (Penguin Books USA Inc.,1960), Foreword 9–10.

23. Carl Weiseth writing about Pinecone Symbology, "Third Eye Symbolism of the Pinecone," http://ournewearth.tv/news_details.php?id=88.

24. The dangers of fluoride, http://healthspectator.com/2008/06/01/fluoride-still-not-safe-despite-tooth-decay-data/.

25. "Frankincense and Myrrh Essential Oils," http://www.auracacia.com/auracacia/aclearn/eo_frankmyrrh.html.

26. Health conditions benefited by meditation, http://1stho listic.com/meditation/hol_meditation_benefits_health_conditions.htm.

27. Ibid.

28. Benefits of mindful meditation with cancer patients, Cary Barbor, "The Science of Meditation," *Psychology Today*, May 1, 2001, http://www.psychologytoday.com/articles/200105/the-science-meditation?page=2.

29. Infinity symbol illustrations, http://photobucket.com/images/infinity%20symbol/?page=2.

30. Arden Mahlberg, "Getting the Ego Humming," in *Music and Miracles*, Comp. Don G. Campbell (Wheaton, Illinois: Quest Books 1992), 219–229.

31. Don G. Campbell, *The Roar of Silence* (Wheaton, Illinois: The Theosophical Publishing House, 1989), 47.

32. Robert Masters and Jean Houston, *Listening To The Body* (New

York: Delacorte Press, 1978), 169–181.

33. "The Beatles, the Maharishi and Meditation," The Beatles in India, http://thebeatlesinindia.com/stories/beatlesmedit.html.

34. "The Beatles,the Maharishi, Sex and Money," http://thebeatlesinindia.com/stories/sexmoney.html.

Chapter Twenty: Counteracting Societal Mind Conditioning

1. Disney Subliminal Messages on YouTube, January 4, 2008, http://www.youtube.com/watch?v=ydqP25N7TBY.

2. http://www.brainyquote.com/quotes/authors/w/winston_churchill.html.

3. Yvonne Raley and Robert Talisse, "Getting Duped: How the Media Messes with Your Mind," *Scientific American*, January 31,2008, http://www.sciam.com/article.cfm?id=getting-duped.

4. Ibid.

5. Ibid.

6. Mary McNamara, "John Edwards' Highly Scripted 'Nightline' Interview " *Los Angeles Times*, Entertainment section, August 9, 2008, http://latimesblogs.latimes.com/showtracker/2008/08/john-edwards-on/comments/page/3/.

7. "With God on Our Side" is a song written by Bob Dylan and released in 1964, *Wikpedia*, http://en.wikipedia.org/wiki/With_God_on_Our_Side.

8. http://www.youtube.com/watch?v=vuEQixrBKCc.

9. Definition and examples of Euphemism, *Wikpedia*, http://en.wikipedia.org/wiki/Euphemism.

10. President Bush's address to congress on ABC news live coverage, September 20,2001, http://www.youtube.com/watch?v=cpPABLW6F_A.

11. Definition and examples of glittering generalities, SourceWatch, August 10, 2008, http://www.sourcewatch.org/index.php?title=Glittering_generalities.

12. Definition and examples of distraction by phenomenon, SourceWatch, September 4, 2010, http://www.sourcewatch.org/index.php?title=Distraction#Distraction_by_phenomenon.

13. "Media Manipulation," Distraction by Phenomenon is summarized in David Mamet's 1997 film, 'Wag the Dog,' *Wikpedia*, http://en.wikipedia.org/wiki/Media_manipulation.

14. Distraction from bombing of Iraq in 1998 with President Clinton's sex scandal, *Wikpedia*, http://en.wikipedia.org.

15. The timing of missle attacks and Lewinsky's testimony lead to accusations of a "Wag the Dog" situation, Ibid.

16. " Recognizing Propaganda," on SourceWatch, February 3, 2012, http://www.sourcewatch.org/index.php?title=Propaganda.

17. Seth Finkelstein, "Alan Dershowitz's Tortuous Torturous Argument," in *The Ethical Spectacle,* February 2002, http://www.spectacle.org/0202/seth.html.

18. Synopsis of TV series, "The Chair," 2002, http://movies.msn.com/movies/movie-synopsis/the-chair-tv-series/.

19. Overview of TV game show "The Chamber," *Wikpedia*, 2002, http://en.wikipedia.org/wiki/The_Chamber_%28game_show%29.

20. Abu Graib torture and prisoner abuse, *Wikpedia*, http://en.wikipedia.org/wiki/Abu_Ghraib_prisoner_abuse.

21. Andrew Buncombe, "US Military Tells Jack Bauer: Cut Out the Torture Scenes…or Else," *The Independent,* February 13, 2007, http://www.independent.co.uk/news/world/americas/us-military-tells-jack-bauer-cut-out-the-torture-scenes--or-else-436143.html.

22. Alex Cruden, "24's Torture Methods Criticized By Military," Yahoo!, February 14, 2007, http://www.associatedcontent.com/article/150781/24s_torture_methods_criticized_by_military.html.

23. Daniel Eggen, "Bush Announces Veto of Waterboarding Ban," *Washington Post*, March 8, 2008, http://www.washingtonpost.com/wp-dyn/content/article/2008/03/08/AR2008030800304.html.

24. Ritsuko Ando, "Waterboarding an Attraction at Amusement Park," LiveLeak, August 10, 2008, http://www.liveleak.com//view?i=357_1218419850.

25. Liz Thomas, "Now TV Contestants Face Water Torture in the Most Sickening Reality Show Yet," MailOnline, October 6, 2008, http://www.dailymail.co.uk/news/article-1069333/Now-TV-contestants-face-water-torture-sickening-reality-yet.html.

26. "Tasers-Potentially Lethal and Easy to Abuse,"December 16, 2008, http://www.amnesty.org/en/news-and-updates/report/tasers-potentially-lethal-and-easy-abuse-20081216.

27. "Taser Torture in America-A Call for Congressional Hearings," Petition 2 Congress, http://www.petition2congress.com/2/1822/taser-torture-in-a-+merica-call-congressional-hearings/.

Chapter Twenty-one: Global High-Velocity Consciousness

1. http://www.elyrics.net/read/l/leonard-cohen-lyrics/anthem-lyrics.html.

INDEX

G

H

www.ingramcontent.com/pod-product-compliance
Lightning Source LLC
Chambersburg PA
CBHW031424270326
41930CB00007B/568